MOUNT RUSHMORE

MOUNT RUSHMORE

Gilbert C. Fite

Lincoln Borglum Collection

MOUNT RUSHMORE BOOKSTORES
MOUNT RUSHMORE NATIONAL MEMORIAL
13036 HIGHWAY 244, • KEYSTONE, SD 57751
WWW.MOUNTRUSHMORESOCIETY.COM

By Gilbert C. Fite

Peter Norbeck: Prairie Statesman (1948)
Mount Rushmore (1952)
George N. Peek and the Fight for Farm Parity (1954)
The Agricultural Regions of the United States
(with Ladd Haystead) (1955)
An Economic History of the United States (with Jim Reese) (1959)
The Farmers' Frontier, 1865–1900 (1966)
American Farmers: The New Minority (1981)
Cotton Fields No More: Southern Agriculture, 1865–1983 (1984)
Richard B. Russell, Senator from Georgia (1991)
From Vision to Reality: A History of Bella Vista Village, 1915–1993 (1993)

Copyright ©1980 by Gilbert C. Fite. Published by the Mount Rushmore History Association, 2005. First edition, 1952; second printing, 1964; third printing, 1971; fourth printing, 1977; fifth printing, 1980; sixth printing, 1984; seventh printing, 1989; eighth printing, 2003; ninth printing, 2005; tenth printing, 2008; eleventh printing, 2014; twelfth printing, 2016; thirteenth printing, 2020

ISBN 13: 978-0-9646798-5-6

Library of Congress Cataloging-in-Publication Data

Fite, Gilbert Courtland, 1918–
  Mount Rushmore / by Gilbert C. Fite.
    p. cm.
  1952 ed. with minor corrections and additions.
  Includes bibliographical references and index.
  ISBN 0-9646798-5-X(alk. paper)
1. Borglum, Gutzon, 1867–1941. 2. Mount Rushmore National
Memorial (S.D.)—History. I. Mount Rushmore History
Association. II. Title.
NB237.B6F5 2005
730'.92--dc22

                                        2005005565

∞ The paper used in this publication meets the minimum requirements of the American National Standard for Information Sciences— Permanence of Paper for Printed Library Materials, ANSI Z39.48-1992.

TO
June, Jim and Jack

Contents

Contents

Illustrations

Illustrations

Map

PREFACE

Mount Rushmore National Memorial is one of the outstanding cultural and patriotic achievements produced in the United States in the twentieth century. It is typically American: a massive sculptural project corresponding to the nation's other manifestations of bigness and power. Sculptor Gutzon Borglum believed that art in the United States was not thoroughly American. It was not, he said, sufficiently large or meaningful to represent or typify the dreams, ambitions and accomplishments of this robust republic. Thus on a granite mountainside, high up among the clouds, he set out in 1927 to carve a national shrine dedicated to the principles and ideals of America. For that purpose he carved the faces of George Washington, Thomas Jefferson, Abraham Lincoln and Theodore Roosevelt in the everlasting granite of Mount Rushmore in the Black Hills of South Dakota. These four presidents embodied the traits, character and achievements that Borglum believed represented the greatness of the United States of America.

This book was first published by the University of Oklahoma Press in 1952 and has been out of print since 1996. However, the Mount Rushmore History Association believed that it was important to have a history of the origin and development of the monument, with all of its problems and struggles, available for readers. With the support of the MRHA the reprinting of this book, with a few corrections and minor additions, fulfills that need.

In earlier printings I expressed my appreciation to all of those who originally were so helpful in making the book possible. Now I want to add my gratitude to Brenda Hill, Managing Director, and the Board of Directors of the Mount Rushmore History Association and to James G. Popovich, former Chief of Interpretation for the National Park Service at Mount Rushmore National Memorial. Together, they have helped make this edition possible. As in the case of all my writing, I am especially appreciative of my wife, June, whose support and inspiration are always present.

Gilbert C. Fite

The National Park Service maintenance staff conducts an annual inspection of the faces to ensure long-term protection of the sculpture.

Constructed in 1957, the Memorial View Building (concession) served visitors with dining and gift shop services until it was removed in 1996.

*Constructed in 1963, the Mount Rushmore Visitor Center provided informa-
tion services and National Park Service administrative offices until its removal
in 1994.*

National Park Service

The Mount Rushmore Visitor Center and view terrace were constructed in 1963.

Aerial view of the memorial in the early 1970s: parking lot at top center with the visitor center immediately below it; concession and concession dormitory to the right; Borglum View Terrace in the center; Sculptor's Studio at lower left and the amphitheater at lower right.

The entrance, constructed in 1994, provides a grand introduction to the memorial grounds while dramatically framing the four great American presidents carved on Mount Rushmore.

Opposite: The Avenue of Flags, dedicated in 1998, displays flags of all fifty states, one district, and five territories and commonwealths of the United States of America.

The Lincoln Borglum Museum, completed in 1998, provides 5,200 square feet of exhibit space, the Mount Rushmore Bookstore, and two 125-seat theaters.

Listed on the National Register of Historic Places, the 1939 Sculptor's Studio houses tools and the scale model of the carving.

Freedom: America's Lasting Legacy, *a movie detailing the selection of the four presidents, is shown at the memorial amphitheater prior to the dramatic lighting of the sculpture. The Lincoln Borglum Museum is located at the top of the amphitheater and below the Grand View Terrace.*

Excellent views of the sculpted faces are found along the half-mile Presidential Trail.

CHAPTER ONE

In the Beginning

A UGUST 10, 1927, was clear and cool in the Black Hills. Nature had provided an ideal day for the official beginning of carving on Mount Rushmore. Sculptor Gutzon Borglum's "mad determination" to carve a mountain into a gigantic national shrine was about to be realized. A great celebration had been planned in which governors, senators, representatives, and even the president of the United States would participate. South Dakotans had seldom witnessed anything comparable.

It was shortly after noon when President Calvin Coolidge left his automobile at Keystone and mounted a horse for the three-mile ride to the base of Mount Rushmore. Above all else, Coolidge was not a cowboy. A ten-gallon hat, boots, and other western attire could not camouflage this true son of Vermont. Yet, although he appeared uneasy in his new paraphernalia, there was a glow of enthusiasm on his thin, pale face as his mount leisurely plodded up the steep incline of the rough logging road. Whatever discomfort he may have felt was submerged in his enjoyment of the magnificent scenery.

Tall, rugged pine and spruce interspersed with lithe and graceful paper birch and aspen lined the trail. Patches of pure blue sky dotted with soft, fleecy clouds were visible through the treetops. An occasional deer bounded off into the underbrush, startled by the president and his party as they rode along.

The central Black Hills abounded in natural wonders. Strange and interesting granite formations, heavily timbered mountains, clear, swift-flowing streams, and grassy meadows combined to create a majestic grandeur. Unique were the great granite spires, known as the "Needles," jutting hundreds of feet heavenward. Harney Peak, towering 7,242 feet high and outstripping any mountain east of the Rockies, seemed to stand guard over the entire area.

Of the many granite outcrops and mountains, it was the nearly 6,000-foot Mount Rushmore that Borglum had selected for his colossal sculpture. There was room on this bold mass of rock, he said, for gigantic figures of George Washington, Thomas Jefferson, Abraham Lincoln, and Theodore Roosevelt—American leaders who personified to the sculptor the founding, expansion, and preservation of the republic. Borglum had determined to carve a memorial whose size and significance would stir the patriotic and nationalistic impulses of every American heart.

About seventeen hundred people waited nervously for the ceremonies to commence. Following brief preliminaries, Coolidge began in his best Puritan manner: "We have come here to dedicate a cornerstone that was laid by the hand of the Almighty." Commenting on the conception of the idea, he continued, "It is but natural that such a design should begin with George Washington, for with him begins that which is truly characteristic of America. He represents our independence, our constitution, our liberty. He formed the highest aspirations that were entertained by any people into permanent institutions of our government. He stands as the foremost disciple of ordered liberty, a statesman with an inspired vision who is not outranked by any mortal.

"Next to him will come Thomas Jefferson, whose wisdom insured that the government which Washington had formed should be entrusted to the administration of the people. He emphasized the element of self government which had been enshrined in American institutions in such a way as to demonstrate that it was practical and would be permanent. In him, likewise, was embodied the spirit of American expansion . . .

"After our country had been established, enlarged from sea to sea and dedicated to popular government, the next great task was to demonstrate the permanency of our union and to extend the principle of freedom to all the inhabitants of our land. The master of this supreme accomplishment was Abraham Lincoln . . .

"That the principles for which these three men stood might be still more firmly established, destiny raised up Theodore Roosevelt. To political freedom, he strove to add economic freedom. By building the Panama Canal he brought into closer relationship the east and west and realized the vision that inspired Columbus in his search for a new passage to the Orient.

"The union of these four presidents carved on the face of the everlasting hills of South Dakota will constitute a distinctly national monument. It will be decidedly American in its conception, in its magnitude, in its meaning and altogether worthy of our country . . ."

After a few other remarks, the president handed Borglum a set of drills. The sculptor quickly ascended Mount Rushmore and began drilling the master points for the face of George Washington. The carving of the world's most colossal sculpture had begun.

The notion of commemorating some phases of American history by carving a gigantic monument in the Black Hills was born in the fertile and imaginative mind of Doane Robinson, the state historian. In 1923, when Robinson first conceived the idea, he was in his twenty-second year as secretary and superintendent of the State Historical Society of South Dakota. At sixty-seven, he was a vigorous administrator, scholar, and writer and was widely known for his works on Indians, particularly the Sioux. Few had contributed as much to South Dakota history.

Robinson was born in Sparta, Wisconsin, in 1856. He was christened Jonah Leroy, but since childhood he had been known as "Doane." As a young man he had homesteaded in Minnesota, but farming did not appeal to him. Next he turned to law, was admitted to the bar in the early 1880s, and began practicing at Watertown, Dakota Territory. In the 1890s, Robinson won recognition in the Northwest as a poet and speaker. Many of his poems appeared in such journals as *McClure's, Arena*, and *Century*. In 1898 he traveled under the auspices of the Northwest Lyceum Bureau of Minneapolis. He interpreted his poems in dialect and was popularly known as the "Dakota Poet and Humorist." His literary interests led to the establishment of *Monthly South Dakota*, a magazine devoted to history and literature. Out of this grew the State Historical Society of South Dakota of which Robinson became the first secretary in 1901. Through the years, South Dakotans had come to respect and love Doane Robinson.

Just when or how Robinson first conceived the idea that such colossal sculpture might be undertaken is unknown. He was, of course, fully aware of ancient sculpture on a grand scale. In the early 1920s he had marveled with millions of Americans at the concept and imagination of Gutzon Borglum who had recently begun to carve a Confederate memorial on Stone Mountain near Atlanta, Georgia. In any event, late in December 1923, Robinson wrote to sculptor Lorado Taft about the idea of carving massive figures on some of the granite pinnacles in the Black Hills. "I am thinking of some notable Sioux, as Red Cloud, who lived and died in the shadow of these peaks," he asserted. "If one was found practicable perhaps others would ultimately follow." He later told Taft, "In my imagination, I can see all the old heroes of the West peering out from them [the mountains] —Lewis and Clark, Frémont, Jed Smith, Bridger, Sa-kaka-wea [Sacagawea], Red Cloud, and, in an equestrian statue, Cody and the overland mail." Robinson asked Taft's opinion about the practicability of such carving, concluding, "I am sure that an artist of vision and imagination could work out a wonderful scheme."

Because of ill health, Taft could not leave Chicago to examine the Black Hills granite. It is not clear why Robinson did not first consult Borglum, who was then carving the head of Robert E. Lee on Stone Mountain. In fact, after Taft refused to visit South Dakota, Robinson asked him to recommend an artist capable of dealing in gigantic sculpture. Perhaps the historian thought Borglum was so absorbed in the Stone Mountain project that no other colossal carving would interest him.

Robinson did not think it wise to make his idea public just then—not, at least, until he had obtained influential support. For this support he turned to his friend, United States Senator Peter Norbeck. For nearly twenty years Norbeck had been the leading advocate of park and game development in the Black Hills.

In many respects the account of Peter Norbeck's career reads like pages from Horatio Alger. Born amid hardship and poverty on a Dakota Territory homestead in 1870, he rose to fame and some fortune through hard work and shrewd management. His father, George Norbeck, was a preacher and farmer who had emigrated from Norway after the Civil War. The Norbecks lived on a farm where Peter experienced the rigors and privations of pioneering. By working at odd jobs, he was able to attend three short terms at the University of Dakota (which became the University of South Dakota in 1889) in Vermillion.

Young Norbeck, who detested the drudgery and loneliness of farm life, entered the business of drilling artesian wells. By 1894 he and a cousin had developed a rig to drill deep, small-bore wells at the reasonable price of about $300 to $500. Within another five years, Norbeck had built a gasoline-powered rig which had no equal in the Dakotas. He could drill faster and more economically than his competitors, and shortly after the turn of the century he and his partner, Charles Nicholson, dominated the artesian well-drilling business in the state. In 1908 Norbeck estimated his company's worth and other personal assets at more than $300,000. Within another decade his Wyoming oil interests raised his fortune to nearly $500,000.

Norbeck was a large, ruggedly built, 225-pound man. His head was covered with a heavy mop of wavy brown hair, and a reddish, ragged mustache adorned his upper lip. His expression was easy and cordial, and his lineage was revealed by a very pronounced Norwegian accent. He was friendly, democratic, and honest, and people had confidence in him and his ability to get things done. He had boundless energy and enthusiasm for whatever he undertook, and his dominating personality was likely to engender undying loyalty or bitter hatred.

Having established himself in business, Norbeck turned to politics during the insurgency of Theodore Roosevelt. In 1908 he was elected on the Republican ticket to the state senate, where he served for three terms. With both business and political connections, he was in a strong position to bid for higher office. He accepted the nomination for lieutenant governor in 1914 and won handily. Two years later he was elected South Dakota's first native-born governor.

Norbeck's four years in Pierre were packed with stirring events. Almost simultaneously with his election, the Nonpartisan League of North Dakota began penetrating the state. Partly in order to turn back the League, and partly because of his desire to help the farmers, he urged a state-in-business program. A state-sponsored rural credit act and a state hail insurance law were passed, a state coal mine was opened, and a state-owned cement plant was provided for. This program aroused antagonism and opposition among conservatives, but Norbeck was strong enough to override them. He was elected to the United States Senate in 1920. Norbeck's political prowess was epitomized in the story of the Scandinavian voter who was asked at the primary voting booth whether he wanted a Republican or a Democratic ballot. "I don't know about that," he replied, "but I want to vote the Peter Norbeck ticket."

Norbeck's interest in the Black Hills region began in 1905 when he and Ole Iverson drove the first automobile over the prairie between Fort Pierre and Rapid City. While touring the area, he conceived the idea of establishing a state park and game sanctuary in the southern Hills. As a state senator, he worked to create a game preserve, and in 1913 some 61,400 acres of land were set aside for this purpose. Six years later, Governor Norbeck influenced the legislature to make a permanent state park in this region, and in the following year, 1920, federal legislation placed an additional 30,000 acres in the custody of the Custer State Park Board. This was designated the Custer State Park Game Sanctuary. The park was stocked with buffalo, elk, mountain sheep, and deer. After Norbeck went to the United States Senate, he had several moose put in the Hills, but, unfortunately, the caretaker let them escape.

So for nearly twenty years Norbeck had taken the lead in developing the country's largest state park. Indeed, it was well known throughout South Dakota that he was vitally interested in game preservation, park development, and road construction. He desired to conserve the natural beauty of the region and to build scenic roads for tourists. There was something incongruous about this rough well driller and politician. He loved and understood art, both natural and man-made. When visiting a large city he generally spent several hours at the art gallery, and his knowledge and appreciation of art and artists both ancient and modern surprised even the professionals. But most of all he loved the art and beauty of nature. He felt personally responsible for the destiny of Custer State Park and was determined that nature's handiwork should not be butchered or commercialized. Norbeck remained on the park board after he went to Washington in 1921 and kept in close touch with Black Hills developments.

To Senator Norbeck, then, went a copy of Robinson's first letter suggesting massive sculpture in the Black Hills. Norbeck reacted cautiously as he did to most new suggestions. His strength lay not so much in originality of thought as in his ability to move the ideas and plans of others to success. He wanted time to study a program of action. Once converted to any plan or idea, however, he was a tenacious fighter who usually achieved what he sought. Aware of this, Robinson wanted the senator's support.

"It is a new suggestion entirely: I had never thought of it," Norbeck replied. He added, however, that there was a "wonderful opportunity to work out among the Black Hills Needles the very thing you suggest." The Needles were beautiful, sharp granite shafts jutting up in the Harney mountain range like cathedral spires. Since the most suitable granite outcrops were in Custer State Park, Robinson wished to present his ideas formally to the park board. "I am certain there are wonderful possibilities in the proposition if it should fall into the hands of an artist big enough to handle it," he enthusiastically told the senator. But, he warned, "The fellow who does it must be something more than a stone carver."

After enlisting Norbeck's support, Robinson felt that the time was ripe to present his plan to the South Dakota citizenry. He intimated something of what he had in mind at a Huron meeting of the Black and Yellow Trail Association on January 22, 1924. The topic of his address was "The Pull of the Historic Place." He emphasized the desirability of stimulating tourist traffic by improving the state's scenic attractions. Every community, he concluded, should have something to draw tourists. Robinson later declared that in the course of his address he specifically mentioned the carving of some unique monument in the Black Hills. The local press, however, mentioned nothing of the kind. Perhaps he did allude to it in passing. If so, it evidently did not make the impression on his listeners that might have been expected.

On February 1, a few days following the Huron meeting, the Associated Press carried a story from Pierre outlining in some detail Robinson's ideas as they had developed thus far. "A definite project of converting a group of Black Hills 'Needles' into massive and spectacular figures of sculpture emblematic of the outstanding historical life of the state, has been conceived by Doane Robinson," the article said. The reporter quoted Robinson at length, asserting that such a spectacle would attract tourists as nothing else could. "Hundreds of visitors would be drawn into the state to view such a landmark," he said. This was Robinson's primary objective. His letters and public statements throughout the early part of 1924 indicate that he was primarily considering the commercial value of the project. At least, he was shrewd enough to know that in the business-dominated era of the 1920s, he spoke a language everyone understood. Debt-ridden farmers and hard-bitten businessmen would hardly be interested in gigantic sculpture for its own sake or for the sake of history. Regardless of his ultimate purpose, Robinson had to speak in commercial terms to arouse interest among the rank and file, and even this approach might not succeed.

Robinson's interview of February 1 was carried by most of the leading newspapers of the state. Undoubtedly, the historian meant to send up a trial balloon to test popular reaction. He did not have long to wait. The *Sioux Falls Daily Argus Leader,* South Dakota's largest newspaper, called his idea "excellent," and the *Press* of that city also gave it hearty approval. No doubt the editors saw advantages for their community if the plan succeeded. Sioux Falls was located on U.S. Highway 16, a principal tourist route from the East to the Black Hills.

Other South Dakota newspapers east of the Missouri River were hostile to the project. The *Yankton Press and Dakotan* declared, "The idea is not likely to meet with unanimous favor. . . . We who live out on the plains are quite satisfied with the beauties of our great Black Hills as bequeathed to us by nature. . . . It would seem rather presumptuous to attempt to improve on the scenic beauties . . . however accomplished the artist or perfect the design." Any attempt to beautify and add attractiveness to the Black Hills would be "painting a lily," exclaimed the indignant editor. The practical question of "expending a large sum of money in such a way" was also raised. Echoes of disapproval resounded from the offices of the *Vermillion Dakota Republican,* the *Evening Huronite,* and others. Doane Robinson's "brainstorm" is "the bunk!" said the Vermillion scribe. Summing up the general attitude, the *Evening Huronite* asserted that the suggestion of working over granite spires "with chisel and mallet . . . is not meeting with general approval."

Sentiment was, if possible, even less favorable in the Black Hills area. The *Rapid City Daily Journal,* the most influential paper in the region, surprisingly did not at first editorialize on the idea. It did, however, reprint a critical account from the *Queen City Mail.* The *Mail* answered the commercial argument by saying that the Black Hills would sell themselves without any "alteration on nature's handiwork." The strongest opposition from any Black Hills resident came from Mrs. Cora B. Johnson, wife of the editor of the *Hot Springs Star.* Her editorial columns censured the idea bitterly. "We view with alarm Doane Robinson's proposal to carve the Needles into statues. Man makes statues but God made the Needles. Let them alone." This was typical of Mrs. Johnson's rebukes.

The scoffing, indignant protests and bitter opposition only stirred Robinson to more vigorous action. He wrote scores of letters explaining his idea, answering critics, and seeking additional support. He could count on help from only a small segment of the press, Senator Norbeck, and the Rapid City Commercial Club. A few Rapid City businessmen envisioned what a sculptured mountain would mean to their community, the eastern gateway to the Hills. J. B. Greene, secretary of the Commercial Club, was happy about "the great amount of absolutely free publicity with which the proposition has been attended."

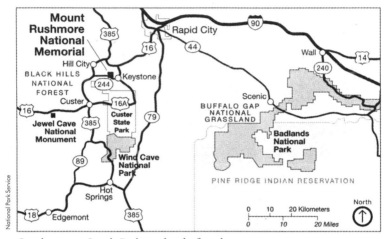

Southwestern South Dakota, land of parks.

Six months had passed since Robinson made his initial suggestions. "Hostility," he later recorded, "seemed to become more intense and took on a personal aspect." He realized fully that something more definite must be done if he were to build up and hold the public interest. Until midsummer 1924 he "had no definite plan of action," he said, "other than to continue agitation until the subconscious and some person of artistic sense and financial ability should take it up and carry it to success."

The time had come for positive action. After receiving an especially abusive letter, Robinson directly approached Gutzon Borglum, a man he knew could carve mountains. On August 20 he wrote Borglum at Stone Mountain, Georgia, telling him that the Black Hills offered unique opportunities for "heroic sculpture of unusual character." Then he came specifically to the point and asked, "Would it be possible for you to design and supervise a massive sculpture there. The proposal has not passed beyond the mere suggestion, but if it be possible for you to undertake the matter I feel quite sure we could arrange to finance such an enterprise."

Borglum was visiting his home at Stamford, Connecticut, when Robinson's letter reached Stone Mountain. Major Jesse G. Tucker, his assistant, opened it and, after digesting the contents, wrote across the top before forwarding, "Here it is, Borglum; Let's go." Borglum, who had great enthusiasm for the unique, telegraphed Robinson on August 28 that he was very much interested in the proposal. He could visit the Black Hills sometime in September, he added. At last, here was a promise of active aid. But who was Borglum, breaker of tradition and carver of mountains? Robinson did not know. He was only sure that here was a daring, imaginative, and intensely patriotic artist who might implement his vision.

Gutzon Borglum in 1934.

The Needles: Granite outcroppings in the Black Hills where Doane Robinson first visualized the carving of giant sculpture.

Washington and Lincoln as Gutzon Borglum first sketched them to be carved on the Needles.

The southeastern face of Mount Rushmore as it appeared before carving began.

Rise Studio

Gutzon Borglum unfurls the American flag on the crest of Mount Rushmore for the first time in 1925.

Lincoln Borglum Collection

Dedication–1927: Calvin Coolidge, "the cowboy from Vermont," delivers an address at Mount Rushmore on August 10, 1927.

Borglum at work on his early models.

Illustration of area newspapers debating the Mount Rushmore controversy.

CHAPTER TWO

Mountain Sculptor

I T is said that when Dean Andrew West of Princeton University conferred an honorary degree on Gutzon Borglum in 1909, he referred to the recipient as "trained but not tamed." This statement is descriptive of Borglum's entire life. Recent American history has seen few more fascinating or controversial figures. He was one of the most colorful men ever to move on the stage of American art.

John Gutzon de la Mothe Borglum was born in the frontier country of Bear Lake, Idaho, on March 25, 1867. His father was a Dane who had emigrated from Denmark in 1864. The elder Borglum settled in Omaha and later in Fremont, Nebraska, where he practiced medicine. Gutzon attended the public schools of those towns, and later his parents sent him to St. Mary's College, a Catholic boarding school in Kansas. Earlier he had tried to run away from home, demonstrating an independence of thought and action which grew with maturity. At St. Mary's he displayed an artistic talent observed previously by his parents, and school officials were pleased with his pictures and models of the saints and Madonnas. But Gutzon was more interested in western subjects—horses, cowboys, and Indians—than he was in the appurtenances of religion.

The confining spirit of a church boarding school was repugnant to this young iconoclast. Suddenly and unceremoniously he left for the West and San Francisco. His interest and talent led him to the Art Association in which Virgil Williams was a prominent leader. However, it was William Kieth, a California landscape artist who greatly influenced Borglum in those early years. His tendency toward the dramatic and romantic in art was due as much to Kieth's influence as it was to his own temperament.

In 1890 Borglum went to Paris to study at the Julian Academy and the École des Beaux-Arts. After only six months he sent a sample of his sculpture to the Paris Salon. He was drawn to western themes, and his first outstanding piece showed a horse standing guard over a dead Indian master. For this he was awarded a membership in the Société Nationale des Beaux-Arts. Shortly afterwards, he exhibited work in Spain. There he also worked on a large painting, "The Conquest of Mexico," which was never completed.

While in Paris Borglum became a close friend and student of Auguste Rodin to whom traditional concepts of art meant little. He often visited Rodin's studio and came almost to worship the great French artist. Borglum considered Rodin's "Hand of God" one of the world's greatest works of art.

In 1893 Borglum returned to the United States. Back home, his most significant works were a painting of John C. Frémont and a bust of Jessie Benton Frémont, the western Pathfinder's charming wife. Most of the next two years, however, he spent with his brother Solon in the Sierra Madres of California where they absorbed local color and studied wildlife firsthand. Solon had previously managed one of his father's ranches, but after demonstrating a marked natural ability for sculpture, he decided to seek formal instruction. The two brothers parted in 1895, Solon going to the Art School of Cincinnati and Gutzon to England a year later.

Gutzon opened a small studio in London. Within a year he was showing his work in the Hanover galleries. Queen Victoria was attracted to the exhibit, and he was invited to display some paintings before Her Majesty. One success led to another, and in 1898 he was commissioned to paint murals for the Queen's Hotel at Leeds. During this period he was elected to the Royal Society of British Artists.

Meanwhile, he was winning acclaim at home. Exhibitions of his work were held in Chicago, Los Angeles, Boston, and New York. Late in 1897 a group of his western paintings were shown at O'Brien's, a commercial art gallery, and at the Art Institute in Chicago. Such landscapes as "Arizona Cowboy," "Mexican Bandits," "Sierra Madre," and "Staging in California" commanded praise from writers and critics. "Nowhere on the continent is there such a kaleidoscopic revel of exuberant color," said one reviewer. Borglum's painting was direct, frank and naturalistic.

Borglum soon tired of Europe, and in 1901 he returned to New York City where he set up a studio. He painted several murals and also did some sculpture which soon began to attract national attention. One of his principal creations was a small statuette, "Apaches

Pursued," which depicted two wild, leaping horses ridden by naked Indians. His "Mares of Diomedes" won the gold medal at the St. Louis Exposition in 1904. This work consisted of a group of seven horses charging wildly over a rock, with the figure of a man clinging to the back of the leading mare. It was vigorously and powerfully modeled and reflected Borglum at his best. Banker James Stillman later bought the piece for the Metropolitan Museum of Art, where it stood for many years in the main hallway. From this time Borglum turned more and more to sculpture, and after 1910 he painted very little.

The horse was the favorite sculptural subject of both Gutzon and Solon, but Solon achieved national recognition earlier than his elder brother. While Gutzon was in England, Solon began to exhibit such noted sculpture as "Lassoing Wild Horses" and "Stampede of Wild Horses." The latter won recognition at the Paris Exposition in 1900. After the turn of the century, Solon produced "On the Border of White Man's Land," "Burial on the Plains," and other notable works. Although Gutzon's sculpture was also influenced by the West, it was not so completely dominated by western themes as was Solon's.

Borglum now began a prodigious output which was soon to place him among America's foremost sculptors. In 1905 he completed figures of the twelve apostles and many other characters, including angels, for Manhattan's Cathedral of St. John the Divine. Two years later he carved his heroic marble head of Lincoln which rests in the rotunda of the national Capitol. He was then commissioned to do the great Sheridan bronze in Washington, D. C., and in 1911 he finished the magnificent seated Lincoln in Newark.

His art expressed intensity and emotion. John Edward Chamberlain said in the *New York Mail* that Borglum sought to realize "the moment of intensity" in his work. "He seems to be looking in all things for the apex . . . that typifies and expresses all that is in them." Borglum was a strong exponent of sculptural impressionism. Faithful to actuality, he was contemptuous of the so called mod ern and ~~~~~~~~~~, as they were of him. His subjects, men and horses, appeared vividly alive. A significant compliment came from Theodore Roosevelt, who, after looking at his Lincoln in Newark, remarked, "Why[,] this doesn't look like a monument at all."

Yet in 1910, despite ten years of solid work in sculpture, Borglum was not considered one of the nation's greatest sculptors. The

Encyclopedia Britannica of that year mentioned him only in connection with Solon. "His elder brother, Gutzon Borglum," the account related, "also showed himself an artist of some originality." Time, however, increased appreciation for his early work, and later productions enhanced his reputation.

It is too early to make any final judgment of Borglum's relative position in the history of American art. Furthermore, because of his personality and character, he tended, like Norbeck, to win loyal friends or to make bitter enemies. Thus there are few unbiased judgments of his work. He was always considered highly competent, but contemporary critics and judges did not rank him with Saint-Gaudens, Daniel Chester French, or George Grey Barnard. In his book *The History of American Sculpture*, published in 1930, Lorado Taft scarcely mentions Gutzon Borglum. Charles H. Caffin devotes a chapter to Solon and his work in the volume *American Masters of Sculpture* (1913) but gives Gutzon only passing mention. J. Walker McSpadden writes more fully of Borglum in his *Famous Sculptors of America* (1927), but even McSpadden does not rank Borglum at the very top of his profession. Most qualified judges considered Gutzon Borglum exceptionally good, but not great.

Regardless of how contemporary professionals rated him, the general public liked Borglum's work because most of it was naturalistic and could be easily understood and appreciated by the average citizen. Increased demand for his talents came from all sections of the United States. The impartial observer must conclude, however, that it was mountain-carving which was to bring Borglum his greatest fame.

Borglum was an apostle of distinctively American art. In 1908 he wrote that American artists were too reliant upon Europe and that monuments in the United States lacked "reverence, sincerity, and individuality." Past traditions did not bind the sculptor; rather, they were something to be shattered. He believed that classical forms had no place in the art of America and argued that it was foolish to tie American art to Europe. "Art in America should be American, drawn from American sources, memorializing American achievement," he wrote. He declared ironically that strong opposition always developed against anyone who believed that "a sweet, young, American child in all her natural charm and unrestraint is more lovely to look upon than a sleepy-eyed Assyrian or Greek rubbed from some wine cup or jug." With biting satire he accused Americans of refusing to "look at anything unless it wears a helmet or Greek sandals." He added, "The greatest stories of the world, the stories of America, go unrecorded in our public parks and galleries."

Borglum was an intensely nationalistic and patriotic artist. To him, Americanism was a sort of religion. He argued that America's epic splendors should be expressed vigorously and independently. "American artists should be seers and should give, serve and complete the spirit and concept of Washington—of Lincoln," he declared. Late in life he conceived the idea of lining a proposed inter-American highway with statuary. "Think of a series of statues running from Washington to Laredo," he enthusiastically exclaimed, "in which the history of the New World could be depicted."

In 1910 Borglum moved to Stamford, Connecticut, where he built a huge studio on the banks of the Rippowan. He did much of his work there during the next ten years, but he also maintained a studio at 166 East Thirty-eighth Street in New York. A year earlier Mary Williams Montgomery, the daughter of the Reverend Giles Montgomery, a noted missionary and educator, had become his second wife. Mrs. Borglum was a charming and talented woman. She was born in Marash, Turkey, attended Wellesley College, and afterward received a Ph.D. degree from the University of Berlin. She was a modest, gentle person who lived largely in the reflected glory of her distinguished husband. The Borglums had a four hundred–acre estate near Stamford known as Borgland, where they lived comfortably on his substantial income. They had two children, James Lincoln and Mary Ellis.

Borglum was a man of manifold interests and ideas. Unlike many artists, he did not withdraw solely to his major interest or ignore the rest of the world. "I'm not the average American who does one damned thing," he once told a reporter. "I do everything, boxing, fencing, wrestling, horseback riding. . . . A man should do everything, turn handsprings, somersaults. The trouble with American life is that it is not vigorous enough. We talk vigor, we patronize sports, but we are not ourselves sportsmen." He admonished and practiced the strenuous life. An ardent boxing fan, he witnessed the Dempsey-Willard fight in 1919 as a representative of the International Sporting Club, an organization of which he became president two years later. He served for a time on the New York Boxing Commission, and on one occasion he sparred in a friendly but serious manner with Bob

Fitzsimmons. In this informal bout Borglum caught Fitzsimmons a punishing blow but saved himself from damage at the hands of the former champion by suddenly disappearing through a trick door.

Aircraft were another of Borglum's major interests. He witnessed some of the Wright brothers' early flights as an observer for the Aero Club of America and was also on hand to see some of the original experiments of Samuel P. Langley of the Smithsonian Institution. His ideas regarding airplane design were far advanced, and one of his fuselage models, made in 1917, still exists. It is tubular-shaped and closely resembles the forms later adopted by modern designers. He also made blueprints for an improved propeller.

Borglum felt a strong personal responsibility for democracy and citizenship which prompted him to engage actively in public life. He was initiated into practical politics when he served for one term in the Connecticut Legislature. In 1912 he campaigned vigorously for Theodore Roosevelt, and four years later he acted as an intermediary between Roosevelt and the conservative Republicans. Roosevelt's moderate progressivism appealed to him as did the Bull Mooser's personality. Borglum thought the country's business was his concern, and he often took a problem directly to the President. White House conferences were no novelty to him—he had free and easy access to every president from Theodore Roosevelt to Franklin D. Roosevelt, with the sole exception of Hoover.

This sense of public responsibility is also illustrated by his aircraft industry investigations during World War I. He insisted that the industry was shot through with graft and corruption in government contracts. In Washington he hired lawyers at his own expense and sent his confidential reports directly to President Wilson. When the Nonpartisan League roared through North Dakota, Borglum campaigned for its candidates and was especially helpful in securing the election of Edwin F. Ladd to the United States Senate. In 1920 the South Dakota branch of the league endorsed Ladd for vice president as a running mate for Robert M. LaFollette.

Near the end of World War I, Borglum established a camp on his Stamford estate for the training of Czechoslovakian volunteers. He was a close friend of Thomas G. Masaryk and had contributed ideas to the first Czechoslovakian constitution. In 1923 Borglum entered the Edward W. Bok Peace Plan competition, and his essay was one of the twelve published of more than twenty-two thousand submitted.

Borglum was a clear and expressive writer. His style had force and simplicity; it was terse, direct, and convincing. As early as 1908 he had published articles on art and related subjects, but a man of such wide interests could hardly confine his writings to his own field. A strong friend of organized labor, he published several pamphlets on the labor problem, and his articles appeared in both professional and popular journals. He was an avid reader and possessed a large library of substantial books. He read particularly widely on the life of Lincoln.

Physically, Borglum was of stocky build and medium height. He did not appear at all like the stage-portrayed artist. Neither cape nor beard and long, flowing, unkempt hair was part of his apparel. In fact, he had scarcely any hair, and his bald pate contrasted sharply with a heavy, bristling mustache which adorned a rugged face. His eyes were piercing, and he had a nervous habit of alternately removing and putting on his pince-nez which dangled from their button on a black ribbon. He spoke rapidly in a booming, resonant voice with great intensity and many gestures, clipping his words in sharp precision. Those with whom Borglum talked were usually won to his views. It seemed futile to disagree with one who spoke with such certainty and authority. He was a super-salesman.

Borglum's whole character was positive and dominating. He was born to command, not to obey; to lead, not to follow. When members of the commission in charge of it criticized his statue of Governor Peter Altgeld, he exclaimed, "I forget more about sculptural art overnight than the commission knows in a lifetime." In 1932, when Joseph Hergesheimer asserted that Borglum's bronze of Sheridan in Washington was inaccurate, Borglum shot back, "He's crazy." He was blunt, pugnacious and outspoken; indeed, he was possessed of most characteristics attributed to the artistic temperament—he was changeable, unstable, inconsistent, unpredictable, and egotistical. But by any standard, he was a dynamic and striking personality.

Unusually energetic and vigorous, Borglum seldom limited himself to any single activity. He was a many-sided man, and he has been characterized as an artist in politics, in business, and always in contention! Generally a personable and lovable man, he commanded deep devotion. If crossed or frustrated, however, he could be bitter, cruel, and ruthless. His temper was easily aroused, but it subsided even more quickly. He thrived on praise and public acclaim and had qualities of showmanship which kept him in the limelight. Whatever he did was attended by considerable fanfare. But beneath all of his brashness there was a generosity and humility of spirit which showed the marked contradiction of his character and personality. Yet Borglum had no intention of dying and waiting a generation or a century for recognition. He would have it now.

Borglum was often in the midst of hot controversies. His strong individualism, crusading spirit, and confident and dominating manner were bound to bring conflict—and he flourished on conflict. His ability to publicize himself and his work generally left him the victor in almost any dispute. He first received national headlines when church authorities objected to the femininity of his angels carved for the Cathedral of St. John the Divine. Irritated, he summarily defaced his models. Borglum was so outspoken and critical of contemporary art and artists that he was frequently engaged in newspaper quarrels with members of his craft. His word-battles became almost as famous as his statues. In 1908 he created a sensation in art circles when he charged that American art lacked sincerity. Most of America's art schools, he said, were worthless and should be closed. Naturally, such statements brought sharp retorts from his fellow artists.

A few years later he again commanded the headlines in art news by resigning as vice-president of the Association of American Painters and Sculptors. This organization had been formed by an insurgent group protesting the methods of the National Academy. Borglum quit the association in a controversy about the manner in which works were chosen for a projected exhibition. He declared that only the "miserable works of favorites are surreptitiously invited." Here Borglum displayed insurgency among insurgents. Nor did he stop needling the New York coterie. About a year after resigning the art association position, he described the unhappy plight of genius in America when he told a group that much sculpture which bore the names of well-known sculptors had been done by struggling young artists for a mere pittance. He damned the work of "imposters" and "artistic prostitutes." When one New York sculptor was asked to comment on Borglum's charges of commercialism, he retorted, "Borglum! I won't discuss him. That man is too much in the newspapers. He's always seeking publicity."

But Borglum had only begun. He leveled an attack on the Washington and Lincoln monuments in Washington, D.C. Discounting their conception and effect, he said that if money were available, *he* would build a monument to Washington and Lincoln in keeping with American ideals. "In the Lincoln Memorial," he said, "we will have nothing but marble, marble, marble."

No one was spared. The Metropolitan Museum, he asserted, was not comparable to the Art Institute of Chicago, and he added that New Yorkers were "victims of shop-culture." The National Academy came in for its share of criticism. Borglum said that it was hidebound and utterly failed in its opportunities and responsibilities. Thus, time and again, this versatile genius was in conflict with others. He commonly wrote long letters to the newspapers expressing his ideas and ideals. One might conclude that these controversies would adversely affect his income, but his public and private battles actually led progressively to more lucrative commissions.

"My life has been a one-man war from beginning to date," said Borglum on his seventy-first birthday. No one who knew him disagreed with this self-analysis. Whether he was defacing angels, investigating the aircraft industry, or carving on Stone Mountain or Mount Rushmore, Borglum demonstrated his two-fisted, hard-fighting qualities. He once told his friend Rupert Hughes, who was about to write a Borglum story, "I ask only one favor: for God's sake don't cover me with the twaddle and gush usually written about artists." This then was the man who said he would go to the Black Hills of South Dakota to help plan a great national monument carved and blasted from the imperishable granite.

CHAPTER THREE

A Garden of the Gods

ORGLUM'S only condition for making the South Dakota trip was that "there shall be no publicity not released by me." Therefore, Robinson informed only Governor McMaster and Senator Norbeck of the famous sculptor's visit. Plans were made for the three of them to meet Borglum in Rapid City on the morning of September 24, 1924.

Norbeck and McMaster were delayed at the last minute, so Robinson alone met Borglum on the train as it approached Rapid City. Although the sculptor's trip was supposedly secret, a large crowd greeted him at the station. Somewhat nonplussed, Robinson later learned that a local relative of one of Borglum's Stone Mountain employees had told when he would arrive. Borglum, who feasted on attention and publicity, was, according to Robinson, "tickled to death."

At noon Borglum was entertained at a wild game dinner, after which his party was driven to the Harney Peak area by Paul Bellamy, a local businessman. The artist was accompanied by his twelve-year-old son Lincoln and Major Tucker. Rapid City citizens who traveled with the Borglum group included C. C. O'Hara, president of the State School of Mines, and Joseph P. Connolly, professor of mineralogy. After touring part of Custer State Park, the party spent the night at Sylvan Lake. The next morning they set out to climb 7,242-foot Harney Peak. As Borglum reached a place where he could get a full view of the massive Needles and other granite outcrops, he exclaimed, "There's the place to carve a great national memorial. American history shall march along that skyline." This is "a veritable garden of the gods," he added.

He continued to the top of Harney Peak, and from there he surveyed the surrounding granite spires and mountains. This was not his first journey to the Black Hills. In 1909 he had visited his brother-in-law, the Reverend Marshall F. Montgomery, in Lead. It is possible that Borglum might not have made the trip to South Dakota fifteen years later if he had not been slightly acquainted with the area. In any event, he was visibly impressed with the magnificent scenery, and after cursory observation he concluded that the great piles of granite were susceptible to gigantic sculpture.

The Black Hills, the area of about sixty by one hundred miles over which Borglum walked and rode, were closely identified with the history and romance of the Last Frontier. A treaty with the Sioux in 1868 had closed the region to white settlement, and for a few years the Indian preserve had been respected by white settlers. It was General George A. Custer's glowing report of 1874 which stimulated treaty-breaking migration. Custer told of rich pasturage, pure water, farm advantages, and most important, gold. "I have upon my table forty or fifty small particles of pure gold . . . most of it obtained today from one panful of earth," he wrote his superiors in St. Paul.

As this news flashed across the country, gold seekers rushed headlong for a new mining bonanza. After some halfhearted effort to restrain white intruders, the federal government ceased military action and thousands of people poured into the Hills. By 1876 some fifteen thousand whites had entered the territory, and the mining boom was on. First on French Creek at Custer, and then in the northern Hills at Deadwood and Lead, the yellow dust drew hundreds and thousands of reckless, fighting, cursing men. As had been true of other frontier regions, placer mining soon gave way to corporation-controlled quartz mines which required expensive machinery and a stable labor force. The Homestake Mining Company, the largest and most productive in the United States, was organized at Lead in 1877.

Much has been written about the territory's "incredible characters"—Wild Bill Hickok, Calamity Jane, and others. Certain glamour and sensationalism surround the lives of these careless women and gun-toting outlaws. They have attracted writers and tourists who seek a vicarious freedom and independence which they themselves can never find.

But lawlessness and reckless living were of short duration in the Hills. People of whom little has been recorded built the foundations on which their communities advanced and prospered. It was men like Robert H. Driscoll—Harvard graduate, school teacher, public servant, and frontier banker—who really developed the region. Others were W. E. Adams, wholesale grocer; Julius Deetkin, pioneer druggist; Dr. D. K. Dickinson, physician and surgeon; Richard C. Lake, hardware dealer and banker; Abram C. Boland, merchant; David H. Clark, rancher; and James Halley, banker. These are only a few of the leaders whose contributions to Black Hills society have been overlooked by the sensationalists.

By the 1920s few, if any, reminders of the frontier were evident in the Hills. A healthy economic life prevailed based on mining, lumber, ranching, and agriculture, and the region's scenic beauties were drawing many people. In fact, the tourist business, although undeveloped, was growing rapidly. Senator Norbeck's work in Custer State Park was attracting state and regional attention. There was a real probability that if Robinson's idea of colossal sculpture could be worked out, the Black Hills would become a mecca for tourists.

The Hills rise like a mountainous island of trees in the midst of endless, grassy plains. A marked blue-black haze first tells the traveler that he is approaching a heavily timbered region. Proximity reveals the prairie grass creeping up the foothills where it is met by an army of white spruce and ponderosa pine.

The Black Hills represent contrast and variety in scenery and geological structure. There are wooded hills, grassy meadows, bubbling brooks lined with birch and aspen, and barren granite pinnacles crowned by majestic Mount Harney. The magnificent Harney Peak range surpasses anything in the region. The giant granite fingers reaching heavenward have caused visitors to gaze in awe ever since the days of General Custer.

N. W. Winchell, state geologist of Minnesota, who accompanied Custer, vividly described the Harney section with unrestrained enthusiasm. "To the northeast," he wrote, "was the grandest sight I ever beheld. This was a truly alpine view. Here was Pelion on Ossa. . . . Very near us, and cutting off our view north, was a series of spindled peaks which, though massive and imposing, proved to be mere pigmies to the giants of the same shape and character that rose in the distance. . . . In the valley below us . . . granitic sugar-loaves, in the background of which, rising nearly as high as old Harney himself, was a perfect nest of organ-pipe peaks, whose sharp spindling tops immediately suggested the name Organ Peaks."

The sharp perpendicular granite outcroppings had been labeled "Needles" and were the pride of the local citizenry. The idea of carving on these points which God had sculptured was fiercely resented by most residents. The higher and rougher range which Winchell referred to as organ pipes is known to modern tourists as the Cathedral Spires.

When the sculptor returned to Rapid City on the evening of September 25, he was entertained by a group of local citizens at the A. & F. Café. He talked enthusiastically about his plans for a great national memorial, and while they were seated around the table, he drew a hasty sketch of Washington and Lincoln as they might appear carved in granite. After handing reporters a lengthy statement, he boarded the evening train, not to return for nearly a year.

"For several years," his statement read, "since the Stone Mountain Memorial has proved a practical possibility and an undertaking awakening and gripping world interest, there has been a constant desire in the north that some sculptural work of equal importance be undertaken, and several suggestions have been made to me with inducement to encourage and undertake some such sculpture in the north, but in every instance those proposing their plans have not realized either the uniqueness nor the dimensions of the southern sculpture and I have been obliged to report against and otherwise discourage their proposals.

"My visit here has been at the earnest request of men interested in the history of our country and its founders. . . . We walked through the veritable garden of the gods, up Mount Harney. . . . I know of no grouping of rock formations that equals those found about this mountain in the Black Hills of South Dakota, nor do I know of any so near the center of our country that is so available to the nation or so suitable for colossal sculpture. . . .

"My present thought is that the opportunity South Dakota has is as real as practical. It is unique; the lesser outcroppings of stone near and along the road should not be disturbed; the large ledges to the rear, near and to the south of Mount Harney are available and should be examined for definite historical portrait characters, preferably national in the largest sense. . . . It would relate itself at once with our national impulse which is greater than a state development."

Borglum's visit produced important results. It encouraged Robinson, who had carried on virtually alone for seven or eight months against strong opposition. Borglum also gave the struggling idea much-needed publicity. Such headlines as GUTZON BORGLUM

VISITS RAPID CITY AND BLACK HILLS and STONE MOUNTAIN GENIUS
LAUDS BLACK HILLS NEEDLE WONDERS FOR HUGE MEMORIAL PROJECT
were not lost on the public. Borglum used the press to great advantage, and his personal enthusiasm was contagious. He convinced
Robinson and several local businessmen that after preliminary
expenses were raised he could solicit funds in the East to complete
any national monument. "I can hardly believe this wonderful thing is
to be handed to us," Robinson wrote.

Naturally, Borglum and Robinson discussed the type of memori-
al that would be carved. The sculptor showed no interest in
Robinson's plan to memorialize a local western hero. From the
beginning he insisted that a monument of merely state or regional
importance would not suit him. He would not agree to carve Red
Cloud or any other Indian chief, or a notable explorer of the region.
There would be no granite statues of Frémont, Bridger, or Lewis and
Clark. The sculptured figures must be of national importance,
Borglum argued. He suggested two great statues of Washington and
Lincoln, certain that these two figures would attract national atten-
tion and support. One of Borglum's first rough sketches showed
Washington and Lincoln carved in the round to the waist. He told
Robinson that such a monument would stir the imagination of peo-
ple throughout the entire world.

The possibility of including other figures was also discussed by the
two men at their first meeting. Robinson, however, opposed the
carving of more than two statues, and he wanted them in the round
rather than in relief. "The more I consider the matter," he wrote, "the
more strongly I feel that the Washington and Lincoln busts should
form the complete preliminary scheme." Then he added, somewhat
reluctantly, "If after they are completed we want to extend the enterprise there will be an abundance of rock left." Borglum wired his
agreement with this tentative plan and declared that these two figures, carved high and alone among the peaks of the Black Hills,
would be an incomparable scheme.

Borglum had come and gone. In spite of the enthusiasm gener-
ated by his visit, concrete plans for beginning the monument were
vague. Money had to be raised, detailed surveys of the granite had
to be made, and state and federal permission to carve in the Harney
National Forest and Custer State Park had to be obtained. Upon
his return to Stone Mountain, Borglum wrote that a complete

examination of the best cliffs was essential. He was ready to return to the Hills for six weeks with Tucker, several assistants, and a photographer. First, however, he thought the Custer State Park Board should appropriate $10,000 for his preliminary survey. He insisted again that no real problem existed regarding finances. But after telling Robinson that only $10,000 would be expected from the state, Borglum suggested that the legislature provide $200,000 to finance a three-year program of carving.

This was Robinson's first contact with Borglum's irresponsible attitude toward finance. He was soon to learn that the sculptor had little interest in money aside from spending it, and that his estimates and calculations were invariably wrong. In any event, Robinson realized the futility of asking the legislature for any such sum. The legislators had been elected on platforms of strict economy and were in no mood to finance new and expensive enterprises. There was not even $10,000 available in the Custer State Park Board fund. Robinson thought some money might be raised from private organizations and suggested the Daughters of the American Revolution. It was obvious from the beginning that it would be a serious problem to raise any substantial funds for the project.

Borglum's visit did not silence opposition to the idea of colossal sculpture in the Hills. He had been careful to assure local people that the Needles near the highway would not be molested. Robinson also insisted that any sculpture would be done at some point distant from the main traveled road. But this did not satisfy Mrs. Johnson and others holding her views. In December 1924, she wrote that she could not agree to carving in the Needles or on any Black Hills mountain. Any human touch, she said, would spoil the "absolutely cosmic" effect. One editor insisted that sculpture was completely out of place "where God's statuary surpasses any possible conception of mere man. . . . Statuary among the Needles or on Harney Peak would be as incongruous and ridiculous as keeping a cow in the rotunda of the capitol building at Pierre."

As he had maintained earlier, Robinson answered that this was a great opportunity for the state. "God makes an Angelo or a Borglum but once in a thousand years," he declared. "Their works are undying. Borglum is now almost sixty years of age, and has not much longer to work." During the autumn Robinson traveled about the state, speaking before the State Federation of Women's Clubs, State Parent-Teachers' Associations, Daughters of the American Revolution, and other organizations. He gained only lukewarm support, and indeed, the women's clubs positively opposed his plans.

But Doane Robinson was not easily discouraged. The vision of the giant sculpture and its potential value to South Dakota only increased his determination. "The project would be of tremendous artistic value," he told Norbeck. "It will 'sell' the Black Hills and the Game Park as nothing else could. The moment Borglum sets chisel into the granite there we have accomplished a publicity; a grip upon American consciousness that we have spent money to secure unavailingly. . . . Money cannot buy the good advertising this thing will give us. . . . Senator, we simply cannot afford to fail in getting this thing started, and South Dakota will bless us for it as soon as they once realize its significance." Then he added that even if the work was not finished, "the wreck of it would bring the world running to see where he [Borglum] had left his mark." Why more people did not see this can be explained only by the fact that few people thought Robinson's ideas would materialize. He accepted this lack of interest philosophically. As a historian, he knew that novel ideas were not readily accepted by the rank and file.

Although Norbeck had given the project active support, he had not done so publicly. Close friends knew of his interest, but he had not made the Black Hills sculpture a major issue. In fact, he did not meet Borglum until early in December 1924. The well driller and the sculptor met in Washington, and immediately respect and affection developed between them. Norbeck's knowledge and appreciation of art surprised and pleased Borglum, and the fact that Borglum was a significant artist was sufficient to win Norbeck's admiration and esteem. Time proved them to be a good working team. Both were men of tremendous energy and ambition, and each held the talents and abilities of the other in high regard.

By the end of 1924 the time had come when either a definite program of action must be taken or the project must be abandoned. Prompt action was necessary, said Norbeck, because such an opportunity might not come again for a century. Robinson and Norbeck agreed that the first step should be to seek permissive state and national legislation. The state legislature was to meet the following

January, so Norbeck asked William Williamson to draw up both state and federal bills.

Both Scandinavians, Norbeck and Williamson had been personal and political friends for many years. In some respects their careers had run a parallel course, although law rather than business had been Williamson's avenue to success and leadership. Born in 1875 on an Iowa farm, he came from an old Norwegian line which he could trace to the mid-eighteenth century. A few years later his family moved to south-central South Dakota, not many miles from the Norbeck homestead. William developed traits of diligence and resourcefulness typical in frontier areas.

During his first eighteen years in South Dakota, Williamson worked on the farm, attended short terms at a rural school, and took a short hitch at country-school teaching. He wanted a college education, and aided by a driving ambition and studious habits, he worked his way through the University of South Dakota, from which he graduated in 1903. Meanwhile, he had moved to Lyman County, west of the Missouri River, where he had entered the newspaper business with his brother.

Even before leaving the university, Williamson had become active in local politics and had stumped his county for the "law and order" ticket in 1902. Law, however, was his main interest. After studying independently, he planned to return to the university in the fall of 1904 to pursue a law degree. But in the meantime, he was nominated for state's attorney on the Republican ticket. Before the election he took the bar examination, passed, and was admitted to practice. Law violators found Williamson a crusading prosecutor who viewed cattle rustling as an especially odious sin. His greatest triumph was the conviction of "Buffalo" (William) George, the most brazen and notorious cattle thief in western South Dakota.

Williamson built up an enviable reputation and a thriving practice. In 1911 he was appointed judge of the Eleventh Circuit where he served until his election to Congress in 1920. In Washington Judge Williamson, as he was known after his appointment to the bench, was a moderately progressive Republican. He and Norbeck cooperated on legislative matters affecting South Dakota, and the Senator depended on the judge's broad legal knowledge and general counsel. When he wrote the first Rushmore legislation, Williamson began an association with the project which lasted until carving was stopped in

1941. Aside from Borglum, he was connected with the work in an active and official way longer than any other person.

The bill he introduced in Congress asked only for permission to carve giant statues in the Harney National Forest. It did not name Borglum as sculptor, specify the figures to be carved, or contain other limiting restrictions. At first the measure called for submitting plans to the Commission on Fine Arts, but this provision was stricken out at Borglum's insistence. Borglum showed early that he would brook no interference, especially from the commission, which had criticized some of his work in connection with Stone Mountain.

Norbeck and Williamson had no trouble getting their bill approved, and it became law on March 3, 1925. But the situation in the state legislature was entirely different. Few lawmakers had any interest in the project, and there was much outright opposition, particularly since the original bill included an appropriation of $10,000. It was hard to get anyone to introduce the measure, but at last Senator J. L. Robbins was induced to take charge of it. In submitting a draft of the bill, Williamson asserted that even if it should not become law, it would publicize the project.

The whole situation was aggravated by the opposition of Governor Carl Gunderson and by differences between the governor and Norbeck. Although Norbeck and Gunderson were both Republicans, their Republicanism differed as much as that of Theodore Roosevelt and Calvin Coolidge. They had become alienated during the bitter primary election campaign of 1924. Norbeck had supported progressive Governor McMaster for the senatorial nomination, while Gunderson, who was the gubernatorial candidate, aided the incumbent, Thomas Sterling. With McMaster's victory, relations between Gunderson and Norbeck became strained. When Norbeck asked the governor to lend his influence to the bill permitting gigantic sculpture, Gunderson refused. Although he told the senator that he would not oppose the measure, it seems that he secretly encouraged the enemies of the bill, Paul Bellamy, a close friend of both men and who went to obtain Gunderson's blessing, but to no avail.

In mid-February the measure was killed by an adverse committee report. Depressed, but full of fight, Robinson called Norbeck in Washington and asked what to do next. Norbeck advised introducing the bill in the senate and, if necessary, lowering the appropriation to $5,000. The Reverend C. D. Erskine of Sturgis now took the lead and offered a new measure which was defeated on February 24. Thus the program was in jeopardy because a parsimonious legislature would not appropriate a sum of $5,000. The lawmakers were to be criticized for not assisting a project which later was to bring both material and cultural benefit to the state. Obviously, the idea had not gripped the imagination of more than a handful of Dakota citizens. Indifference was a greater enemy than positive opposition.

Robinson and Erskine now sought reconsideration for a bill carrying no appropriation. This was passed and received the reluctant approval of Governor Gunderson. The law permitted carving under the supervision of an executive committee, the governor, and two appointees. Washington and Lincoln were specifically designated as the figures to be carved. Robinson, who wanted to confine the memorial to statues of those men, was responsible for that portion of the law.

Under any circumstances, it would have been difficult to get a legislature made up of businessmen, lawyers, and farmers to see the importance of the proposed monument. But a legislative demand for economy was basically responsible for the lawmakers' failure to appropriate any money for the work. This, however, was only part of the trouble. Late in February, when Robinson thought $5,000 might be appropriated, newspaper headlines told of Borglum's dismissal from the Stone Mountain project. Before Robinson was fully aware of what had happened, Borglum's enemies in Georgia had "simply plastered the state with propaganda" against him. "So far as I can learn," Robinson wrote, "every professional man and banker has received the stuff. A cart load of it has been forwarded to me." He might have added that legislative desks, too, were piled high with anti-Borglum charges. For the first time South Dakotans began paying close attention to press dispatches coming from Atlanta. What sort of man was this Borglum who had broken his models and left Stone Mountain in a huff?

Buildings, stairways, and equipment on top of Mount Rushmore.

Taking every opportunity to tell the world of his monumental dream, sculptor Gutzon Borglum speaks to the crowd at the dedication of the Washington figure July 4, 1930. Shown below the building on p. 41 is a flat, smooth area where the inscription was to be carved. The Lincoln head was eventually carved in that area instead.

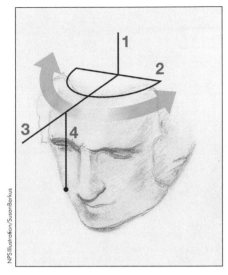

NPS Illustration/Susan Barkus

The Pointing System

The differences between the models in the Sculptor's Studio and the heads on the mountain show how Borglum fine-tuned the four granite giants into true works of art.

The models were sized at a ratio of 1:12—one inch on the model would equal one foot on the mountain. A metal shaft (1) was placed upright at the center of the model's head. Attached at the base of the shaft was a protractor plate (2), marked in degrees, and a horizontal ruled bar (3) that pivoted to measure the angle from the central axis. A weighted plumb line (4) hung from the bar. It slid back and forth to measure the distance from the central head point and raised and lowered to measure vertical distance from the top of the head. Thus, each point on the model received three separate measurements. The numbers were then multiplied by 12 (angles remained the same) and transferred to the granite face via a large-scale pointing mechanism anchored at the top of the mountain.

Opposite: Gutzon Borglum, wearing his customary scarf, directs drillers in work on the granite faces. Bell Photo

Borglum's conception of the entablature and inscription superimposed on a photograph of the mountain. The first two sections were written by Calvin Coolidge and modified by Borglum. This phase of the project was never completed.

CHAPTER FOUR

Stone Mountain

EARLY in 1915 Jack T. Graves, a Georgia newspaperman, suggested the possibility of carving some monument on Stone Mountain. Graves did not push his idea, but his editorial aroused the imagination of Mrs. C. Helen Plane, the elderly leader of the United Daughters of the Confederacy. Mrs. Plane wrote to Borglum about carving a Confederate memorial. Among other things, she suggested "a great tablet cut into the side of the mountain carrying some record of the war between the states."

Always attracted by the colossal and the unusual, Borglum consented to investigate the matter. He arrived in Atlanta on August 17, where he was entertained at the home of Samuel H. Venable, owner of the mountain. It was first suggested to Borglum that a memorial to Robert E. Lee might be appropriate. Could the head of Lee be carved on the side of Stone Mountain, asked his hosts? Borglum studied the rock. There before him was a most unique formation: a crescent-shaped granite mountain, nine hundred feet high and three thousand feet long, rising sharply out of the rolling countryside some sixteen miles from Atlanta. To carve the head of Lee or to inscribe a tablet on a working face eight hundred by fifteen hundred feet would be like "pasting a postage stamp on the side of a house. . . . It must be something grander than that," he declared. Mrs. Plane had been right about the availability of Stone Mountain, but her ideas for a memorial were cramped and lacked imagination. Borglum possessed an abundance of imagination.

During the three days he spent at Stone Mountain and Atlanta, a tremendous thought seized him. Why not carve the legions of Lee on the march? Borglum's design would "portray the mobilization of the mental and physical energy of the South, which should indicate all branches of the Confederate army on the march with a central group of such leaders as Lee, Davis, Jackson, Johnston, Forrest and

45

Stuart." Carved in granite, such a monument would preserve the record of southern glory for thousands of years. Here was something that should arouse the interest and win the backing of every loyal southerner.

So enthusiastic were those to whom Borglum talked that the next month a Stone Mountain Confederate Monumental Association was formed. Samuel H. Venable, a wealthy Atlantan, gave to the association the face of the rock and an area around the base. (He reportedly had traded a mule for the mountain many years before.) A formal dedication was held in May 1916.

Borglum's conception was magnificent. It called for carving a panorama of Southern military might trailing across the mountainside for nearly 1,500 feet—more than a quarter of a mile of marching men, stamping horses, and rolling guns. Lee, Jefferson Davis, and Stonewall Jackson were to be the central and dominating figures. Carved in bold bas-relief, these leaders would be followed by cavalry, artillery, and foot soldiers shown in simple relief or sketched in by chisel. The frieze was so designed that the figures would all *appear* in full relief, moving over the surface of the mountain, not across its side. Borglum planned a 20-foot head of Lee, and the distance from the top of the general's head to his horse Traveler's knee would be about 150 feet.

In addition to the giant figures, he intended to hew a great hall of records in the base of the mountain. It would be 180 feet long, 60 feet wide, and 40 feet high. This vast vault was to serve as a museum and archive for Confederate records. A large open amphitheater would complete the plan.

No modern artist had conceived or executed so vast a design. Borglum's vision overshadowed anything accomplished by the ancients. He was thoroughly familiar with the sculptural art of antiquity and was greatly influenced by it. Nothing indicates, however, that he knew of a suggestion by Thomas Hart Benton that a great statue of Columbus be carved on some granite peak in the Rocky Mountains. Speaking in favor of a national road from Washington to San Francisco in 1849, Benton had declared in his best spread-eagle style that the road "shall be adorned with its crowning honor— the colossal statue to the great Columbus—whose design it accomplished, hewn from a granite mass or a peak on the Rocky Mountains overlooking the road—the mountain itself a pedestal and the statue a part of the mountain—pointing with outstretched arm to the western horizon, and saying to the flying passengers—'There is the East; there is India.'"

Probably the nearest thing to Borglum's idea was the Persian Behistun relief. In the late sixth century B.C., Darius the Great had a bas-relief of himself carved on a lofty cliff at Behistun. He is posed standing with his foot on a fallen enemy, his hand raised toward approaching prisoners. Behind him stand two attendants. As traders journeyed between Babylonia and the Iranian Plains they passed this monument, 50 feet wide, 25 feet high, and 155 feet above the valley below. A great inscription in three languages records for all time the exploits of an ambitious and egotistical king.

The Egyptians, Greeks, and Romans were all creators of gigantic monuments. In Egypt the Great Sphinx of Gizeh, which is 200 feet tall, has inspired awe and wonder for nearly five thousand years. This is thought to be the portrait of King Khafre, Egyptian monarch and builder of the Second Pyramid. The twin Memnon Colossi, which are seated portraits of Amenophis III, tower 60 feet in height as they guard the king's tomb. Mountain-carving was not unknown in this ancient country, for in the mountains of Nubia great temple courts were hewn out by Rameses II. Four great statues, 75 feet high, guard the entrance to the mammoth rock temple at Abu Simbel.

The Greeks and Romans did not undertake mountain sculpture, although the artist Stasicrates, a man of rare boldness and imagination, suggested the idea to Alexander the Great. "If . . . Alexander should so order," he said, "he [Stasicrates] would make out of Mount Athos a most enduring and most conspicuous statue of the kings, which in its left hand should hold a city of ten thousand inhabitants, and with its right should pour forth a river running with generous current into the sea."

Alexander declined Stasicrates' suggestion, but gigantic bronzes were quite common in Greece and Rome. The Colossus of Rhodes, a tremendous bronze built to the Greek God Helios, was completed by Chares in 280 B.C. after twelve years. The Colossus was considered one of the Seven Wonders of the World. Scholars have estimated that it was approximately 120 feet tall. Nor were the Romans to be outdone. In the first century, the infamous Nero commissioned the sculptor Zenodoras to do a figure of himself. Zenodoras produced a colossal bronze statue 100 feet high.

These are some of the more familiar great monuments of ancient times to which Borglum often referred.* He was impressed by sheer size, but he insisted that no real cause or spiritual value was represented in any of these works. They had been produced to satisfy the egotism of a Rameses, a Darius, or a Nero, or perhaps to glorify some god. At Stone Mountain Borglum saw an opportunity to carve the largest monument in history. Moreover, he sensed a chance to immortalize himself.

Borglum once told reporter Joe Beckley of the *New York Evening Mail* that he had always wanted to "remodel a state or make over a mountain range or something like that." Certainly, if this conception could be realized, it would give the sculptor a chance to work off some of his imprisoned energies. It would also give him an opportunity to build a monument to a cause or an ideal. "I am celebrating an idea," he said of Stone Mountain, "the idea of strength, courage, self-sacrifice and love. These men who fought for a lost cause went forth fearlessly to do their best as they saw it. That is the idea I want to perpetuate on that rock—the going forward to meet the unknown at the call of right and truth as one sees it." He expressed the hope that statues of individuals, dedicated to a "Dr. Cooper or a Bill Smith," would soon cease to exist in the United States.

During 1916 and 1917 some preliminary work was done. Borglum made his models, completed some surveys, and had a stairway built. He spoke throughout the South and more than anyone else helped to quicken public interest. Borglum and Venable paid these early expenses to the extent of nearly $25,000.

World War I interrupted the work. It was not until 1922 that the Stone Mountain Monumental Association was reorganized and definite plans were made to begin. In this reorganization the United Daughters of the Confederacy lost their voice in the project, and control fell into the hands of a group of Atlanta businessmen. The next year the association contracted with Borglum to do seven equestrian figures for $250,000. The sculptor was to furnish the models, the labor, and part of the equipment.

Borglum later admitted that he had not foreseen the tremendous engineering difficulties of mountain sculpture. Since there were no modern precedents, he had to proceed by trial and error. The first

---

*Borlgum gave no indication that he had heard of the 196-foot Buddha which was carved about 700 A.D. in a cliff rising from the Min River near Kiating, China.

problem was to determine a suitable location. Since he must depend on the sun for lighting, it was essential to select rock which would show up best from the point of vision below. Borglum had always been intensely concerned with the effect of light and shade on sculptural forms. After months of study, he chose the northeast side for carving. In this position, light would constantly strike the upper part of his mounted figures.

The second problem was purely mechanical. Working on a mountainside was hazardous. How could he get to his "canvas" and work there with ease and safety? After much experiment, walks were built and anchored in the mountain with steel pins, and then hoists, sheds, and tool shops were constructed. Workmen were lowered over the sharp mountain precipice in leather-steel swing seats fastened to flexible cables. The seats were lowered and raised by hand-operated hoists or winches.

Outlining the figures on the mountain preparatory to actual carving posed an additional problem. Borglum first thought of sketching the figures in white paint while lowered in a swing seat. But this proved too slow and difficult. So he worked out a scheme for throwing a sketch of his model on the rock surface with a powerful projecting lamp. After eliminating distortions and solving other technical problems, he had his workmen outline the figures with paint at night.

Finally, there was the matter of actual carving. Borglum originally thought in terms of handwork, but he soon realized that this would be too slow and costly. There was so much useless stone to be removed that a faster and cheaper method must be devised. Dynamite was the solution. He hesitated to employ explosives, however, without knowing the exact effect of the blast. Necessary stone might be cracked or crumbled unless he could control the measure of the explosion. It was not until he was encouraged by a Belgian engineer that Borglum turned to this rapid method of stone removal. From that time onward he carved with pneumatic drills and dynamite.

With the historical difficulties overcome, and several hundred thousand dollars in cash and pledges (mostly pledges), carving now proceeded. The twenty-foot head of Lee was unveiled on January 19, 1924. Borglum arranged an elaborate ceremony and in his dramatic manner personally carried ninety-four-year-old Mrs. Plane to the platform. Devoted followers of Lee sat on the front row of the observation platform and watched tearfully as the flag slipped from the face of their old commander. "My God, it's Lee," one reverently murmured.

But progress on the monument was of short duration. Soon after the head was unveiled, Borglum and his supervisory association began having trouble. Difficulty arose over lack of understanding between the sculptor and Hollins N. Randolph, president of the association. The duties of Randolph and his group were to raise money and administer the project generally, while Borglum had the responsibility of making the designs and models and supervising the actual carving. Neither Borglum nor Randolph would confine himself to his own business. Randolph charged that Borglum was absent from the mountain, engaged in other activities during much of 1924. The trip to South Dakota and the time spent at Stamford working out plans for a statue of Mustapha Kemal, the president of Turkey, were cited as examples. As a result, Randolph declared, the work had been retarded. A more serious complaint against the sculptor was that he had received money out of proportion to his accomplishments. After reportedly spending about $185,000, the association found only one-third of the work roughed out, although Borglum had said he could finish the central group for $250,000.

On the other hand, Borglum argued that the association had not raised sufficient funds and that it had no "firm or fast plans." He charged that the South was not really behind the memorial. One report asserted that the Ku Klux Klan was attempting to gain control of the project and that this was hurting prospective support. Randolph, so Borglum charged, was trying to use the monument for political purposes and was handling the funds in a careless manner.

The situation became explosive early in 1925. Dissatisfied with the association's administration, Borglum wrote complainingly to President Coolidge on January 21. He urged the President to appoint a committee of twelve or fifteen national leaders as an advisory committee for the Stone Mountain Monumental Association. This attempt to bypass Randolph and the association added to the strain between the sculptor and his supervisors. On February 25 the association's executive committee dismissed Borglum.

While the committee was in session, Borglum arrived in Atlanta and was met at the station by Mrs. Borglum and his chief engineer,

Jesse G. Tucker. Venable also joined the party. As this group motored to the mountain, Venable, a member of the committee, informed Borglum that plans were being made to seize his models and designs. By the time Borglum arrived at his studio, he had concluded that only by breaking his models could he protect the integrity of his art. He could not permit any other artist to use them. Without consulting anyone, he ordered his choreboy to smash the large plaster head of Lee. Then he ascended the mountain and ordered the head of Jackson and Lee's shoulders pushed over the ledge. This accomplished, he hastily departed.

The officers of the association were furious. They swore out a warrant for Borglum's arrest, claiming that he had committed "malicious mischief" in destroying his models. A suit was filed against him for $50,000. Almost at once a court order was obtained enjoining Borglum from entering his studio or climbing the mountain, but officers arrived too late to apprehend him. The shattered remains of Lee's head littering the studio floor told of Borglum's recent departure. For several days his whereabouts were undisclosed. Although Borglum was protected by the governor of North Carolina, news releases compared him to a bank robber and told how police from four states searched for him.

Borglum, while in North Carolina, hurled vitriolic accusations against the association. He was reported as saying, "I'll rot in jail forever before I will give the key to my design . . . to that committee." He expressed a willingness to complete the memorial but refused to work with the group in charge. He added that if he had been left free he could have raised sufficient money to complete the monument. Repeatedly he charged Randolph with loose and irregular financial practices. Writing in *Plain Talk*, Craig F. Thompson later asserted that strong evidence existed to substantiate these charges against the association.

The fight was basically over whether Borglum or the association was to control the project. The *New York Times* declared that must of the trouble could have been avoided. Borglum had committed himself to carving. When he sought to raise money and undertook additional responsibility, he developed a sense of ownership that was resented by those under whom he was supposedly working. A local Georgia editor took much the same view. "The longer Randolph was in charge the more firmly convinced he became that he was not only a great business manager, but a great sculptor, and the more Borglum saw the memorial business methods the surer he became that he not only was a great sculptor but a great business manager."

Borglum found it impossible to work "under," or be subordinate to, anyone, and it was not easy for him to cooperate with others. Senator Norbeck once said of him, "His enthusiasm knows no bounds and his originality is marvelous . . . but his unwillingness to cooperate with anyone else is simply astonishing." Left alone, Borglum could accomplish wonders, but in a project where give-and-take was essential, he was sadly deficient. His attitude is shown by a statement made some five years later: "I was dismissed by the Stone Mountain Association," he said, "because it was charged I dominated the entire project. I do not deny this. But I am going back and dominate the project without interference." It should be added that Randolph failed completely to understand the sculptor.

Both Borglum and Randolph sought public support, and their controversy made front-page news all over the nation. The resolution that discharged Borglum stated, "His loudly professional admiration for the valor of the soldiers of the South begins and ends at the door of the association's treasury. . . . His inordinate demands for money not due him, his offensive egotism and his delusions of grandeur render it impossible to deal with him." Many Atlanta officials and civic clubs agreed with the association. But it was difficult, if not impossible, to best Borglum in a newspaper controversy.

Within a few days it became clear that most of the editorial comment was sympathetic to Borglum. The *New York Times* was openly friendly. It asserted that both sides shared the blame, "but by far the greater part of it is going to those who, by standing on petty rights, have driven away from a great artistic undertaking a man whose exceptional competency to carry it to successful completion is recognized by all qualified judges." The editor admitted that Borglum was difficult but asked, "What of it?" The newspaper said on another occasion, "That he is not like other men is not a fault since upon the difference largely depends his competency." Later the *Times* argued that if Randoph and his committee could not "forget their grievances against the temperamental genius and take him back, then they should gracefully retire." The *Chicago Tribune* said that Borglum's temperament was an "artistic prerogative" that should be ignored. The editor praised his conception and concluded by saying,

"Dixie had better get Gutzon back." In a survey of several leading newspapers, the *Literary Digest* found a friendly attitude toward Borglum.

Not even the sympathetic *New York Times* denied that many of the charges made against Borglum "have more or less foundation in fact." But the general belief seemed to be that the committee was under a heavier obligation to "get along with Mr. Borglum than he was to get along with them." The *Times* declared that the officials should not have quarreled with him over "miserable money matters" or insisted that he work so many hours a day like a bricklayer. This was Borglum's contention and his justification for being absent from the work.

While Borglum's popularity continued high, the association was forced on the defensive. In March it issued an eight-page booklet justifying the sculptor's discharge. He was accused of gross neglect of work, attempts to use the memorial for personal profit, a desire to assume the association's responsibilities, absence from his job, and "lust for money." Influential people throughout the United States were bombarded with copies of this statement, and South Dakotans seemed to be at the top of the mailing list. Senator Norbeck was only one of many who received a copy. Randoph also distributed a form letter which carried nearly the same charges. The propaganda seemed to have little effect in South Dakota. Norbeck replied philosophically, "I admit it would be just as easy to prove that a good artist was not even an average business man, as it would be to prove that a good business man was not even an average artist."

Nothing came of the association's attempt to jail Borglum, and the governors of Georgia and North Carolina acted as peacemakers. Borglum had the last word when early in March he announced triumphantly that he had contracted to carve the figures of Washington and Lincoln in the Black Hills. No contract had been signed, but it was clearly understood that Borglum would do any work undertaken. He apparently became uneasy, however, for within a few weeks he wrote to Norbeck asking if those interested in the Black Hills project were in a position to retain him.

What was the truth of the Stone Mountain controversy? The unfortunate outcome was ultimately regretted by almost everyone, including Borglum. Most people realized that a golden opportunity had been muffed. Although financial problems had at first retarded the work, Congress authorized the coining of five million memorial half dollars to be sold at one dollar each. These were just going on sale and promised adequate financing.

Borglum and Randolph, who spoke most frequently for the association, must share responsibility for the disaster. It is true that Borglum was absent from the work for long periods, that he made demands for money beyond the terms of his agreement, and that he did not always abide by a strict legal interpretation of his contract. On the other hand, Randolph failed to see that it was needless for Borglum to be constantly on hand. His models and designs were being carried out largely by engineers. So long as he produced the designs and supervised the work, he should have been free for other tasks. The *New York Times* was right in saying that it was unreasonable to expect Borglum to punch a time clock like an ordinary miner or mason. He needed and deserved time to dream his dreams and to be free from ordinary cares.

When the whole problem is considered, most of Randolph's complaints seem petty, with the exception of Borglum's demands for money. Moreover, the association never allowed the sculptor credit for the vast publicity he had given the memorial. As the *Richmond Times-Dispatch* asserted, Borglum, not the association, was "stirring the flame of enthusiasm for the Stone Mountain project." There is no available evidence that the association made a real effort to understand Borglum and his problems or to make allowances for the temperament and idiosyncrasies that were a part of his genius. That Borglum was hard to deal with, there is no doubt. But the association should have shown greater cooperation and understanding. In not doing so, it ruined the chances for the Stone Mountain memorial.

After Borglum was dismissed he was free for other work. There was little likelihood that he would be recalled to Georgia in the fore-seeable future. He had the support of many friends and constantly talked about returning, but the re-election of Randoph as president of the association meant continued control by the anti-Borglum faction. In April, Augustus Lukeman of New York (who reportedly feared high places) was selected to finish the memorial. After partially destroying Borglum's head of Lee, Lukeman carved another which was unveiled in 1928. At that point the whole project miserably collapsed for lack of funds. Artistically, Lukeman could not compare with Borglum. At the time of Borglum's dismissal the *Chicago Tribune* had warned, "To start a monumental work and then to change sculptors is heading straight for failure. A great sculptor will not undertake the second hand job; and a mediocrity will spoil it." These were prophetic words.*

But the tragedy in Georgia was not a total loss. Without the Stone Mountain fiasco there would have been no Mount Rushmore Memorial. Even before he was dismissed, Borglum explained to Robinson that if he had not solved difficult engineering problems at Stone Mountain, he could not have launched the Black Hills project. Moreover, those in charge of the South Dakota work learned early that Borglum was difficult to work with and that they must go beyond the line of ordinary patience and cooperation to succeed with him. Stone Mountain also had its effect upon Borglum. On many a trying occasion he might have quit at Mount Rushmore had not the specter of Stone Mountain haunted him. He frankly admitted that he wanted to vindicate himself elsewhere. Departing from Georgia, Borglum haughtily indicated that the citizens of the South could now stew in their own juice for a time.

---

*From 1928 until 1964 no carving occurred at Stone Mountain. Early in 1964 Walker Hancock, a Massachusetts sculptor, was employed to complete a Confederate memorial consisting of the figures of Jefferson Davis, Robert E. Lee, and Thomas J. ("Stonewall") Jackson. The Stone Mountain Memorial was completed and dedicated in May 1970.

CHAPTER FIVE

"We'll Call the Damn Thing Rushmore"

"WHATEVER comes of the Stone Mountain affair I have much faith in Borglum and in his capacity for doing things." Thus Robinson wrote during the difficulties in Georgia. Now someone had to do something to get the South Dakota project started. Legislation to permit carving was on the statute books, but without money the law seemed unworkable. Financing was the crux of the whole affair. Robinson's idea would live or die on the ability of those interested to raise funds for the sculpture.

Robinson had no pipeline to the bank accounts of wealthy art patrons, and Norbeck's official position made it embarrassing for him to approach the sources of great wealth. Perhaps a small amount could be solicited in South Dakota, but no one believed it would exceed $25,000, or at the most, $50,000. Could Borglum tap the purses of his rich friends? He believed that he could. He told Norbeck in January 1925 that he knew where $100,000 could be raised for the proposed monument. In fact, Borglum startled Norbeck with his confidence and enthusiasm in regard to soliciting funds. "This stuff sounds too dreamy for a man like me who has been bumped ten thousand times by stern realities," the senator confided.

In April Borglum wrote that he was free to go to South Dakota to get the project started. But Norbeck had to reply that funds were not yet available for any preliminary work. Robinson was trying to obtain some financial backing, but this was not easy in a state where 140 banks were closed. Norbeck, however, hoped for better things. He expressed the wish that Borglum would not get "tied up" with other work so that he could not undertake the South Dakota memorial. Borglum promised to remain available.

If no surveying or carving could be undertaken, at least plans for the sculptural group might be developed. Robinson's idea of carving two presidents in the round was gradually abandoned during the early part of 1925. Norbeck was the first to urge that Washington and Lincoln, standing alone sentinel-like in the Hills, would not be appropriate. "I did not dare tell Doane Robinson that I am trying to talk Borglum out of his Washington-Lincoln Siamese Twins idea," he wrote a friend. The senator insisted that a statue of Theodore Roosevelt would be much more suitable. Borglum admitted that Norbeck was responsible for his consideration of Roosevelt, but he was not at first convinced that the Trustbuster should be included in the group, and he expressed strong opposition to carving the Roosevelt statue first.

Yet it is not surprising that Roosevelt was ultimately added. Borglum and Norbeck had both been militant Bull Moosers and were devoted to the former President's political ideals. Roosevelt had a direct connection with the West in spite of his long career in an eastern metropolis. Many people viewed him as a westerner because he had lived for a time on a Dakota ranch and possessed many western characteristics. Furthermore, Borglum was thinking more and more of a monument of "Empire Builders" or "Nation Builders." Through Roosevelt the United States had acquired the Panama Canal Zone, which ultimately provided a waterway connecting the two oceans washing American shores. In Borglum's eyes this achievement completed the national expansion of the United States—reasoning which did not impress Norbeck. The senator argued that Roosevelt should be included because of his trust-busting activities and his leadership in demanding a higher standard of political morality.

The sculptor claimed that his personal feeling did not enter into the selection of Roosevelt. Yet if Borglum and Norbeck had not been loyal Roosevelt men, it is unlikely that his face would appear on Mount Rushmore today. Considering Borglum's idea of a memorial to "Empire Builders," a much better case might have been made for expansionist James K. Polk, and if progressivism and political morality were to be the criteria, the followers of Woodrow Wilson could logically claim a place for their leader.

After Borglum decided to include Theodore Roosevelt, he considered for a time carving only those figures whose careers touched the West or the frontier. He asked Norbeck's reaction to confining the sculpture to Lincoln and Roosevelt, both of whom were connected with frontier life. But as late as April 1925, Borglum's ideas were still vague. He simply wrote to Robinson that he would like to place two or three colossal figures on Mount Harney.

Gradually, the image of an incomparable national shrine took form in the artist's mind. Two elements dominated his thoughts. First of all, the monument must be large. For nearly a quarter of a century Borglum had been urging gigantic American art. Upon his return from Europe in 1901, he concluded that "the amazing and expanding character" of American civilization "clearly demands an enlarged dimension—a new scale." "We are living in an age of the colossal," he once said. "Our age will some day . . . be called the 'Colossal Age.'" Borglum had asserted in 1916, "There is not a monument in this country as big as a snuff box."

Borglum was impressed with the bigness of America, its buildings, bridges, factories, farms, and other manifestations of its greatness. To correspond with these developments, American art must be of magnitude. "My big mission in life is to get the American people to look at art in a big way and to get away from this petty stuff," he told Norbeck. Borglum had reached the stage in life where he wanted to engage in the largest type of artwork in the world and leave behind him a monument which would stand for all time as a record of supreme achievement—a monument to the nation and to himself. Borglum would stun his onlookers by sculpturing huge masses and awe them with the epic subject represented. He repeatedly declared, "A monument's dimensions should be determined by the importance to civilization of the events commemorated."

It was equally important to Borglum that the memorial represent the spirit and ideals of American geographical expansion and political development. Borglum was proud of his country's growth, and he gloried in its democratic ideals and institutions. Nothing gripped his imagination or motivated his life more than the westward sweep of American civilization. The romance and adventure of American history were to him a thrilling and significant story. Here he saw an opportunity to symbolize and portray the material progress of a people who, in his judgment, were unequalled in world history. He would pay no monument to a dead king or a vain military conqueror, but to the living ideals embodied in America. Therefore, his memorial would be large, in keeping with his country's emphasis on, and respect for, bigness. The sculptured portraits would include those who, in his estimation, contributed most to the nation's "creation and preservation."

It is not known exactly when he finally chose Washington, Jefferson, Lincoln, and Theodore Roosevelt for his group. By the middle of 1925, however, newspapers were referring to this plan, and Borglum was writing about it. For a time the scheme was temporarily revised to include only three statues. In addition to the colossal figures, Borglum planned a vast entablature, eighty by one hundred feet, on which would be carved what he considered the nine great events in American history: independence, the establishment of the republic under the Constitution, the Louisiana Purchase, the admission of Texas, and the acquisition of Florida, California, Oregon, Alaska, and the Panama Canal Zone. Engraved in three-foot letters on the mountainside would be a permanent account of the creation and expansion of the republic. Lewis and Clark, Sam Houston, John C. Frémont, William Seward, Theodore Roosevelt, and Marcus Whitman were among the names Borglum intended to place on the tablet. If these ideas could be realized, it would be the most flamboyant gesture ever made by man in the name of art.

Then and afterward, Borglum was obliged to defend his selection of American leaders. He argued that Washington had contributed so much to independence, the Constitutional Convention, and the establishment of the government that he must be the leading and dominant figure. No one seriously disagreed. Jefferson's purchase of Louisiana typified to Borglum the entire spirit of American continental growth. There was little objection to memorializing this expansionist and great political philosopher. Lincoln could lay claim to preserving the Union.

Borglum's inclusion of Roosevelt brought the greatest amount of criticism and controversy. Many people felt that he did not deserve permanent enshrinement since too little time had elapsed since his death to allow a mature judgment of his life based upon historical perspective. But the sculptor argued that he could "think of none more fitting." Roosevelt, he asserted, was "preeminently an all-American President" and reflected the "restless Anglo-Saxon spirit that made the ocean-to-ocean republic" inevitable. Though historians might criticize Borglum's choices, he never claimed to be selecting the four greatest men in American history.

Robinson was never completely reconciled to Borglum's plans. He displayed his dissatisfaction when he wrote, "In the determination of the final form of the memorial I sometimes think that the solitary figure of Washington . . . would be the most effective thing we could do." But Borglum would not hear of this. He replied that they must stick to the idea of building a great national memorial—and there was no use arguing with Borglum.

What the Black Hills project lacked in actual support, Borglum supplied in enthusiasm. He was not easily discouraged, for he looked upon discouragement as a weakness, almost as a disease. Even with no money at hand, he volunteered to go to South Dakota and make a survey of the granite peaks to find the one which would lend itself to his ideas of colossal sculpture. And only by a more detailed examination could he determine whether or not a granite of suitable texture existed.

No sooner had he arrived in South Dakota than newspaper reporters began following his every move. Borglum liked this attention. Representatives of the press soon learned what eastern and southern newsmen already knew: Borglum made news. He arrived in Pierre on August 10 en route to the Black Hills and there conferred with Robinson, and also with Governor Gunderson who was not yet sympathetic to mountain carving. Borglum gave no indication of being disheartened by the bleak financial outlook or the governor's indifference. Once the monument was started and took on a national character, he said, the state would be deluged with eager and curious tourists. He told Gunderson that hard surface highways would be required to meet increased traffic needs.

The next morning the *Rapid City Daily Journal* announced in headlines an inch high: GUTZON BORGLUM HERE TO CHART HARNEY PEAK. Senator Norbeck accompanied him. At noon Borglum attended a Lions Club luncheon and afterward spoke to a group of interested citizens in the Baptist church. He again stated positively that there would be no carving in the Needles. He had no intention of "making totem poles of these wonderful spires." He went on to say, "Instead, we want to go back into the Hills, find some now unknown mountain, and carve these figures upon them. They must be high. The statuary must be simple and possessed of dignity." Borglum explained to his somewhat skeptical audience that he intended to locate a suitable mountain, measure it, and prepare sketches for the proposed work. "We should know within the next ten days whether the project will be attempted," he concluded.

Borglum indicated that South Dakotans should congratulate themselves on his decision to carve in their state. "You have a unique opportunity," he declared. "I have been asked by seven different states to carve some statuary." Stone Mountain, he emphasized, was becoming a major tourist attraction in Georgia, and he suggested that if statues of three or four "great empire builders" were carved, "the whole world will speak of South Dakota."

Following his informal talk, Borglum and Norbeck left for the Game Lodge in Custer State Park, where Borglum planned to headquarter while seeking granite suitable for his supreme artistic achievement. Norbeck, who was thoroughly familiar with the area, intended to ride with Borglum but was called to the eastern part of the state on business. Therefore, before he left, the senator engaged Theodore Shoemaker, state forester and resident of the Hills since 1885, to guide the artist. Shoemaker promised to show Borglum every mountain suitable to sculpture in gigantic proportions.

The next day Borglum, his son Lincoln, and Ray Sanders, a horseman at the Game Lodge, rode toward Harney Peak. Borglum made a striking figure as he trailed off over the pine-covered hills. He was garbed in golfing knickers, knitted sweater, flowing black ascot tie, and sneakers which gave him secure footing on mountain slopes. His dark eyes peered searchingly from under the narrow brim of his black Stetson. A heavy, ragged mustache added to his unique appearance.

Several miles from the lodge, Shoemaker met Borglum and guided him to the heart of the great granite pinnacles. Since the idea of carving among the Needles had been abandoned, he led the party a considerable distance from the highway into a rugged and remote section. After showing Borglum several unsatisfactory cliffs and spires, Shoemaker approached a large granite mountain northeast of Harney Peak. As they neared the giant mass of sullen rock, he asked Borglum not to look until they reached a certain vantage point. When the artist opened his eyes, there before him in all its rugged grandeur stood Mount Rushmore, towering 5,725 feet above sea level. It was capped with a solid granite head about 1,000 feet long and 400 feet wide, and its east side presented a 300-foot perpendicular slab.

For a moment, Borglum shifted his gaze from Mount Rushmore and caught a glimpse of Old Baldy about a half-mile to the north. Jubilantly, he exclaimed, "I would like to carve a statue of Roosevelt on horseback on that mountain." But even from that distance he could see the deep cracks and crevices which scarred the mountain. Mount Rushmore, however, was another matter. To be sure, the mountain was rough and had obvious blemishes—natural seams, the result of millions of years of weathering and erosion. The layman might consider it impossible to carve on such a surface, but Borglum did not believe the imperfections were so deep that the granite was unusable. Hastily he pulled a notebook from his pocket and sketched the head of Washington as it might appear on the mountain in full relief. A day later he made a record of how he thought the entablature might look.

During the next two days Borglum examined other structures, but none seemed as suitable as Mount Rushmore. He was assisted by Colonel M. L. Shade, C. C. Gideon, and others. The following week a larger party made a more detailed survey of the mountain. The Reverend C. H. Loocke of Rapid City took several pictures of Mount Rushmore to be used by Borglum in making sketches and plans. The artist scaled the mountain several times and tentatively concluded that the stone was satisfactory. Writing in his diary, Borglum admitted that he had doubted ever to find suitable granite in sufficient proportions. But here was a mountain which would permit the carving of colossal figures. He was happy and encouraged.

The surface of the mountain which was adaptable to sculpture was ideally located from the viewpoint of lighting. Borglum had always insisted that light was a factor of utmost importance in any sculpture. Lengthwise, the mountain stood in a north-south direction. The bold chunk of granite composing the southeast shoulder was situated so that the sun would light it much of the day. In this respect, Rushmore was superior to any other mountain examined.

When Borglum returned to Rapid City, he bubbled with enthusiasm. There was no mountain of granite in the United States comparable to Rushmore, he said. More detailed engineering tests would be necessary, of course, but he added, "It looks good, I believe it's all right."

The mountain which seemed so promising to Borglum was northeast of Harney Peak and about three miles southwest of Keystone, a small mining village. It was situated in a strikingly scenic part of the Hills, isolated and alone in its natural majesty. No one inhabited the immediate area around the peak, there were no roads leading to it other than logging trails, and it could be approached only with great difficulty on foot or horseback.

The Keystone region was rich in history and tradition. It was typical of hundreds of small mining communities throughout the West whose fortunes had risen and fallen on the vagaries of fate. Ever since gold had first been panned from Grizzly and Battle Creeks in 1876, the area had tottered between poverty and prosperity. The village had begun as a row of shabby prospectors' cabins at the confluence of the two creeks, had grown to a population of about two thousand in the 1890s, and then had declined to between three and four hundred souls. One of the most famous and profitable mines was the Holy Terror, which contributed to the boom period of the late nineteenth century.

But grizzled prospectors discovered that gold was not the only valuable mineral in the vicinity. There were mica, spodumene, amblygonite, feldspar, tourmaline, beryl, cassiterite, and others. In 1883 a tin mine, the Etta, was opened, which caused excitement among eastern investors. Shortly after, James Wilson, a New York mining promoter, engaged Professor Gilbert E. Bailey, state geologist of Wyoming, to examine mining claims in the area where Keystone was later located. In need of legal talent as well as geological advice, Wilson hired Charles E. Rushmore, a young but able New York attorney, to check the titles to properties on which Bailey reported favorably.

Although an easterner, Rushmore quickly made friends among the miners and prospectors. One day he was returning to the headquarters of the Harney Peak Consolidated Tin Company, Ltd., located at Pine Camp, which was north of the great granite peak soon to bear his name. With him were David N. Swanzey, a local businessman, and William W. Challis, a prospector and guide. As they neared this spectacular mountain, Rushmore turned to Challis and asked its name. Challis jestingly replied: "Never had any, but it has now—we'll call the damn thing Rushmore."[*] Thus, in 1885, the chance remark of a rough miner to a visiting lawyer fastened a permanent name to the mountain. No one imagined that within half a century the world's greatest memorial would be carved upon it. Whether or not the name seemed suitable in later years, no amount of agitation could change it. Rushmore would be permanent.

---

[*]Another account quoted Challis saying, "Twain't got no name, but from now on we'll call her Rushmore by God-damn." The United States Board of Geographic Names officially recognized the name "Mount Rushmore" in June 1930.

Geologically, Mount Rushmore is one of the oldest outcroppings in the world. The Harney Range of which Rushmore is a part represents the most exposed view of the granite core of the Black Hills. Millions of years of erosion have swept away the rocks which once overlaid the Black Hills, leaving exposed the bare granite outcrops. The mountain is chiefly a biotite-muscovite granite interlaced with pegmatitic veins. These veins have an abundance of such accessory minerals as tourmaline and beryl. However, Rushmore granite is not as typically pegmatitic or coarse-grained as most of the Harney Range. Because of its smoother grain and finer texture, Mount Rushmore is more suitable for carving than most of the surrounding peaks.

How long will Mount Rushmore National Memorial last? Geologists estimate that the mountain weathers one inch every ten thousand years. Physical weathering depends partly on how the memorial is maintained by the National Park Service.

Borglum did not leave Rapid City until after Senator Norbeck returned. Meanwhile, he fished in Rapid Creek and gave constant interviews to news-hungry reporters. Arriving on August 23, Norbeck went over tentative plans with the artist, and together they again visited Mount Rushmore as well as other peaks. Norbeck wished to ascertain personally that Rushmore was the best possible selection.

During his stay in the Hills, Borglum explained that it would be necessary to bring his engineer Jesse G. Tucker and other assistants to test the rock before final plans could be drawn. But his preliminary surveys had convinced him that Rushmore was suitable. "We are delighted with the entire outlook," he said, "and we are determined to make this project tell the story of the country." At this time Borglum usually spoke of carving only three figures, Jefferson, Lincoln, and Roosevelt. These presidents had all been in some way connected with the West. However, he never seriously considered omitting Washington. The first president was the only figure sketched in his original notebook. In any event, before boarding the train on August 26, he assured his well-wishers that the memorial would be "the greatest thing of its character in the entire world." He promised to return with helpers within two weeks to study the subsurface granite. The departing sculptor was handed a check for $250 by the Rapid City Commercial Club, the first money raised and spent on the mighty Rushmore project. At that time there were skeptics in Rapid City who believed that even this small amount was being wasted.

Borglum's two-week visit stimulated another flurry of criticism and opposition to the proposal. Mrs. Johnson was especially agitated and turned directly to the governor for help. She was more excited than she had been earlier because the time did not seem far off when carving would actually get under way. She stressed the danger of entering into any contract with Borglum because of his uncertain temperament and his experience at Stone Mountain. Mrs. Johnson told Gunderson that the bitterest letter she had ever received had recently arrived from Atlanta. This had convinced her of the sculptor's complete unreliability. She considered it very strange that Borglum should be pushing the South Dakota project personally.

Others also appealed to the governor to stop the movement. One citizen had received statements from the Stone Mountain Monumental Association and was at least partly convinced of their veracity. "If true," he asserted, "it seems to me this man should have very little encouragement in our state." Gunderson told the critics of the project that he had never favored the undertaking. It was his belief, too, that only meager sentiment existed for such carving, and he added that the state could not afford to expend any money for such purposes.

The *Deadwood Pioneer-Times* editorialized on the question: "To Carve or Not to Carve." It admitted that colossal sculpture might have aesthetic and commercial value, but wanted to know from what sources money for such a gigantic undertaking would come. Only a few newspapers had the interest or courage to come out vigorously for the work. The *Rapid City Daily Journal* did not yet actively support the proposal editorially. The *Sioux Falls Press*, however, pulled no punches. The editor charged that Black Hillers were "shortsighted if they continued to sneer at this vision of gigantic statues of Washington and Lincoln along Mount Harney. . . . The Black Hills has nothing to lose and a vast amount to gain by the Borglum project."

Borglum cared little whether or not public opinion at the time favored his idea. He believed that its realization would eventually win support not only from the state, but from the entire nation. Rumbles of dissatisfaction meant nothing to him. He was busy in the East assembling his rig and gear for another trip to Mount Rushmore. This time he would make the final decision on the suitability and texture of the granite.

CHAPTER SIX

Dedication—1925

THE interest and enthusiasm excited by Borglum's August 1925 trip were not allowed to ebb and die. Following a pattern set at Stone Mountain, Borglum urged an elaborate dedication ceremony at Mount Rushmore. He wired Robinson early in September that such a dedication must be held while public attention was centered on the project. Borglum estimated that about $5,000 was necessary to complete further surveys and to finance some kind of dramatic exercise which would rivet the attention of the state on Rushmore.

Norbeck and Robinson were both concerned over Borglum's casual reference to $5,000 or more. The sculptor offered to donate $500 himself and thought that there were at least nineteen other interested citizens who would contribute as much. This, indeed, seemed logical to a man who had scarcely known want for more than twenty years. But Norbeck knew that South Dakotans were not likely to match Borglum's financial generosity. Referring to his plans, the senator expressed fear that the artist might "run up an expense of several thousand dollars, by bringing out his men. I have no idea how he expects this is going to be paid." He added, "Possibly he expects to pay it himself." Norbeck admitted that Borglum's visit gave the project valuable publicity, but he was obviously worried over the very real possibility of "a bunch of unpaid bills." He recognized that Borglum should not act as business manager. But how could he be kept in check? Borglum was inclined to go right ahead without constraint.

Borglum and his party arrived in Rapid City on September 25 and soon established an operations camp at the base of Mount Rushmore. The Commercial Club of Rapid City once again came to the rescue financially and provided $1,000 for his expenses. During the next three days Borglum and his assistants measured and tested the granite. Suspended over the precipice in a chair, Borglum studied the potential carving surface. He appeared to be a human fly dangling in mid-air 250 feet over the cliff, dwarfed by the immensity of the forbidding mountain wall. Absolutely without fear, he went up and down while shouting instructions to his tackle operator above. More timid souls watched in awe and amazement as the stocky little figure waved nonchalantly at photographers. After a rather cursory examination, he confidently announced that "the dimensions are highly satisfactory, there being twice as much face space than will be needed for the heroic figures."

But Borglum seemed more interested in the approaching dedication, set for October 1, than in the drilling and measurement procedure. He busied himself arranging a program and creating facilities to accommodate a hoped-for crowd of ten thousand people. Even President Coolidge was invited, but he could not attend. Borglum was a crack showman. He knew how to win and hold public attention, and he gloried in his grasp of mass psychology. The dedication was presented as a tremendous event in local history. People from far and near were urged to attend. The *Rapid City Daily Journal* ran a boxed, front-page editorial declaring that citizens who stayed at home would "miss the opportunity to participate in the greatest historical event. . . in the state." The editor continued, "The carving of Rushmore is not a thing of today but of the ages. . . . It is the most stupendous undertaking of its kind in all history. . . . It is epoch making."

October 1 proved to be a beautiful, quiet, sunny fall day in the Black Hills. At noon, prior to the ceremonies, the men of Keystone served an elk dinner to more than a thousand hungry people, many of whom had traveled over nearly impassable roads from Rapid City. By mid-afternoon three times that number had made their way to a prominence across the canyon east of Mount Rushmore, a place later named Doane Mountain.

No one was disappointed by Borglum's show. Band music blared, and salutes were fired by a troop of cavalry from Fort Meade at Sturgis. There were speeches by Borglum, Norbeck, Robinson, and others. A colorful flag-raising ceremony climaxed the dedication. On the mountain stood a Sioux Indian in full native dress alongside impersonators of the French, the Spanish, and the English. Then in succession, the flags of France, Spain, and the Thirteen Colonies, and finally Old Glory, were raised and lowered. This ceremony was meant to symbolize the mountain's various owners. Of course, the Thirteen Colonies never owned the territory, but Borglum's artistic license permitted a certain carelessness with history. The vivid colors of the flags against the background of an azure sky dotted with fleecy white clouds made a striking and impressive picture. People applauded. "It seems to me," Borglum told his attentive and enraptured audience, "that the hand of providence is seen decreeing that a national memorial like this shall be erected before a monument shall be built to any one section." He promised that if his audience would meet him there a year from that day, they would see the first completed figure.

Local citizens now began to realize the meaning of the memorial and its potential importance. The *Rapid City Daily Journal* declared, "Never in its history has the city been so profoundly moved as it has been in connection with the carving of the memorial on Rushmore." "Just the idea," concluded the editor, "has given us a better perspective upon our national ideals, our national history and our world wide mission. It has turned our minds from the small things of today and given us a vision of the great things of the past and of the future."

"The Great American Memorial is not an advertising scheme," said the *Lead Daily Call.* "It is a great ideal. How many tourists it will bring to the Hills should be calculated in the interest of great art, and not the profits that will incidentally come from Borglum's work. . . . It will express the ideals of the United States people. It should be more than a commercial proposition to the Hills. It should be their ideal too."

Dedication of the mountain had publicity value, but little more. As the Stars and Stripes floated lazily atop the rugged peak, as Borglum spoke in his confident, enthusiastic manner, imaginations were excited and emotions were stirred. Newspaper editors rushed to their desks to pen lyrical columns about the importance of aesthetic achievement. This was all well and good, but there were still no plans. Nor was there any money on hand or much in prospect. The more mundane aspects of the project rudely disrupted the beautiful dream.

After the dedication, a group of Rapid City businessmen held a dinner for Borglum. Already they had contributed $1,250 for the sculptor's personal expenses, and now they were anxious to learn how much more would be expected of them. From what sources were to come the large amounts necessary for the actual carving?

Admittedly, these businessmen were only incidentally interested in art. They wanted more tourists. Many of them were frankly skeptical of Borglum's ability to complete his vision, but they were ready to gamble a small amount. Nothing ventured, nothing gained. Perhaps Robinson had been right when he said that the moment Borglum began carving, tourist traffic would boom. These practical men of affairs wanted Borglum's estimate of what the Black Hills should contribute.

Borglum's hosts were quickly aroused from their reverie when he said that $50,000 must be raised by the Black Hills community. This might be only a molehill to Borglum, but it was a mountain to most Rapid Citians. They simply did not make drives for such amounts. "We are unable to do anything," some protested. "We have gone out and assured the Black Hills people that the money was all available, providing we start with $5,000." Others claimed that Robinson and Borglum had promised eastern contributions if the necessary preliminary expenses were raised in South Dakota. Now Borglum was asking local residents to provide for the entire Washington figure. What kind of a man are we dealing with? wondered the hard-bitten merchants.

Robinson was flabbergasted by Borglum's demand. He had repeatedly assured his fellow citizens that not more than $10,000 would be expected from within the state. How could he reconcile his own and Borglum's statements? He was so disturbed that for a time he considered quitting the whole affair. But then he wrote to Norbeck that he would "continue to support Borglum, and to defend him against the charges . . . at Atlanta and any prejudice he had incurred at Rapid. I guess I will have to take the blame and keep my mouth shut," he concluded. He learned early that it was essential that someone act as the artist's buffer.

Borglum intimated that money could not be raised among wealthy benefactors unless South Dakota did its part. This was entirely reasonable. But he had created a bad psychological condition previously by carelessly saying that South Dakota's contribution would be small. Only about six weeks earlier he had told people in Rapid City, "You're not asked to spend a dollar on the project." Unfortunately, this and similar statements appeared in the press. Such an unrealistic approach may have temporarily encouraged local residents, but it proved harmful in the long run. It is true that

Borglum knew many wealthy people. Some of these friends had contributed generously to his other projects. On the basis of past experience he doubtless believed sincerely that once the great national memorial was started, he could solicit large sums. Even so, a man with more business judgment would not have publicly indicated the possibility of getting funds elsewhere until he had obtained every available penny in South Dakota. To suggest sources of money outside the state was to invite South Dakotans to close their purses and leave it all to Borglum. He even made the rash statement that he did not want "one cent" for his labors, except expenses. Careless and imprudent words of this kind were bound to cause misunderstandings later. The greatest mistake Borglum made in financing the memorial was his assumption that he could raise thousands of dollars among rich friends. He made the situation worse by constantly repeating this publicly. The gravest error South Dakotans made was to take seriously the sculptor's statements about finances. Norbeck was right when he said, "Mr. Borglum can not be the artist and also the business manager." Borglum's inconsistent and optimistic remarks about money were to cause endless trouble until the monument was completed some fifteen years later.

For several months Robinson had been insisting that it should be possible to interest some rich individual in financing one figure, or perhaps the entire memorial. Borglum estimated the total cost at between $400,000 and $800,000. The general opinion was that $100,000 for each figure was the minimum, plus a substantial sum for the entablature. Of course, no one really knew. Carving on such a scale had never before been attempted. There were many imponderables, any one of which could disastrously affect a budget. One practical way existed to determine costs: raise some money and begin to carve.

There was no effective statewide organization to supervise and promote the work. The law of 1925 had created a Mount Harney Memorial Association and clothed it with power to carry out the act. An executive committee of three with the governor as ex-officio chairman was designated to administer the law. An impotent and ineffective organization was formed in 1925, but it did little except authorize a committee of Rapid City businessmen to solicit funds locally. Governor Gunderson was chairman by law, Norbeck was elected vice-chairman, Joseph W. Parmley, secretary, and George P.

Bennett, treasurer. Under this arrangement, it is not surprising that the association accomplished nothing during Gunderson's term. The governor remained opposed to any carving, and he and Norbeck continued to be politically unfriendly. Consequently, the Mount Harney Memorial Association was virtually dead until 1927. In that year the new governor, Democrat William J. Bulow, became chairman. Norbeck continued as vice-chairman, Robinson was elected secretary, and George F. Schneider became treasurer. An advisory committee was also created. Meanwhile, progress depended mainly upon the individual efforts of Robinson, Borglum, Norbeck, and a few others scattered about the state. Miscellaneous contributions helped the financial problem very little.

Robinson continued to believe that someone could be found who would contribute at least $100,000. Late in 1925 he sent a number of letters to wealthy easterners. He wrote Edward W. Bok of Pennyslvania, "I can think of no other way in which one could render a greater patriotic service to his country and produce a wonderful art, at the same time perpetuating his own name and fame to the centuries." Bok, however, was not interested. His and other replies to Robinson seemed to confirm the belief of Norbeck and Borglum that it was futile to expect assistance from outside the state until South Dakota had raised a substantial sum. Borglum gained the support of S. S. McClure but only to the extent that McClure gave the project publicity.

Yet the three promoters would not give up. They were periodically discouraged, but they maintained faith in the final outcome. During the winter and early spring of 1925–1926, Borglum made models, photographed them, and traveled widely throughout the Midwest giving illustrated lectures on the Black Hills and Mount Rushmore. He spoke in Kansas City, Chicago, and other cities, emphasizing the importance of getting the Washington figure started in 1926.

Borglum had striking popular appeal. He could go to almost any city and at a private club or public gathering command the interest and attention of all those present. His international reputation, captivating personal charm, and versatile conversational ability caused those in his presence to feel honored and flattered by his attention. He talked to scores of people in small, informal groups and won many friends for the project.

The publicity which Borglum gave the memorial from beginning to end was invaluable. He, more than anyone else, made the country aware of this unique proposal. It was he who fanned the flames of support and enthusiasm. Without Borglum's ability to obtain and hold public attention, the Mount Rushmore National Memorial might have remained only a vision and a dream. This was not a task for an ordinary man. It took a person of unusual audacity to succeed in such a venture—one who did not hesitate to rush in where timid men feared to tread.

Throughout 1926 little was actually accomplished on any phase of the work. All, however, was not disheartening. Perhaps the most important development came when the support of Herbert Myrick of Boston was won. It was through Borglum's influence that Myrick became a booster for Mount Rushmore.

Herbert Myrick was one of the great men of his generation. He began a long publishing career in his father's printing shop at Fort Collins, Colorado. He had always loved the Black Hills, and during the gold rush of 1876 he urged his father to join the stampede and start the first newspaper in the Hills. Had his father heeded his impetuous young son's advice, Herbert might never have achieved fame as an international leader in agriculture. Later he moved to Massachusetts and began organizing farm co-operatives. He was a vigorous advocate of rural free delivery, federal farm credit, and tobacco and dairy cooperatives. He built up a chain of agricultural journals, among them the *New England Homestead*, the *American Agriculturalist, Orange Judd Farmer,* and the *Dakota Farmer*.

Myrick first became interested in colossal art when he contributed to the undertaking at Stone Mountain. He had known Borglum for many years and considered him "the Michelangelo of our era." He wrote, "Every time I think of or serve him, I have a feeling that I am ministering unto the spirit of good old Michelangelo himself." He later contributed $2,500 to the Rushmore project, and he wrote to many prospective donors with whom South Dakotans had no influence. His paper carried several stories on the Black Hills work. Late in 1928 the *Dakota Farmer* published a rather lyrical account of the proposed monument, and the cover picture showed Borglum's Washington model. Norbeck and other local promoters recognized his great help. "Well, Myrick," Norbeck wrote, "we wouldn't even have had a start yet except for your wonderful interest and great help."

Another wealthy easterner who came to look favorably upon the memorial was Arthur L. Humphrey, president of the Westinghouse Air Brake Company. He was also a director in Andrew Mellon's Pittsburgh bank. In August 1926, he visited his brother, I. M. Humphrey, in Rapid City. One evening during his stay, a small dinner party was held at which Mr. and Mrs. John A. Boland and the Humphreys were present. I. M. Humphrey and Boland gave their guest an enthusiastic sales talk on mountain-carving. He was evidently impressed. In concluding his address before the Lions Club the following day, Humphrey turned to Borglum and said, "I am completely sold for a national memorial on Rushmore mountain and I pledge you every assistance in my power."

A new local spirit came to add to Myrick's and Humphrey's support. C. C. Warren, a prominent Rapid City businessman, wrote to Norbeck early in 1926 that he believed $25,000 could be raised in South Dakota. This was the first time that a responsible Black Hills citizen had expressed such confidence. Norbeck believed that if this amount could be collected, and if the state highway department would build a road to Mount Rushmore and construct some cabins to house workmen, preliminary work might be undertaken. Then he and Williamson could ask Congress for a special fifty-cent memorial coin, similar to that minted for the Stone Mountain memorial. The sculptor relied more heavily on a special coin issue than did Norbeck. The senator did not doubt the value of the scheme, but he questioned whether such a a bill could be put through Congress. In any event, Norbeck knew South Dakota had to do something before he could successfully approach Congress.

Later in the year Robinson suggested that large corporations with South Dakota interests should be asked to contribute. He thought a committee ought to approach the Burlington, Chicago and North Western, and Milwaukee Railroads, as well as the Standard Oil Company and the Homestake Mine. "They might go so far as five or ten thousand each," he asserted. Norbeck agreed in principle but found himself in a difficult position. "I doubt the propriety . . . of my joining in a personal appeal to the railroad companies or the big oil companies," he wrote. "It is likely to create an embarrassing situation because they will later expect favors from me which they won't get." Thus more delay resulted. Everybody seemed to be depending on Norbeck or Borglum.

The artist returned to Rapid City late in August. Much of his time since his visit in 1925 had been devoted to designing and completing a monument in San Antonio for the Texas Trail Drivers Association. Another major work was his "Wars of America" memorial for the city of Newark, New Jersey, which was dedicated on May 31, 1926. Back in the Hills for the fourth time, Borglum moved his family into Keystone. He and Tucker took more measurements and painted tentative locations of the figures on the mountain. A few marks of white paint stirred local writers to predict that "before the bitter blasts of another year" arrive, "the air drills . . . will have chiseled away many tons of the solid pile."

After this survey Borglum prepared a report for the Mount Harney Memorial Association. For the first time, he made a complete summary of the project as he envisioned it. He planned for the four faces to be of colossal dimensions, each scaled to the proportion of a man 465 feet tall, and he proposed that the entablature be 80 by 120 feet. A major change appeared in his plans when he declared that the inscription should be on the mountain's west wall. "No lettering of any kind should appear with the sculpture on the east wall," he wrote. Borglum had originally intended to place the entablature on the east cliff, slightly north of the figures. His diary of 1925 shows this plan, and his correspondence otherwise corroborates it. He predicted that five years would be sufficient to complete the work, estimating that one working season would be required for each face and the entablature. Borglum said nothing in this report about a hall of records, sometimes referred to as a museum, or the grand stairway, which were to be a part of the overall plan developed later.

The sculptor stated, surprisingly, that he did not intend to carve with dynamite, indicating how little he then realized the tremendous amount of rock that must be removed. Light explosive charges, he said, were used at Stone Mountain to blast away surplus granite many feet from the finished surface. But to use dynamite at Rushmore, he believed, was "unnecessary and unsafe , , . as we are actually carving in the round on a projecting mass." He stated that he was ready to begin work just as soon as money was available.

After leaving the Black Hills, Borglum made another speaking tour to publicize the project. He visited Pittsburgh where he called on Humphrey, Kansas City, Detroit, Minneapolis, and Chicago. He interviewed many financial leaders during these visits and consulted representatives of the press concerning the proposed work. The Chicago papers carried a number of stories about Mount Rushmore.

But Borglum felt that he was working alone. Less help was coming from South Dakota than he had a right to expect. Robinson admitted that "we have utterly failed in our support of you," but he hoped for better things because Norbeck had promised to "get things going" in Rapid City. "The Rapid City boys" will "get active," he predicated, "when Pete gets after them." Robinson continued, "We are up against a stone wall with the Governor. He would ruin the whole movement if he could." But Gunderson had been recently defeated, and the Democratic governor-elect, Bulow, was friendly to the project. Indeed, Gunderson had lost the 1926 election partly because he had opposed some of Norbeck's plans for Custer State Park and the Black Hills area. Many of Norbeck's Republican friends openly supported Bulow.

Borglum was more irritated than discouraged. He was especially annoyed that no one from South Dakota had met him in Chicago or Minneapolis to help solicit funds from leading financiers. He recognized that publicity in itself was not enough. Men of means must be approached directly, and Borglum felt that the interested citizens of South Dakota should help him. Spicing a letter to Robinson with mild profanity, he impatiently declared that they should do something besides talk about the work.

CHAPTER SEVEN

President Coolidge Visits

T HERE was little to buoy the sagging spirits of Mount Rushmore's leading supporters early in 1927. Even the persevering Borglum and Norbeck were discouraged and nearly at their wits' end. A few private subscriptions dribbled in, but no substantial contributions. Norbeck accepted the situation more philosophically than did Borglum because he had learned from long years of public service that success often comes slowly. Borglum, on the other hand, was impatient and eager to find short cuts. By 1927 his early optimism about raising funds had turned sour.

One source of help had not been studied—the federal government. Congress had appropriated millions of dollars for statues, monuments, and memorials of various kinds since 1789. More than $3,000,000 had been provided for the Lincoln Memorial in Washington, D.C. What about tapping this reservoir?

On January 15 Borglum, Norbeck, and Williamson held a long conference in the senator's office, discussing tactics by which they might get federal support. Borglum still argued that their best bet was to ask Congress to authorize a special memorial coin. He recommended a fifty-cent piece which could be sold for one dollar. His experience with the Stone Mountain coin had convinced him that large sums could be raised in this manner. Norbeck and Williamson agreed in theory but replied that Congress would be unwilling to permit additional memorial coins.

To counter Borglum's proposal, Norbeck suggested asking Congress for an outright appropriation. He and Williamson were in a good position to get such a measure enacted. The senator was popular among conservationists and supporters of state and national park development. If necessary, he could probably obtain their help. Furthermore, he had a knack for getting bills through the Senate by unanimous consent. Indeed, his success had led the National Park Service and other agencies to lean heavily upon him. And Williamson had achieved real success in the Coolidge administration. He was chairman of the Committee of Expenditures in the Executive Department, a position which gave him close contact with the comptroller general. He knew the president well, and he was often called into conference on fiscal problems.

Norbeck and Williamson believed their chances of getting a direct appropriation were good if Secretary of the Treasury Andrew Mellon did not oppose it. The senator suggested that Borglum go to Mellon, discuss the project with him, and ask for his support. If anyone could sell Mellon on mountain-carving, it was Borglum. Once Mellon's approval was secured, Norbeck and Williamson could introduce their bills with a reasonable chance of success. It is not clear whether Norbeck suggested that Borglum ask for the entire $500,000, the estimated cost of the project, or for only $250,000, which would be matched by private funds. Evidence indicates that the senator originally hoped to get all the money from the federal government. He wrote in February that as an alternate plan, they would accept $250,000 and try to match it with money raised elsewhere.

After the discussion, Borglum left for Mellon's office. The secretary was out, but he had a satisfactory conference with Undersecretary Ogden Mills, an old personal friend. The Treasury Department, Mills said, would vigorously oppose any special coin issue but was willing to support a direct appropriation. He could not commit Mellon, but he gave Borglum strong encouragement. If Mellon would support the program, only the president remained to be won to the project. While there would be some opposition in Congress, administration support would probably carry the day.

It was about a month later, on February 17, that Borglum saw the secretary and obtained his support for an appropriation on a matching basis. It would seem that Arthur L. Humphrey had helped prepare Mellon on this matter. He had been interested in Mount Rushmore since his visit to the Black Hills the previous summer. Borglum, who did not ask full participation by the federal government, never revealed why he so readily settled for $250,000. Perhaps he thought there was no chance to get more. Norbeck, however, wrote at the time that Borglum did not want the national government to finance the whole project because "control would pass into other hands." Borglum evidently wanted no federal checks on his activity.

With the hazard of an adverse report from the Treasury Department eliminated, Norbeck and Williamson moved swiftly to obtain government help. Williamson had prepared bills which were now introduced by himself and Senator McMaster because at the time, Norbeck was hospitalized from a taxicab accident. The season was not ripe, however, and McMaster's bill never returned from the committee. In the meantime, McMaster had introduced a measure authorizing the treasury to issue five million fifty-cent pieces to be sold by the Mount Harney Memorial Association. No one expected this to pass. Norbeck frankly admitted that it was only a blind to draw attention from his real purpose of getting a direct appropriation. Too, it would help publicize the Rushmore project.

While Norbeck and Williamson were busy in Washington, Rapid City businessmen made their first significant promise of financial aid. John Boland wrote early in February that $15,000 might be raised. However, this prediction was too optimistic and money came in slowly. Only $1,900 had been solicited by late March. Norbeck continued to blame the project's condition on the failure of the Black Hills community to support it.

The lack of progress irked Borglum and made him harder and harder to deal with. And there was some cause for his annoyance. He had spent much time and a lot of money promoting the project. He claimed that $5,950 was due him for promotional expenses, but the businessmen of Rapid City were reluctant to expend any of their meager funds for this purpose. There was a strong feeling among them that during the initial stages, money should be spent only at the mountain. In any event, Borglum got no reimbursement, and only his faith in Norbeck and Robinson, he said, kept him going. Another grievance was the lack of a formal contract.

Faced with an empty treasury, it seemed foolhardy to enter into a contract with the sculptor, but late in February, Williamson, Norbeck, and M___ ___ ___ ___ ___ ___ ___ ___ ___ ___ on March 1. Borglum was given "full, final and complete freedom and authority" for the work's "artistic excellence." Changes in the design could be made at his discretion, although Washington's head was to be sixty feet long. The sculptor was personally to carve the finishing features in order to perfect the monument, and the models and designs were to remain his property. He wanted to avoid another Stone Mountain experience.

For supervising the work, making models, and assuming responsibility for the artistic development, Borglum was to receive 25 percent of the total expenditures. Outlays for labor, materials, machinery, and most other expenses were items on which he would get a commission or honorarium. Under no circumstances, however, was he to be paid more than $87,500. The estimated cost of the figures and the entablature was $437,500. It was believed that $38,000 would install a suitable plant, and that $312,000 was enough for the actual carving of four faces and the inscription. Work was to begin in 1927, and one figure was to be completed each year. Borglum was also to receive an extra $5,900 for expenses which he had advanced, and if at any time the association could not pay the sculptor's fee, the unpaid balance was to draw 6 percent interest.

It was also agreed that Borglum should be paid on a percentage basis as the work advanced. For instance, when one-tenth of the carving was completed, not more than 10 percent of $87,500 should be paid to him. This part of the contract was never adhered to. Finally, Borglum placed complete reliance for his honorarium on monies in the treasury, and the officers of the association were in no way financially responsible. The plant and machinery were to be the property of the association.

At the same time, a contract was made with Major Jesse G. Tucker of Bradenton, Florida, Borglum's former assistant at Stone Mountain. Borglum had never intended to remain constantly at Mount Rushmore. He desired freedom to undertake other work. Consequently, he wanted someone on the job who could follow his instructions. Tucker agreed to act as contractor and to construct the memorial from Borglum's designs and under his supervision. He was to receive $10,000 a year. In light of the bleak financial outlook, it was perhaps less rash to make a percentage contract with Borglum than to promise Tucker a fixed salary. He would not leave Florida, however, for a smaller sum. Both contracts were based mostly on faith and hope.

Myrick was anxious to compensate Borglum for his out-of-pocket expenses, and within a week after the agreement was signed, he gave $1,000 to the project through his paper, the *Dakota Farmer*. This, together with some funds raised in Rapid City, paid a part of

Borglum's claim and restored his old confidence and enthusiasm. Nothing depressed his spirits more or made him more irritable than to be short of cash.

The whole picture was suddenly changed for the better when on May 25 news flashed across the nation that President Coolidge would spend his summer vacation in the Black Hills. The friends of the Mount Rushmore project realized that this was their first real break in the struggle to create a great national monument. Besides the tremendous publicity which the president's visit would give them, there was always the chance of obtaining his outright support. South Dakotans had been urging Coolidge to spend a summer in the Hills for over a year. After reading a report early in 1926 that the president was looking for a mountain retreat, Francis Case, editor of the *Hot Springs Star*, promptly sent a telegram to Congressman Williamson, urging that every effort be made to bring Coolidge to South Dakota. At about the same time Robinson wrote to Senator Norbeck stressing the importance of a presidential visit to the Rushmore work. Although the South Dakota congressional delegation called on Coolidge in April 1926, the President declined its invitation. However, nothing was left undone to win his favor for the following season.

In January 1927 Governor Bulow and the South Dakota Legislature sent the president formal invitations. Williamson and Norbeck made many calls at the White House where they extolled the wonders of the Black Hills to the taciturn Coolidge. The best pictures of the region were laid before him, and good trout fishing was presented as an added lure. Adequate accommodations were promised the presidential party at the Game Lodge in Custer State Park. Others were also urging Coolidge to make South Dakota his summer home. Herbert Myrick made a special trip to Washington to talk with him on this matter. "Coolidge must summer in Black Hills," he wired Norbeck. Borglum became almost overbearing and pestered Coolidge with letters and telegrams. He offered to carve a bust of the President, strike a medallion, and do almost anything to tie the president to the memorial in some way.

Early in the year Norbeck declared, "We have a very good chance of getting the President out there for the summer and a good chance for the appropriation to make the memorial an assured thing." These two developments were directly connected. If Coolidge should go to the Black Hills, he might become sufficiently interested in the monument to support a federal aid bill. Without his blessing it probably would not pass. McMaster's bill was still buried in committee.

However, Coolidge was not going to South Dakota merely because the Mount Rushmore enthusiasts invited him. He was chiefly interested in sounding out public opinion on farm relief. Late in February he had vetoed the McNary-Haugen bill, a farm measure demanded by many midwesterners, including Norbeck. An extended stay in South Dakota, which was a McNary-Haugen stronghold, would give him an ideal opportunity to study agricultural problems and to feel out political attitudes. And it was no empty chamber of commerce propaganda—the Black Hills was a wonderful vacation spot. This combination of circumstances was responsible for his final decision. His friendship with Williamson and Norbeck probably had some influence. In an impulsive moment, Borglum said that Norbeck deserved the credit for the president's South Dakota visit.

The announcement that Coolidge would arrive in June caused another spurt of money-raising among the sponsors of Mount Rushmore. If they expected to win Coolidge's support, some actual progress must be shown by summer. Great effort was exerted by Robinson, Norbeck, Borglum, Boland, Warren, and others to gather funds, get machinery installed, and begin carving. Robinson mailed another bundle of letters to prospective contributors, including Charles E. Rushmore. Williamson called on Nicholas Longworth to suggest that the Roosevelt family give at least $10,000 toward the memorial. A little later Norbeck and Boland obtained a $5,000 gift from the Homestake Mine officials in Lead.

Also, a drive was started to get substantial donations from Black Hills businessmen, particularly those of Rapid City. The campaign there was the result of some very plain talk by Norbeck. Early in June he called on Boland and spoke "very frank" with him. "I . . . had to tell him that if the indifference of the Black Hills people continued that there was nothing . . . to do but drop the whole thing," he said. Money could not be solicited elsewhere, he argued, unless people "dig up at home." He concluded by assuring Boland "that I would not permit Borglum to come to the Black Hills for any purpose until their . . . subscription [was] fixed up."

The senator may have been unjustly blunt with Boland since he had been active in soliciting funds. In any event, Boland went into action. Shortly afterward, many individuals and firms in Rapid City gave from $50 to $500 each. The First National Bank donated a total of $1,450. By July 1 Boland had arranged for ten businessmen to guarantee or underwrite $25,000 for Mount Rushmore. It was understood that if this amount was not raised during the summer campaign, the guarantors would make up the difference on a prorata basis.

Now the time seemed opportune to press for substantial donations from the three railroads which did business in the Black Hills. In Chicago, Norbeck, Robinson, and Borglum met with officials of the Chicago and Northwestern, the Burlington, and the Milwaukee Railroads. W. G. Edens, vice-president of the Central Trust Company, took the lead in urging these corporations to aid the Rushmore project. At Norbeck's request, General Charles G. Dawes invited a group of businessmen to a Union League Club luncheon where the memorial's finances were discussed. Only friendship for the senator prompted this interest, Dawes said. Each of the lines finally agreed to give $5,000. This $15,000, plus $5,000 each from the Homestake Mining Company, Charles E. Rushmore, and Senator Coleman Du Pont of Delaware, and cash and pledges from the Black Hills community, made a total of over $50,000. Norbeck and Robinson had agreed that if a few thousand more could be obtained and some machinery acquired, work might begin with assurance of success.

Meanwhile, Tucker and Borglum were seeking a suitable power plant for the work. Borglum first approached Samuel Insull, but without success. Finally, however, he and Tucker arranged for the permanent loan of a 200-horsepower diesel engine from the Northwestern Public Service Company of Huron, a subsidiary of the far-flung Insull utility empire. The engine, valued at between $15,000 and $20,000, was given to the Mount Harney Memorial Association.

In spite of these bright prospects, Borglum was complaining about failure to start the actual carving. He told Norbeck in April that if the association officials had his courage, they would put Tucker to work on the mountain at once. He argued that enough money was available to run for sixty days and that if no more could be raised during that time, they should abandon the project. This incensed Norbeck. "I am frank to say," he declared, "that Mr. Borglum tries my patience . . . when he talks about courage in starting the work, for courage alone won't do it—it takes money."

Norbeck and Robinson had difficulty in restraining Borglum's enthusiasm. He wanted to order machinery and incur other debts in order to start work immediately. Robinson, secretary of the association, warned him repeatedly that "propositions involving cash outlay" must be submitted for the executive committee's approval. In fact, Robinson so distrusted the sculptor's business ability that he did not want him to buy anything on the association's account. Above all, Norbeck and Robinson opposed installing heavy and expensive equipment until there was assurance of enough money to operate it. "I do hope that Borglum doesn't just ignore the committee and start operations or buying of machinery on his motion," Norbeck declared. "It would be just like him. If we are to have any trouble with him over . . . business matters we might as well have it at the front."

On June 15 President Coolidge's special train puffed across the South Dakota prairies toward the Black Hills. Senator Norbeck, Governor Bulow, and other state leaders joined the presidential party for the final lap of the journey. As the train sped westward, farm problems were the main topic of conversation. Apparently Mount Rushmore was not even mentioned. But with a coterie of the nation's newsmen accompanying Coolidge, there was little doubt that column after column would be written about the Rushmore project before the summer ended.

Less than a week later, Borglum arrived in the Black Hills from San Antonio. He announced that Tucker would be on hand shortly and predicted that actual carving would begin within a month. "We will rush through with the work this summer in an effort to get as much of the Washington figure completed as can be done before President Coolidge departs," he said.

The sculptor spared nothing in appealing to Coolidge. A great showman under any conditions, he flew low in an airplane over the summer White House, dropping a wreath of flowers on the lawn.* Who but Gutzon Borglum would have made such a flamboyant gesture?

A few days later Major Tucker arrived and took charge of installing the plant preparatory to beginning work. The first machinery was unloaded on July 10, and on the following day ground was broken in Keystone for a building to house the large diesel engine. Compressors, jackhammers (pneumatic drills), and other equipment

*Grace Coolidge later wrote Borglum a note thanking him for the flowers.

were ordered and made ready for drilling. Tucker estimated that about $12,000 would be necessary to provide a complete working plant. The diesel engine set up in Keystone generated electricity which operated compressors at the mountain base. It was necessary to cut through the dense forest between Keystone and Mount Rushmore to make way for the power line. About fourteen hundred feet of three-inch air line was laid to the mountaintop where the individual drills were connected for power. Since there was no road to Mount Rushmore, trees also had to be felled to open the way. A wagon trail went part way from Keystone, and supplies were hauled by teams as far as possible, then carried by hand the remainder of the distance. It was tedious work, but the crew of sixteen men whom Tucker had recruited locally made rapid progress at the mountain.

Activity at the mountain base took on the appearance of a hustling mining camp. Swearing, sweating teamsters hauled lumber, cement, and machinery up the steep slope. Carpenters quickly constructed rough buildings and renovated an old log cabin which Borglum would use for a temporary studio. Every daily report carried the slogan RUSH MORE. By early August, Tucker had increased his crew to twenty-three, and the mountain seemed alive with workmen who were building a stairway and scaffolds, and connecting air pipes. On August 9 the compressor was given a trial run, and the air pipes were tested for leaks. Everything seemed ready for the work to begin.

This rush of activity was aimed at putting things in readiness for the elaborate ceremony which Borglum had set for August 10. He intended that the first drilling should be accompanied by a tremendous celebration, the kind for which Borglum was famous. Borglum, Norbeck, Robinson, and others had planned that the president should play a prominent part in the program. "This," Robinson wrote, "would give the project wonderful publicity."

August 10 was a delightful summer day, cool and pleasant following heavy rains. Coolidge drove from the Game Lodge to Keystone, and from there he ascended the mountain on horseback. Normally a livery, dressed in cowboy boots and a ten gallon hat, he looked ill at ease and completely out of place. For those who had to struggle up the mountain on foot, soft white clouds occasionally brought welcome relief from the sun. The ceremonies were held on Doane Mountain. Coolidge and other dignitaries sat on a rough platform made of native pine while some seventeen hundred visitors stood or sat on the ground, rocks, or tree trunks nearby. Senator Norbeck presided.

Since no cannon was available, the presidential salute consisted of blasting stumps from the right of way for the new road to Rushmore. This was as practical as it was unique. After a few preliminaries, the president was introduced. "We have come here to dedicate a cornerstone that was laid by the hand of the Almighty," he declared in his dry New England manner. Praising Borglum and his conception, he asserted that "the people of the future will see history and art combined to portray the spirit of patriotism . . . This memorial will be another national shrine to which future generations will repair to declare their continuing allegiance to independence, to self government, to freedom and to economic justice." Finally, Coolidge came to the practical problem of financial support. He asserted that the effort and courage of South Dakotans to build a great national monument had been so great that they deserved "the sympathy and support of private beneficence and the national government." He concluded, "Money spent for such a purpose is certain of adequate returns in the nature of increased public welfare."

The president then turned to Borglum and handed him a set of drills. Realizing that this was the opportune moment to guarantee Coolidge's support, Borglum made a brief talk and concluded by saying, "As the first president who has taken part, please write the inscription to go on that mountain. We want your connection known in some other way than by your presence. I want the name of Coolidge on that mountain." The crowd applauded.

Borglum, accompanied by Tucker, then ascended Mount Rushmore, and the crowd watched breathlessly as he was lowered over the cliff. Suddenly the staccato bark of the drills told that the sculptor was drilling master points for the face of George Washington. Senator Norbeck, Robinson, Williamson, and the other promoters watched with pride and satisfaction. Flag-raising ceremonies, even more elaborate than those of 1925, and additional speeches completed the program.

After the ceremony, as Robinson thanked Coolidge for his participation, the president said, "I made the address very brief and explicit for I thought you might want to print it to help you get the money." And, indeed, it might. With presidential support now assured, new bills could be introduced with good chance of success. The project's supporters were greatly encouraged by the outspoken approval of the reticent president. His frank statement was more than even the most optimistic enthusiasts had anticipated.

The president's visit to South Dakota was a turning point in the history of Mount Rushmore. The project benefited not only from Coolidge's outright support, but from the publicity which attended his stay as well—publicity which, Robinson declared, could not have been bought for $1,000,000. The *New York Sun, Times,* and *Herald Tribune* carried long stories during the summer on Borglum and his venture into gigantic sculpture. For the Black Hills in general, the vast flow of news surrounding the presidential visit made millions of people aware for the first time of the area's tourist attractions. The completion of the bridge across the Missouri River at Chamberlain in 1925 and the graveling of U.S. Highway 16 also helped to increase tourist traffic.

During the summer a few people visited Mount Rushmore even though it was still necessary to walk part of the way. The novelist O. E. Rolvaag wrote in September that he had gone to the Black Hills "with only one purpose: to see with my own eyes what was going on on Mount Rushmore." He wrote Norbeck, "Never have I been so impressed with the magnitude of human ideas; what a tremendous figure this man Borglum is!"

The few holes which Borglum drilled in the face of Mount Rushmore on August 10 did not mean the beginning of steady work. That day was nearly two months away. During late August and September, hand-operated winches, which controlled the steel cables used to lower workmen over the mountainside, were set up and fastened with steel pins. A cableway was installed from the canyon below to the top of Rushmore to carry tools and equipment. Borglum's model of Washington and a smaller group-model of Washington, Jefferson, and Lincoln arrived from his San Antonio studio late in August. Things were rapidly being put in order to begin work.

The ominous rumble of an approaching storm was heard during this period of preparation. Borglum's mercurial temperament was much in evidence. His ability to create or destroy on paper rivaled his genius in sculpture, as those who bore the brunt of his pen-and-ink attacks painfully learned. In September he sharply criticized

Robinson and the Mount Harney Memorial Association for inefficient work, poor construction, and trifling economies. He charged
that interference had resulted in a lower quality of work which he
must apologize for or disown. His need for a suitable studio was the
main bone of contention.

These complaints brought a stinging reply from Robinson, who
was usually mild and even-tempered. He reminded Borglum that a studio had not been included in the request for equipment and added, "I
am not worth a damn at divining what a man has in the back of his
head and does not reveal." The sculptor and his contractor were fully
responsible for the character of all work, he continued, and if it were
shiftless, Borglum was at fault. Robinson's charge of "bellyaching"
could have left little doubt in Borglum's mind of the historian's interpretation of these complaints. "You think it is artistic temperament,"
Robinson wrote, "but to me it seems childishness, pettiness, unworthy
of a man of your great gifts." He assured Borglum that the association
would endeavor to provide adequate funds, but at the same time, every
effort would be made to economize.

The character of this letter may have sobered Borglum, who was
unaccustomed to such sharp talk in reply to his rash accusations.
Certainly it put a strain on the relationship between the two men.
Robinson referred to Borglum's "free handed methods" with money
and expressed dislike for the cost-plus feature of his contract. In protecting the association's treasury, Robinson aroused the ire of the
free-spending sculptor.

Another illuminating episode was the fuss over publishing
Coolidge's Mount Rushmore speech. Robinson had several thousand
copies of the address printed on rather ordinary and inexpensive
paper. These were to be included in letters appealing for funds.
Infuriated by this meager economy, Borglum spoke harshly to
Robinson. The argument occurred in Norbeck's presence, and the
senator's timely intervention prevented a serious riff. Looking directly at the two men, Norbeck said, "Doane, you should have printed
the speech on better paper; and Gutzon, you shouldn't have said a
damn thing about it."

Governor Bulow recalls that his first year in office, 1927, was
made miserable by Borglum's unending demands for a road to
Mount Rushmore. Since Borglum considered his project the most
important thing in the world, he chafed at even the briefest delay or

inconvenience. If he requested a road one day, he expected the governor to produce it the next. One day Bulow received a three hundred–word telegram dealing with the road situation. (Borglum habitually used the wires when a letter would have sufficed.) He complained bitterly to the governor that he had muddied a new pair of shoes and white trousers on a recent trip up the mountain. The governor quieted him for a few days by suggesting that "the next time he went to the mountain in the rain he ought to wear a pair of overalls and go barefooted." These minor incidents reflected Borglum's temperament and foreshadowed trouble for those who were to work with him.

The daily report of operations for 1927 presents a detailed account of activities and progress. This was the only time during the fourteen-year drilling period that such a record was kept. The entry for October 4 states, "Today we started the actual drilling on Rushmore. Several holes were drilled and equipment tried out." That was all. There was no fanfare, no celebration. As the delightful October days slipped away, clouds of granite dust raised by the busy jackhammers testified to progress on the Washington figure. Five or six drills were operated most of the time. Although they were not trained to handle such tools, the men quickly learned to operate the jackhammers efficiently. Borglum later boasted that he had taken a group of "forgotten and left over miners," trained them, and welded them into one of the most loyal and efficient outfits he had ever had.

As at Stone Mountain, it soon became evident here that tons of surplus rock must be removed in order to get down to a surface suitable for the finished faces. Dr. O'Hara of the State School of Mines had warned Borglum in the beginning that the fissures in Mount Rushmore were quite deep. But with characteristic self-confidence Borglum had ignored the warnings of a professional geologist and had compared Rushmore with Stone Mountain, a complete mistake. So his estimates of time and cost were generally wrong. Of course, no one knew the exact depth of the fissures, and actual carving was the only way to discover perfect or near perfect granite. It must be said for Borglum that he did not look for courage, and the final result justified his constantly erroneous predictions and calculations.

To drill and break away the rock by hand was slow and expensive, so Borglum again resorted to dynamite, although he had said in 1926 that this would be unnecessary. However, he was obliged in any case to remove the outer rock to the point at which the blemishes diminished or ceased to exist. Late in October Tucker and Borglum were ready to experiment with small charges of blasting powder. The daily report of October 25 reports, "The chief event of today was the trying of dynamite in blasting off rock." It was so successful that the single stonecutter was laid off.

During the first few weeks Borglum refined and improved the engineering techniques which he had developed at Stone Mountain. His experiences in Georgia greatly eased the work in South Dakota. After the sculptor had located the approximate granite mass for the figures, the first overall operation took place, known as pointing. This was the important and technical task of translating the measurements of the model to the mountain. Borglum had thrown pictures of his models on Stone Mountain, but this was not practicable at Rushmore. The granite was too rough and imperfect, and it was impossible to tell in advance where each head could be carved.

The model was first measured by fastening a horizontal bar on the top and center of the head. As this extended out over the face, a plumb bob was dropped to the point of the nose or other projections of the face. Since the model of Washington's face was five feet tall, these measurements were then multiplied by twelve and transferred to the mountain by using a similar but larger device. Instead of a small beam, a thirty-foot swinging boom was used, connected to the stone which would ultimately be the top of Washington's head and extending out over the granite cliff. A plumb bob was lowered from the boom. The problem was to adjust the measurements from the scale of the model to the mountain. The first step was to locate the point of the nose since that was the extreme projection of the face. If it were found that several feet of rock had to be removed to reach the nose point, this was indicated by paint marks. Then other projected points of the face, such as the frontal bones, were located and measured.

After the rough points were established, men suspended in swing seats began the drilling and blasting. The holes for the first process were drilled vertically from two to six feet deep. Charges of dynamite were lowered into the holes and packed with damp sand. The blasting was done in such a way as to leave a great, rough, egg-shaped mass. The oval shaping, while not always achieved, was desirable because it was then possible to shift the position of the face if inferior rock was encountered. The nose, for example, might be moved several feet one way or another.

As the drillers came close to what would be the finished surface, holes three or four inches apart, and sometimes closer, were drilled to the desired depth. A channeling iron was used to break the rock between the drill holes to permit wedging, or splitting off blocks of honeycombed granite. The resulting pockmarked surface was then smoothed by a process called bumping. This was done with a pneumatic tool and a four-point bit which, when bumped against the rock, made it smooth.

It was possible to dynamite within an inch or two of the intended surface, and occasionally this was done at Rushmore. But generally, blasting was not carried on closer than six inches to the surface. It was not practicable to dynamite too near because the charges had to be so small and the holes so near together that little if any labor was saved. Measuring, drilling, blasting, drilling, wedging, and bumping made up the ordinary work cycle. The term "carving" was only a figure of speech in this gigantic project.

The whole task involved cutting away unwanted stone. Borglum took great delight in telling astonished visitors that the faces had always been in the mountain: they only had to be brought out by drilling and dynamiting away the unnecessary granite. The stone must be "relieved . . . from the head," he explained.

On December 7, when the weather reached twenty-two degrees below zero, work on the mountain was halted. Significant progress had been made. Proceeding downward from the top of Washington's forehead, workers had blasted and drilled away rock to a depth of about twenty-five feet, or down to the point where the eyes would be. Drillers had penetrated about six feet from the outer surface, leaving a shelf at the level of Washington's eyes. But to any visitor who might have made his way to the mountain, it appeared to be nothing but a gash in the southeast shoulder of Mount Rushmore.

Available funds had been exhausted when operations were closed down. Tucker had, in fact, borrowed more than $2,000 on his own signature to meet late November payrolls. Again the perennial problem of raising money reared its ugly head. Work was not to be resumed for more than eighteen months. Norbeck had not been over-cautious when he wrote shortly after the August ceremonies, "I shall be greatly surprised if the big showing does not come at the front end and the exasperating delays later on."

Opposition to the project in South Dakota had practically vanished after carving was begun. Several months earlier, the editor of the *Evening Huronite* had written, "All South Dakota should rejoice over the seeming fact that work on the great Rushmore memorial in the Black Hills is soon to start." The memorial's dollar-and-cents value became increasingly apparent although a road to Mount Rushmore suitable for tourist travel had not yet been completed. From other quarters, however, came satire and sneers. In October *Liberty* magazine carried a most eloquent cartoon, portraying Borglum's disturbing influence on America's mountain ranges. It showed a panoramic view of the Rockies with a figure carved on each prominent peak. Devoted followers of Woodrow Wilson frequently cast snide remarks at the project because their own hero had been omitted. Some Democrats continued to demand that the plan be changed to include Wilson. In addition, officers of the Stone Mountain Monumental Association had not ceased in their attempts to discredit Borglum. A pamphlet entitled "The Truth at Last Is Brought to Light" was distributed generously among the friends of Mount Rushmore.

The *London Daily Telegraph* ran a sharply critical and sarcastic editorial. "Imagine our cliffs . . . our hillsides carved with colossal monuments of the heroes and the art of yesterday, Beachy Head shaped into an immense Albert Memorial," commented the editor. "We are bound to condemn the whole plan." But it was indifference, not ridicule, which remained the principal obstacle to the project.

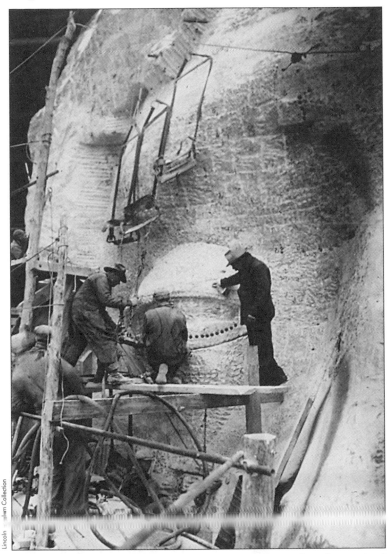

Only the most trusted and skilled workers were allowed to work on the presidents' eyes. Here, Borglum directs work on the eye.

A driller "honeycombs" the rock as crews near the finished surface of Washington's face.

At work on Lincoln's eye. The workman is using a "bumper" to smooth the rock. Note the size of the pupil, which protrudes just above the drill.

The monument as it appeared in 1933. Note the early position of the Jefferson face. The next year it was blasted away and moved north to a position behind the Washington figure.

The Jefferson face near completion. Veins of quartz which line the face can be seen.

CHAPTER EIGHT

Manna from Washington

"I SAW the Chief regarding Rushmore today," Norbeck wrote early in April 1928. "Everything is fine." The senator's call at the White House was part of his and Williamson's renewed campaign to get a law authorizing federal aid. There seemed to be no other hope. During the late winter, Robinson, Boland, and Warren had tried to solicit funds in Sioux Falls and Sioux City. Robinson also went to Minneapolis. Representative business leaders in each of these cities promised to raise $10,000 for Mount Rushmore, but they were only promises, and results were meager.

An interesting sidelight on the campaign was Leonard Imboden's agreement to contribute $100,000 for the Roosevelt figure. Imboden was a mysterious and enigmatic individual about whom neither Norbeck nor Robinson ever learned much. He appeared to be a wealthy New England businessman. In March 1928 Imboden sent Robinson $50,000 of preferred stock in the New England Industrial Corporation with the idea that it be used as security to borrow funds. The stock was only a loan and was to be returned to him when his pledge was paid. Unfortunately, nothing could be borrowed on the stock, and the secretive easterner never honored his commitment. This was the nearest the Mount Rushmore promoters ever came to obtaining a large donation.

Tired of waiting for private subscriptions, Norbeck and Williamson were busy preparing bills for the consideration of Congress, which Senator McMaster and Representative Williamson introduced late in March. These measures called for a twelve-man federal commission appointed by the president and the authorization of $250,000 on a matching basis.

Legislation of this type is often passed by unanimous consent. With only 96 senators to Williamson's 435 congressmen, Norbeck had the simpler task. Nonetheless, he had to deal with some very conservative Republicans, men with whom he had little in common and whose measures he had often opposed. When the bill was being considered in the Committee on the Library, he wrote to all members, pointing out that Secretary Mellon had approved the expenditure and that Coolidge would write the inscription for the entablature. Luckily, Senator Fess, chairman of the committee, had been at Mount Rushmore for the dedication ceremonies. Hiram Bingham and other administration stalwarts were gradually brought into line with the help of Senator Charles Curtis of Kansas. The confidence and good will which Norbeck had built up among his colleagues paid dividends here.

At eleven o'clock on the night of May 16, the bill passed the Senate without objection or debate. Norbeck breathed a sigh of relief and shortly afterward wrote: "That was the hardest day's work I have done since I came to Washington." Norbeck's patience almost snapped the following day, however, when the erratic sculptor wired him that he was not disposed to help if the federal government took control. A million dollars could be raised from private sources, he said, if it were not made a national project. "He does not want the $250,000 from Congress now," the exasperated senator confided to Robinson. "He wants to go to New York, London, Jerusalem, or Heaven and get $1,000,000. He is quite certain that a million is more than $250,000 but that is the only thing he is sure about."

Yet in writing to Borglum, Norbeck showed remarkable patience. He pointed out that he, too, would rather tap private reservoirs, but he reminded the sculptor of their failure thus far. "Really, I think the government appropriation is the only thing that will save us," he concluded. Borglum seemed to feel that it would be more difficult to solicit large sums if people thought the federal government had assumed financial responsibility.

In the House, Williamson was having a difficult time. He told Norbeck early in May that Congressman Robert Luce, chairman of the Committee on the Library, wanted to sidetrack the bill. Yet Luce was easy to convince when compared with Louis Cramton of Michigan. Cramton, a conservative and tight-fisted Republican, was an influential member of the important appropriations committee. The principle involved in federal aid to Mount Rushmore aroused his opposition. It made no difference that Borglum was his personal friend. When Williamson saw that Cramton was determined to object when the bill came up for consideration, he went directly to the White House and asked Coolidge to intercede. Shortly afterward, Cramton showed a change of spirit and called Williamson to discuss the Rushmore matter. He now said he was willing to let the measure pass if certain amendments were added.

He demanded that no charge ever be made to view the memorial, that there must be no salaried secretary, that the state must maintain the monument, and that the commission must not officially solicit funds. Cramton was especially insistent that the memorial should never be commercialized. In 1928 Norbeck, Williamson, and Borglum had discussed charging a small fee to help finance the work. If Cramton's amendment were accepted, that potential income would be eliminated. Since Mount Rushmore was to be a great national shrine, many thought it would be somewhat anomalous to levy an admission charge. Williamson and Norbeck agreed that these amendments would not seriously hurt the bill. Their main concern was the $250,000 authorization, and to overcome Cramton's opposition was in itself a major victory.

But what about the Democrats? Williamson, Norbeck said, demonstrated great political skill in quieting them one by one. Representative Loring M. Black of Brooklyn was almost alone in expressing opposition. With biting satire he denounced the project because Woodrow Wilson was not included and because the cost was high. He was also aroused by an article in the *Springfield (Massachusetts) Republican* which asserted that a bust of Coolidge might also appear on Mount Rushmore. "That would be a bust, indeed!" Black declared. When Coolidge was in the Black Hills, the article said, Borglum had pointed out a space for the president's figure beside that of Theodore Roosevelt. The only fitting memorial to Coolidge, Black explained ironically, would be an "empty space on the tablet." The inscription should read, "The farmers asked of Coolidge bread and he gave them this stone."

Williamson arose at once to assure everyone that there was no thought of including Coolidge in the sculptural group. He then reviewed the project, history, and praised Borglum for his work. The struggle for independence and the romance of that constant progress of our people toward the setting of the sun have gripped his imagination and fired his zeal to construct, in the very heart of the continent, a memorial in keeping with the high ideas and great accomplishments of our people. . . . It idealizes our progress, stimulates our patriotism, and adds luster to our achievements. It will forever remain an inspiration to youth, the pride and hope of full maturity, and the solace of old age. Who can measure its value and influence upon our future citizenship?" Williamson concluded by arguing that the United States had never economized on material things, so why not spend "just a little to advance the spiritual ideals of our great nation."

The measure passed the following day, after Black's statement that he would not object if the people of South Dakota wanted a statue of Coolidge "to look at or laugh at." But time had run out. A few hours later Congress adjourned before the House and Senate conferees could iron out differences in the two bills. The last-minute legislative jam denied success when it seemed almost certain. So there was no recourse but to wait for the next session of Congress, about six months away.

Meanwhile, work on the mountain was at a standstill. Tucker had a skeleton crew of four men working on a water supply and other odd jobs. The Mount Harney Memorial Association was without funds, and Tucker continued to advance small amounts. Creditors bombarded him with letters demanding payment of accounts long overdue, and morale was low among the sponsors. Tucker and Borglum were bickering over seemingly trivial matters, and, perhaps worst of all, the public had lost interest. Boland regretted that even yet the Black Hills community was not willing to do more financially. Although everyone seemed to favor Rushmore, "Only a few expect to do anything about it," Norbeck complained. "I would like to do something to jar the Black Hills people into a realization that Rushmore is important to them and that . . . it is their own responsibility."

But the entire year passed without further carving. "Everything is flat in South Dakota as a result of the year's idleness," Norbeck told Borglum in January 1929. "Previous to this, public sentiment has held up pretty well under our repeated assurances that everything would go right along. But the fact that neither you nor I were able to scare up a few dollars for work during the summer of 1928 has led people to believe that we were just talking hot air and that there was nothing back of our statements. . . . Most people in South Dakota figure that Stone Mountain is dead and that Rushmore is in the same class."

Indeed, the lingering stench from Stone Mountain continued to handicap the Rushmore project. This episode, unfortunately, was still fresh in people's minds, and it had a frightening effect upon prospective donors. Borglum's constant talk of returning to the Georgia work did not help. Many asked if he could be trusted. Would Rushmore be another unfinished monument? Here again Norbeck was almost brutally frank. Failure to proceed in 1928, he wrote the sculptor, left people with the feeling that "Borglum starts a lot of things but doesn't finish them." Conditions at Mount Rushmore, of course, were not Borglum's fault; no one was to blame. But it was true that the project was dead.

When Congress assembled in December, Norbeck found it hard to get a favorable conference report on the Rushmore legislation. Inertia was the great obstacle, and it was not until February 1929 that action was taken. Williamson was away from Washington in January, and his absence contributed to the delay. Senator Fess was slow in reporting the bill back to the Senate. But Norbeck called on Cramton and found him willing to help.

In conference committee the Michigan representative agreed to drop two of his amendments, but he still held that no charge should ever be made to see the memorial and that the commission as a body should not solicit funds. As this had been the only stumbling block, the House accepted the conference report on February 21. The next day it was passed by the Senate. In neither house was there any debate or opposition worth mentioning. Norbeck simply remarked that Washington's birthday was an ideal time to provide for additional work on the figure of the first president. He also explained that South Dakota was ready to provide $200,000 for a highway to the monument, of which $65,000 already had been expended.

When the Senate passed the bill, Williamson recorded in his diary, "The Senator could hardly contain himself with joy that the long agony was over. It will, of course, be signed by the President. The project now seems assured if the vagaries of the sculptor do not wreck it." Norbeck confided to an old friend, "I am very much relieved to have unloaded it on Uncle Sam and stronger shoulders." Two years had elapsed since federal aid had first been sought. If Williamson and Norbeck had not been successful in securing this legislation, Mount Rushmore would, indeed, have been another Stone Mountain. So elated were some local citizens that they suggested adding a fifth figure to the design—that of Peter Norbeck.

Public Law 805 created the Mount Rushmore National Memorial Commission as an independent agency and defined its purposes and powers. This was the basic act under which the project was administered until August 1938. It was very similar to the bills originally drawn up by Williamson in 1927. The law provided for (1) a commission of twelve presidential appointees, (2) an executive committee of five, and (3) a paid secretary. The commission's function was to be the execution of four gigantic figures and an entablature; Coolidge was named to write the inscription; the memorial was to be constructed according to the models and designs of Borglum; all property, rights, contracts, and other assets of the Mount Harney Memorial Association were to be taken over by the commission; the commission was to receive money to complete the work and "exercise such powers and functions as are necessary to carry out the purpose of this act"; and, finally, the national government agreed to furnish not more than half the total cost, or $250,000, on a matching basis.

The law now had to be implemented. Success or failure for the whole project could well have hinged on the commission members selected by the president. Membership had to be more than a mere honorary position, for there was real work to be done. Money needed to be raised—and properly spent—to match federal funds, and the commission would have to work in harmony with Borglum, no small assignment in itself.

As Borglum saw it, the principal qualification for membership should be wealth. He wanted the commission packed with millionaires. Norbeck partly agreed, but he recognized that some South Dakotans must be appointed to handle the day-to-day administration, and South Dakota was ill-supplied with millionaires. Norbeck and Robinson believed that under no circumstances should Borglum be entrusted with the business matters. "There will never be a Rushmore Memorial completed," Norbeck declared, "if Borglum is permitted to handle the business end of it."

The senator planned to recommend to President Coolidge six members from South Dakota, most of whom were of moderate means. For the other half of the commission he was ready to go along with Borglum and support the appointment of wealthy men. He told Robinson that he had "one main thought. Put on somebody that can get the money, and build the monument, regardless of who is entitled to credit for the onerous burden that has been carried for four long years." A few days later he wrote, "I want to put the work in charge of men who have the time and money to accomplish the purpose." Holding to the same theme, he asserted, "I shall be glad to endorse Jews, Gentiles, or Mohammedans if they will only come forward with the necessary money." Norbeck emphasized this point to remove the sting from his failure to recommend Robinson's appointment. By every criteria, except wealth, he deserved appointment. But Norbeck himself refused to be considered, telling the president, "I would not dare accept an appointment, because so many of my South Dakota friends who have sacrificed much for this undertaking desire to be members and must be left off."

Coolidge appointed only three South Dakotans, all of whom Norbeck had recommended. They were John Boland, Charles M. Day, and D. B. Gurney. Day and Gurney were chosen because of their control of effective publicity organs. Gurney owned the Yankton radio station WNAX, and Day published the influential *Sioux Falls Daily Argus Leader*. Other appointments were Charles R. Crane, New York businessman; Joseph S. Cullinan, millionaire Texas oil man; Hale Holden of the Southern Pacific Railroad; Mrs. Lorine J. Spoonts, a Texan and a friend of Borglum's; Frank O. Lowden, wealthy Illinois political leader; Julius Rosenwald, president of Sears, Roebuck and Company; and Fred W. Sargent, a personal friend of Coolidge and president of the Chicago and North Western Railroad. Cullinan, Spoonts, Crane, and Holden had been recommended by Borglum, and, indeed, the commission was "loaded with millionaires."

A striking feature of the commission was the absence of Robinson, Norbeck, and Williamson, who, with Borglum, had done most to develop the project but who had been passed over for richer men. Two vacancies were left for Hoover to fill, and he partly corrected the situation by appointing Williamson and Congressman Royal Johnson, giving South Dakota five of the twelve members. Within another year Robinson was appointed to fill a vacancy.

President Hoover was aggravatingly slow in calling a meeting to organize the commission. Meanwhile, none of the first federal appropriation of $100,000 could be spent. At the mountain, idleness continued. Borglum was characteristically impatient at this delay. He wanted to begin in April or May and put in a full working season on the faces. But it was impossible to begin work with only $20.67 in the Mount Harney Memorial Association treasury. In May the sculptor went to Washington and singlehandedly tried to get Hoover to act quickly. Why he bypassed Norbeck and Williamson can be explained only by his complete self-confidence. He could not forget that through four consecutive administrations, he had enjoyed free and easy access to the White House. But he had little influence with Hoover, so he and Norbeck finally agreed to leave the whole matter to Williamson, who was on close terms with the president. Nevertheless, further inaction was unbearable to Borglum. He went to the White House and got into an argument with a presidential secretary which resulted in the temporary cancellation of Williamson's appointment. This prompted Norbeck to write that Borglum "has made me no end of trouble here." He reminded the sculptor that Williamson must handle the matter and added that Napoleon had once said he would rather have one poor general than two good ones.

It was not until June 6 that the president called the commission to meet in the Cabinet Room of the White House. Boland, Williamson, Cullinan, Day, Gurney, Rosenwald, Sargent, Spoonts, and Johnson were present, along with Norbeck, to whom Hoover had issued a special invitation. The main business of the meeting, which was described by Norbeck as "dignified and impressive," was to elect officers and choose an executive committee. Cullinan, a public-spirited Texan and a personal friend of Borglum's, was elected chairman. Other members frankly hoped that this multimillionaire would assume much of the financial responsibility in providing matching funds. George F. Schneider of the Pennington County Bank in Rapid City was chosen treasurer. Boland, Williamson, Sargent, Gurney, and Rosenwald were elected to the executive committee. The commission instructed its committee to proceed at once with the carving. In accordance with Borglum's wishes, Cullinan was authorized to appoint a committee on design and publicity.

Upon adjournment of the full commission, the executive committee met and selected Boland chairman and Williamson secretary. The next afternoon they called at the office of the secretary of the treasury with their requisition for funds and were assured that payment would be made.

The Mount Harney Memorial Association had spent $54,670.56 on the memorial, most of this amount during 1927. Under the law, this sum was now due the commission from the federal government. With more than $50,000 in prospect, the way seemed clear to get in at least one full working season without further solicitation from private sources. Since he was getting such a late start, Borglum estimated that about $30,000 would carry the work through 1929. However, the huge task confronted the commission of raising nearly $200,000 more to match the federal authorization. In light of past experience, this would be difficult unless wealthy members of the commission decided to make large donations.

But these problems were temporarily shelved or forgotten. The commission had scarcely adjourned when Borglum wired Tucker to resume work on the mountain. The same evening he gave a dinner for some twenty-five important guests and gloried in the praise showered upon him in "about twenty-four speeches." Borglum was a gracious and delightful host, and he loved to entertain. There were no signs of that dejection so visible in the preceding months of inactivity. Mount Rushmore had come to be the most important thing in Borglum's life, and now with assurance of funds for the current working season, he again radiated his unequaled charm and contagious enthusiasm.

Oblivious to most practical problems and confident in the future, Borglum engagingly discussed his plans for the memorial. His captivated guests had no doubt that they were sitting in the presence of genius. Regardless of what he may have said or done in an impulsive or irrational moment, people found it hard not to love Gutzon Borglum at a time like this. Without this dreamer and visionary, this impetuous and impractical idealist, Mount Rushmore would never have been more than a mass of gray granite.

On July 17 the commission held its second meeting in Borglum's unfinished studio on Doane Mountain, across the canyon east of Mount Rushmore. The studio was built of native logs, and a large window looked out toward the mountain, providing the sculptor with an uninterrupted view. Until it became overrun with curious tourists, he would at last have a favorable place to work. At this meeting Boland was made "chief field representative" of the commission, and Gutzon appointed Borglum, Spoonts, and Lowden to the committee on design and publicity. Perhaps the most important business was the assignment of Borglum's contract by the Mount Harney Memorial Association to the new commission. The executive committee was directed to study the document and recommend changes or modifications. The only change made, however, was the exemption of certain small items of expenses such as insurance, on which the 25 percent honorarium was figured.

The commission considered Tucker's $10,000-a-year contract extravagant and refused to assume responsibility for it. Neither did it agree to pay the outstanding obligations of the old state association, which totaled $32,505.71. All but $6,101.29 of this was owed to Borglum and Tucker. Among other creditors, the Mine and Smelter Company of Denver had $3,333 on its books. In effect, the commission officially took over the assets of the Mount Harney Memorial Association, which had been legislated out of existence the preceding March, but refused to guarantee its liabilities. However, Boland and Williamson were insistent that the debts of the old association be paid, and a scheme was worked out whereby money solicited locally would be applied on the earlier obligations. These were all finally settled, due largely to Boland's management.

Carving on the mountain was now progressing rapidly. By the end of the working season in November, Washington's features were clearly perceptible. E. C. Howe, clerk of the works, asserted in September that "Washington is beginning to look quite like himself and the block where Jefferson's head will appear is nearly ready for the sculptor to locate the center." After visiting the work, Norbeck wrote, "The progress this past summer has . . . been not only satisfactory, but almost remarkable." Everyone was greatly encouraged.

Beginning where they had left off in 1927, Borglum's crew carved downward from Washington's eyebrows to the point of his chin. The forehead, from the hair down, was practically completed, and the brows, nose, eyelids, and the eyeballs were drilled to within a few inches of the intended surface. After the roughing out had been completed by workmen in swing seats, finishing was done from scaffolds. Carvers were protected from inclement weather by a tarpaulin spread over the scaffolding.

In contrast to the rosy picture presented by the actual work on the mountain, the long-range financial outlook was still bleak. In July the secretary of the treasury remitted $54,670.56 to the commission to match the money previously spent by the Mount Harney Memorial Association. Miscellaneous receipts brought the total to $54,791.23. Between June and November, $45,864.36 was spent on the project, leaving only $8,926.87 on hand. Analysis of the expenditures shows top-heavy outlays for administration and supervision, the second largest item of expense being a $10,000 payment to Tucker. Borglum was given $2,000 which was only a small part of his honorarium. The entire construction payroll of $13,091.79 was only slightly more than that paid to Borglum and Tucker. Completion of the studio had cost more than $8,000, and nearly that amount had been spent for equipment, explosives, and salaries. In any event, there was less than $9,000 remaining for the fiscal year which began November 1, 1929. The problem of raising matching funds had again become pressing. Actually, money due Tucker and Borglum exceeded the treasury balance.

In retrospect it seems that the commission blundered by not organizing a vigorous fund-raising campaign during the summer of 1929. Conditions were then more favorable than at any time in the history of the project. The United States was on a spending spree. Smart traders, plying the bull market, were becoming millionaires in record time. Stock and bond quotations were soaring. At the White House meeting on June 6, Williamson had urged that funds be sought immediately. Since Gurney had raised large sums for other projects, Williamson suggested sending him into the field on a campaign of personal solicitation. Other members, however, particularly Cullinan and Sargent, believed there was ample time to raise money, and so no action was taken.

The fact that the commission members were businessmen or public servants probably accounts for a part of their inaction. With money in the bank and rapid progress on the work, the need for soliciting funds seemed less urgent. Norbeck's opinion was probably typical when he advised Gurney not to press members of the commission for contributions until they knew more about the work and had become interested in its completion. There was undoubtedly a letdown after the first federal funds were received and a tendency to wait for the wealthy commissioners to make heavy contributions.

An additional factor was the commission's continued faith in Borglum's optimistic promises to raise subscriptions among wealthy friends. Why, after the experience of two years, anyone would believe these confident reports is hard to explain. It would be unfair to criticize Borglum for not raising more money. The publicity given the memorial as a result of his efforts was of incalculable value. His mistake was in continually giving the impression that he was just within reach of funds. Norbeck warned Gurney not to "take Borglum's enthusiasm as being of cash value." The only large contribution for which he had been directly responsible was the $5,000 from Du Pont.

But whatever the reasons for delay, no concentrated effort to raise matching funds occurred in 1929. Before the end of the first working season the stock market crash shook the country, and it entered upon the long, drawn-out era of depression. If any opportunity to assure funds for Mount Rushmore had ever existed, it now vanished. "We lost the finest opportunity we had," Williamson complained.

An otherwise successful year at Mount Rushmore was slightly disturbed in August by the resignation of Major Tucker. He had become disgruntled when the new commission refused to take over his contract, although he was employed in 1929 on a basis of $833.33 per month. After the Mount Harney Memorial Association exhausted its funds, it still had a contractual obligation to Tucker, although he was doing practically no work. During 1928 and early 1929 he had advanced more than $1,500 to purchase materials and $2,300 for payrolls. His unpaid salary amounted to $16,441 by the summer of 1929, making a total due him, including interest, of $20,664. Between June 1928 and the time when the federal commission took control, the old state association had been able to pay him only $2,000. After other payments during the summer of 1929, an audit showed that he had $8,289 due him when he resigned.

During the time Tucker worked for the commission he was paid in full. But now he brought suit to collect what was due him from the extinct state association. Williamson recognized that Tucker had a weak legal case. His contract specifically exempted members of the association from any liability, and he had agreed to rely solely on funds in the treasury. His lawyer wrote to Williamson that neither he nor Tucker had any desire to test the matter in court. Although Williamson wanted to fight the case, Boland believed that some compromise ought to be reached so that Tucker would depart quietly and contentedly. The specter of Stone Mountain was constantly before Boland, and he feared that if Tucker were not paid at once, he would go to the newspapers and give out publicity harmful to the project. So he arranged to make a cash settlement with Tucker for $7,500, although the contractor claimed $11,150. Of the amount paid, Borglum advanced $5,000 and Boland persuaded the Rapid City Chamber of Commerce to put up $2,500. Boland admitted that this was a costly settlement and declared that if Rushmore had been an enterprise of which he was the manager, he would have handled the matter differently. The mistake had been to hire Tucker at such a high salary in the first place and keep him on when there was no work in 1928. This had been unavoidable, however, for Borglum would not undertake the project without him, and Tucker would not go to South Dakota for less. Actually, the employment of Tucker cost $12,500 a year because of Borglum's honorarium on the basic salary of $10,000. Yet all was not lost; Tucker had made some contribution.

Upon learning of Tucker's resignation, Borglum took personal charge of the carving. J. C. Denison was promoted to superintendent at $4,000 a year, saving the commission about $7,500 over the previous arrangement. But now Borglum had to spend more time in South Dakota. He had originally intended to stay only a few weeks each summer at Mount Rushmore, but he soon found the project more and more demanding. To be near his work he bought a ranch not far from Hermosa and about twenty miles from the mountain, and moved his family there. Shortly afterward he remodeled an old building into a large studio in which to do his other commissions. Although the Borglums generally spent the winter months in San Antonio, the sculptor was to make the Black Hills his home during the rest of his lifetime.

CHAPTER NINE

History for the Ages

URING the winter of 1929–1930, Cullinan and Borglum turned to the problem of raising money from private sources. If the Washington figure were to be unveiled on July 4, work had to begin no later than April. Only a little more than $5,000 remained in the treasury on January 1. The commission had failed to develop any plan to meet the fiscal problem. Understandably impatient, Borglum suggested publishing a handsome Mount Rushmore brochure in which advertising space would be sold. The commission approved his scheme, and early in 1930 Borglum's committee on design and publicity prepared and issued an illustrated, thirty-six page brochure of folio size. It contained a historical account of the project, an article by Borglum on the significance of the memorial, Coolidge's 1927 address, important documents and speeches, and several pictures showing the work in progress.

It was a splendid method of advertising. More than forty thousand copies were published and sent to libraries, members of Congress and other government officials, nearly two thousand daily newspapers, and the principal news syndicates. If the sculptor omitted from the mailing list any important person in the United States, it was an oversight. The brochure was also sold at Borglum's Rushmore studio.

This scheme was surprisingly successful in raising funds, and Borglum deserves the credit. Most members of the commission had given him only indifferent support. The Texas Company and the Chicago and North Western Railway, through their presidents Cullinan and Sargent, each ordered ten thousand copies at $5,000. Each firm also took a page of advertising at $1,000, as did the Standard Oil Company of Indiana, making a total of $13,000. When this was matched by federal funds, about $20,000 became available after deducting more than $5,000 for expense of publication.

Meanwhile, Chairman Cullinan was developing another fund-raising plan. In December 1929 he proposed the formation of the Mount Rushmore National Memorial Society to serve as an auxiliary to the commission. He first explained his idea to Borglum, urging "a permanent Rushmore Club composed of individuals contributing say $100, furnishing each an appropriate certificate and membership card signed by you."

When he made his proposal to the commission, the members responded favorably if not eagerly. Boland wrote that he favored the idea and would take ten memberships, but Williamson was less enthusiastic. He still felt that the commission should approach men of means and raise the money directly. However, members were willing to try anything that offered even a faint hope of relieving their financial stringency. The society was incorporated in the District of Columbia on February 24, 1930, along the lines suggested by Cullinan. He was named president, Robinson, secretary, and Boland, treasurer.

The main purpose of the organization was to raise money, handle publicity, assist in plans for landscaping and parking, and help to protect the grounds around the memorial from commercialism and exploitation. Memberships moved out briskly, mostly to members of the commission who presented them to friends and relatives. Certificates signed by Borglum graced an increasing number of office walls. By July 1, fifty-six people had joined the society and $5,600 was turned over to the commission. When this was matched by the federal appropriation, another $11,200 was added to the treasury. Thus, during the spring and early summer of 1930, a budget of over $40,000 became available to continue operations on the mountain.

In the meantime, hearings were being held before the House Committee on Appropriations regarding additional Mount Rushmore funds for the next fiscal year. Williamson was invited to appear before the subcommittee, where he asked that an additional $60,000 be appropriated. He explained that each year $100,000 could be spent efficiently on the project. For the first time his colleagues raised the question that was to be heard continuously throughout the 1930s: Would the federal government be asked for more than the $250,000 authorized in 1929? "No, I do not think it will be necessary," Williamson replied. "I do not anticipate that any further help from the National Government will be asked." Federal lawmakers, however, were skeptical.

Other discussions centered around the length of time necessary to complete the memorial and its accessibility to tourists. Some congressmen wanted to know whether or not additional figures were planned. Williamson told his colleagues that at least four years would be required to complete the work, that the state was building satisfactory roads, and that no figures were contemplated other than those specified by law. It was important to stress the state's willingness to build highways. Congress would not likely appropriate money for a memorial cut off from the traveling public by several miles of impassable wilderness. Some lawmakers felt that the project was too isolated to be of much value to the nation as a whole even if suitable roads were provided. But, satisfied with Williamson's explanation and assurance, Congress appropriated another $60,000, which made more than enough funds available to match private contributions.

At the mountain work now progressed rapidly. Most of the carving was aimed at completing the face of Washington preparatory to the unveiling ceremonies on July 4. Additional finishing work was done, and some of the remaining stone on each side of the face was blown away. This caused the features to appear in greater relief.

Borglum also located and began roughing out the Jefferson head. His first group-model showed Washington, Jefferson, and Lincoln placed from left to right as one faced the mountain. The Roosevelt figure did not appear in the early models, but it was assumed that it would be located to the left of Lincoln at the north end of the group. However, Borglum constantly pointed out that changes in design would probably be required and that the stone must necessarily dictate the final form. From the beginning he was certain of only one thing: Washington must be the central and dominating figure. When the Washington face was located on the extreme southeast shoulder of the mountain, it was thought that Jefferson, Lincoln, and Roosevelt would be placed in that order on Washington's left, and southwest on the cliff. But by 1933, Borglum had decided to place Jefferson slightly lower and to Washington's right, and Lincoln and Roosevelt, from left to right, as viewed from the valley below.

Hundreds of thousands of tourists who visited Mount Rushmore after 1933 were unaware that the rough features of Jefferson had once appeared south of Washington. After spending much time and money and nearly finishing a mask of Jefferson, Borglum found that there was insufficient stone to complete a full head. To make matters worse, a large crack developed in the granite which forced a change of plans. When the road was built to Horse Thief Lake along the south side of the mountain, tourists could see the back of the head, which gave a poor impression of the monument. Consequently, in 1934 Borglum dynamited the Jefferson face away. But by the time Washington was ready to be unveiled, the position of the Jefferson head, as first located, had been blocked, and the features were ready for pointing.

At the same time, Borglum had workmen preparing stone for the entablature. He had modified his plans for its location several times, but he had never given up the idea of including it. His original notebook sketch of the entablature showed it on the mountain's east wall, but in 1926 he said that the inscription should be on the west side, opposite to and completely hidden from the faces. In that case it could be seen only from the west and north. Borglum felt that any text beside the faces would harm the sculptural effect. By 1930 he had again changed his mind and had determined to place the entablature several hundred feet north of Washington's face, at the point where the Lincoln figure was finally located. The entablature surface was to resemble the geographic outline of the Louisiana Purchase.

The memorial would not be complete, in Borglum's judgment, without a permanent inscription. This, he thought, should tell something of the country's history as well as the significance of the monument. If it were to last five hundred thousand years, as some geologists said, the four faces without explanative text might someday be meaningless. Borglum was carving for the ages. At one time he recommended dressing the walls of the canyon back of the faces and carving the nation's principal records, such as the Constitution, in three languages, "English, Latin, and some great Asiatic language—Chinese or Japanese." To undertake such a project, or a similar one, required a strong faith in the permanence of human institutions. But the inscriptions of the ancients had always impressed Borglum. From the time of Darius to the creation of the Lion of Lucerne in Switzerland twenty-four hundred years later, outdoor mountain scribes had been busy with mallet and chisel. Borglum, however, would outdo anything accomplished by his predecessors. They would make poor competitors for they had neither the ideas nor the tools which he possessed.

President Coolidge had promised in 1927 that he would pen an inscription to be carved for posterity, and this provision had been written into the basic law. The choice of Coolidge was primarily a political one since he had no reputation in either literary or historical fields. His single qualification was the terseness and brevity of his style. There was no room for a wordy account. In January 1930 it was announced that the former president was ready to begin his "history á la tabloid," as the *New York Mirror* labeled it. The inscription was to appear on an entablature 80 by 120 feet, carved and gilded in letters five inches deep. It would be seen for a distance of three miles, Borglum said. Although Coolidge was not restricted to any specific number of words, it was clear that he must be extremely brief. Newsmen were soon referring to a five hundred–word history of the United States, and the country generally believed that this limit had been set either by Borglum or by the commission. Nothing had given the project so much publicity as the announcement that the former president would write a manuscript to be permanently inscribed in Black Hills granite. Borglum engaged the McCutcheon-Gerson Service of Chicago to publicize this and related events. During January alone, stories appeared in 317 newspapers of thirty-six states, which had a total circulation of more than thirteen million.

Not to be outdone, the *Chicago Tribune* sponsored a contest of its own, offering a $1,000 prize for the best five hundred–word history of the United States. Professor William W. Sweet of the University of Chicago, an authority on American church history, won the *Tribune*'s award.

Cartoonists and editorial writers filled their columns with suggestions and speculation regarding the project. A major question was whether or not such a short history would be worthy of permanence. But the fact that professional historians were dubious did not deter Borglum. Perhaps he was encouraged by the fact that the author of Genesis had told the story of the creation in less than eight hundred words.

Some writers expressed confidence that Coolidge was equal to the task. Many scribes were convinced that if Coolidge's reminiscences, which were then appearing serially, were any indication of his literary ability, he would not succeed in so responsible a work as the Rushmore inscription. Of course, these critics commented, he was getting a dollar a word for his magazine articles, and he was donating his time to the Mount Rushmore inscription. The *Brooklyn Eagle* carried a cartoon showing Coolidge, dressed as a cook, stirring a large volume of history in a pot of hot water. The caption read: "Boiling It Down." The *Seattle Times* declared that his task demanded "a display of talent for condensation amounting to genius."

Objection to the whole affair was raised by the *New York Post* because Coolidge, although "a grand little president . . . does not rank quite that high in history or literature." Furthermore, the editor added, "We are not at all sure that we like to see 'all God's mountains' messed up with sculpture and inscriptions." The *London Daily Telegraph* chided, "Quite jolly must be the nation which can write its history in five hundred words."

When the press kept pounding on the idea of a five hundred–word history, Borglum explained publicly that he had selected eight events which he considered epochal in the nation's development. The history would be written around these events, which included: the Declaration of Independence, the framing of the Constitution, the purchase of Louisiana, the admission of Texas, the settlement of the Oregon boundary dispute, the admission of California, the conclusion of the Civil War, and the building of the Panama Canal. Such a restricted and imperial view of history was sure to bring critical comment from thoughtful people who had even a slight knowledge of American history. The *Waterbury (Connecticut) Republican* concluded that under these circumstances, Coolidge could not be blamed for a poor job because "any of two hundred historians in the country could have produced a more logical outline." But the former president agreed to follow Borglum's pattern and proceeded to prepare his text. On April 9 the first two "chapters," or paragraphs, were released to the press. They dealt with the Declaration of Independence and the Constitution.

Newspapers all over the country gave voluminous publicity to this initial material. Vigorous comments came from editors who blissfully supposed that they were publishing Coolidge's original text. Suddenly, however, the storm struck. About the middle of May it was revealed that these first portions of the text had been blue-penciled and revised by Borglum without Coolidge's consent. This was first learned by John J. Corbin, a student of the Constitution and a former editorial writer for the *New York Times*. On April 25 he had written a letter to the *Times* severely attacking the so-called history. In response to

Corbin's blistering criticisms, Coolidge privately disclaimed any responsibility for the published accounts. Corbin then wrote another public letter saying that Coolidge's work had been changed. It was not until May 13, after Borglum had admitted tampering with the manuscript, that anyone knew what Coolidge had written. Then practically every major newspaper published the two versions together.

Coolidge wrote: "The Declaration of Independence—The eternal right to seek happiness through self-government and the divine duty to defend that right at any sacrifice." Borglum edited this to read: "In the year of our Lord 1776 the people declared the eternal right to seek happiness, self-government and the divine duty to defend that right at any sacrifice." He explained that he wanted to identify the historical era and put the text in narrative form. He omitted the word "through," believing that happiness did not necessarily depend upon self-government.

Coolidge's next paragraph was subjected to more fundamental changes. He had written: "The constitution—charter of perpetual union of free people of sovereign states establishing a government of limited powers—under an independent President, Congress, and Court, charged to provide security for all citizens in their enjoyment of liberty, equality and justice under the law." Borglum's revision read: "In 1787 assembled in convention they made a charter of perpetual union for free people of sovereign states establishing a government of limited powers under an independent President, Congress, and Court charged to provide security for all citizens in their enjoyment of liberty, equality and justice." He continued his idea of historical narrative by giving the date, but he omitted the word "constitution" and substituted a description of the event. Finally, he struck out the phrase "under the law," arguing that justice and liberty were so fundamental and inalienable that they were above and outside the law.

Most of the country's newspapers emphatically denounced the sculptor for his highhanded action. Headlines such as "Borglum Shows Coolidge How," "Borglum Alters Coolidge's Work," and "Borglum Revises ... History" were typical and stimulated critical editorial pens. After reading Borglum's revised history, the *Waterloo (Iowa) Courier* concluded that he was "an excellent sculptor!" Coolidge's experience would probably prompt him to confine his writing to magazines rather than mountains, said the *Beloit (Wisconsin) News*. "Possibly the Borglum attack upon the Coolidge text may be just another expression of his urge to hack," ventured the *Cleveland (Ohio) Plain Dealer*.

The *Tampa (Florida) Tribune* suggested that Coolidge's difficulty was similar to that of every cub reporter, and added, "If Calvin has got any spirit at all, he'll turn in his resignation." The editor of the *Olympia (Washington) Olympian* said, "To invite him to write it, and then subject this project to the blue pencil . . . seems hardly proper." From Leavenworth, Kansas, came the comment, "Borglum does things with a high hand and if he can't have his own way he won't play." The *Salem (Massachusetts) News* wondered how Borglum would react if Coolidge were to suggest some change in the sculpture. The *Oklahoma City Times* carried a cartoon showing Borglum seated examining a manuscript while Coolidge looks on from across the desk. Borglum is saying, "Cal, you use too many *dollar* words." The *Los Angeles Times* half-humorously concluded that the inscription should bear an accompanying phrase, "Written by Calvin Coolidge and corrected by Gutzon Borglum."

Borglum's strongest support came form the *Boston Transcript*, which declared that the sculptor's revision showed a deeper philosophy and a more universal concept. But this was only an island in a sea of criticism. Grateful for even scant praise, Borglum wired the editor his heartfelt thanks. He added that he did not wish to change the president's ideas, but the inscription must contain broad basic truths. The sculptor consistently argued that his only interest was to have the inscription accurate and written in "beautiful English." Posterity would hold him responsible, he said, whether or not he wrote it.

Coolidge would not immediately comment on Borglum's editing, but his irritation soon became evident. Shortly after the revised text appeared in print, he emphatically told Borglum, "I do not wish to approve the changes that you suggest." He added, "In each instance, it breaks up the thought I was trying to convey." In reply, Borglum reminded Coolidge that he had given permission to make minor changes. Robinson, referring to a conversation in 1927, said that Coolidge had asked Borglum and himself to act as guides in writing the inscription; therefore, he should not be offended by Borglum's action.

Members of the Mount Rushmore Memorial Commission had made every effort to avoid the controversy. Cullinan explained to newsmen that the basic legislation had made Borglum responsible for all plans and designs; therefore, by law he was the final arbiter. "In that case," said the *Los Angeles Times*, "the inscription needs a better arbiter." At any rate, Coolidge wrote sharply to Cullinan. Enclosing copies of his text, he declared, "They were changed and in the changed form without any approval from me published. . . . If your commission wished to publish the proposed inscription, it should have stated . . . that it was not my composition."

Cullinan's correspondence with Coolidge and with members of the commission indicates his sympathy with the sculptor. Since Congress had made Borglum responsible for the work, he told the former president, "It seems to me that Mr. Borglum necessarily should have a voice in everything pertaining to the memorial." This was somewhat beside the point, but it clarified Cullinan's position and showed Coolidge that he could expect no official support from the commission in his embarrassment. Cullinan expressed the hope that Coolidge and Borglum would "reach an early understanding." But this was a vain wish. Coolidge had decided quickly that he was through with manuscripts for mountain-carving.

He was, perhaps, further aggravated by Borglum's public statement intimating that he had approved the changes. Borglum had done this even after Coolidge had specifically disapproved them in writing. The sculptor's real intentions were revealed when he actually started to carve the inscription before he and Coolidge had made any attempt to iron out their differences. The first and only letters ever inscribed were "1776." Since this was not part of the Coolidge manuscript, it was clear that Borglum was determined to suit his own fancy. It is no wonder that Coolidge gave it up as a bad job. These numerals remained until they were carved away several years later when preparation was being made to block out the Lincoln head.

On July 3 the commission passed a resolution requesting Coolidge to prepare his full text for consideration by the commissioners at their November meeting. Later in the month Williamson, one of Coolidge's closest friends on the commission, urged him to proceed with the entire text. He did not seem to realize how miffed Coolidge had become. "It has been a pleasure as you know to try to help along the work at Mount Rushmore particularly on account of yourself and Senator Norbeck," he replied to Williamson. But Coolidge refused to deal further with the project. He made no mention of Borglum. Williamson confided to Boland, "I know enough about him to know that the manner in which his inscription was handled did not set well."

Out of the whole affair came an entertaining story with a typical Coolidge comment. Paul Bellamy, who had become acquainted with Coolidge during the summer of 1927, was visiting the former president at his Northampton home. Finally, the conversation got around to the Black Hills and Mount Rushmore. "Mr. Bellamy," said Coolidge, "do you see Mr. Borglum very often?" Bellamy replied that he frequently saw the sculptor during the summer months. "How far is it from Northampton to Rapid City?" Coolidge asked. "Oh, about two thousand miles, Mr. President," said Bellamy. Coolidge looked pensively out the window, blew a puff of cigar smoke, and said, "You know, Mr. Bellamy, that is just about as close to Mr. Borglum as I want to be."

Most unbiased judges would agree to the superiority of Borglum's text. The Coolidge manuscript did need much revision. This, however, was not the point. What Borglum did was not so bad as the way he did it. Common sense should have told him that Coolidge and the country would react unfavorably regardless of the quality of his own work. Borglum did not intentionally irritate Coolidge, but in his boyish impatience and self-confidence, he probably never even considered the impropriety of his action. Anyway, he considered Mount Rushmore his personal project and felt his ideas must prevail.

From one point of view the outcome was fortunate. The worst blunder of all would have been to carve any history on Mount Rushmore where it might have stood for half a million years. Clio would have forever chafed at the injustice. No history could be written in such brief compass, following Borglum's unbalanced outline, which would justly and accurately portray the spirit and meaning of American development. This is not to say that some inscription was not desirable. But this particular plan would have been a travesty on both art and history. Even Borglum concluded later that his plan should be changed.

The question of a successor for Coolidge was discussed by the commission at its meeting on November 19 in Chicago. But the touchy matter was postponed for a year, partly because most responsible officials believed that the inscription was less important than the faces and that all available money should be expended on the four figures.

The effect and importance of the whole episode was to give the memorial untold publicity. Money could not have bought so much advertising. Millions read about the work who had never heard or seen the name Mount Rushmore. The controversy also stirred the people's desire to see the project and the man who so dramatically conducted it. Borglum was a poor historian and a somewhat better philosopher, but he was nothing short of a genius at publicity.

As Coolidge returned to writing magazine articles at Northampton, Borglum was busily planning elaborate ceremonies to celebrate the unveiling of the Washington head. He would make July 4, 1930, a memorable day in Black Hills history. Fancy invitations had been sent out to hundreds of prominent people, including President Hoover. It was unnecessary to invite local citizens because they had learned that a Borglum dedication was a sight to behold.

By noon about twenty-five hundred people had assembled around Borglum's studio on Doane Mountain. A large flag, seventy-two feet long and forty feet wide, covered Washington's face, thus arousing the curiosity and expectations of those who had not yet seen the sculptural work. Chairman Cullinan presided and in his introductory remarks coined a phrase which, with slight modification, was to give the memorial another name. He referred to the work as "America's Shrine for Political Democracy." From this came "The Shrine of Democracy," a label which some enthusiasts hoped to substitute in later years for "Mount Rushmore."

Doane Robinson, vigorous and erect despite his seventy-four years, gave a brief historical sketch of the project and asserted that even if work were to stop at this stage, the idea had proved itself a success. He expressed halfhearted regret that the plans had been expanded to include the entablature and other figures besides Washington and Lincoln. Following Robinson's talk and one by Dr. O'Hara, Cullinan introduced Borglum, the "foremost artist of the universe in colossal portraiture."

It was Borglum whom the crowd had been waiting to hear, and he was in top form as was always the case on these occasions. Taking up the philosophy and meaning behind the memorial, he said that the Washington head had not been conceived merely to show "bulk form . . . but rather to give form and intimate personal character, while yet being colossal and heroic in dimension." One of the most notable things regarding this art, he declared, was "the human character and vitality that can be given to great mass." Borglum was not content with mere size; the Mount Rushmore figures must have life, vitality, and reality.

Continuing, he said, "Upon Mount Rushmore we are trying to give to the portrait of Washington all the vigor and power that direct modeling makes possible and produce a head in sculpture as vital as one can hold, produced at arm's length. On Mount Rushmore there has been produced a forehead of Washington twenty feet from wig to nose, as animate and carefully constructed as the Houdon mask which I have followed, together with the portraits of Peale and Stewart. The brow has emerged, amazing in mass, vigor and beauty of form; the nose seems better than the Stewart nose. Altogether the face is as vital as it is possible to make it. When the great sockets below the brow were cut to their proper depth the eyes seemed unnecessary; the great face seemed to belong to the mountain; it took on the elemental courage of the mountains surrounding it."

Borglum assured his audience that during the remaining working season "the head of Washington will be continued on down to the knees in vigorous strokes," and that the Jefferson face would be completed by July 1, 1931. He also repeated what he had told Coolidge three years earlier: He was creating a monument which would outlive the government. "In 1927 the man was regarded as a dreamer, a bit impractical, a little disrespectful of the government," said the *Rapid City Daily Journal*; but now he was cheered and applauded. Perhaps one observer was right when he said it was "the first occasion in history equal to the day when the Pharaoh Ptolemy completed the Sphinx of Egypt."

When Borglum finished speaking, the flag was withdrawn from the sixty-foot face of Washington. Riflemen fired salutes, airplanes roared overhead, and spectators watched in awe and amazement. It was a true Borglum exhibition.

The dedication was a marked contrast to the first ceremony held at the mountain nearly five years before. On that day people had laboriously ascended to Mount Rushmore on foot or horseback. There in the midst of nature's majestic grandeur, as yet untouched by man, they had seen Borglum climb Rushmore peak and raise an American flag. They had heard this optimistic genius tell them to meet him there a year later to see the Washington figure. He had been pitting his confidence and energy against a mountain. Faith might move mountains, but faith alone was not enough to carve them. By combining his work and effort with that of others, Borglum had been able to keep his promise, albeit somewhat late. A flag still flew atop Rushmore, but now it waved over winch houses, machinery and equipment, and the unfinished head of George Washington.

By 1930 it was possible to reach Mount Rushmore by automobile. A graded road existed from Rapid City to Keystone and from Keystone to the mountain base. There were days when as many as four hundred cars from all over the nation arrived at the monument—testimony to the rapidly increasing tourist travel. Visitors enjoyed watching Borglum at work on his models or on the mountain. He was a major tourist attraction and usually did not disappoint his visitors. Not infrequently, upon learning of the visit of prominent people, he made it a point to be in a swing seat on the side of the cliff. This properly impressed visiting dignitaries. Sometimes he would dramatically mount the ladder leading to the scale models in front of a wide-eyed crowd. Usually dressed in a business suit, with the characteristic scarf about his neck and his Stetson pulled well down over his eyes, he would take out his tape measure, adopt a serious professional mien, adjust his glasses, and begin to work.

Borglum was completely unpredictable, and this trait increased with the pressure of work. No one knew how he might react to admiring visitors. On one occasion during the depression of the early thirties, a middle-aged farm couple entered the studio. Of Danish ancestry, the couple revealed in their weathered faces the hardships of Dakota farm life. The man was dressed in faded blue denims, his wife in simple calico. The husband timidly told Mrs. O. H. Wilcox, who handled the few concessions permitted by Borglum, that he would like to speak to Mr. Borglum, but felt embarrassed and restrained. Mrs. Wilcox, however, urged him to approach the sculptor who was working on his models. Screwing up his courage, he introduced himself to Borglum as a fellow Dane and complimented him on his wonderful work. Borglum responded magnanimously. He took more than an hour to show the couple everything in the studio.

Sometime later a prominent state citizen came to the studio with a group of friends. As they entered, Borglum was just beginning to climb a ladder to the top of his models. When he started up the first few rungs, the visitor said, "Hello, Mr. Borglum, I'm Mr. ———." Borglum paid no attention whatever, and the man repeated his salutation, "Mr.

Borglum, I'm —— ." By that time the sculptor was at the top of the ladder. He turned around, pushed his pince-nez down his nose so he could look over them, and blurted out, "Well, what of it?"

The celebration at Mount Rushmore in 1930 again called national attention to the monument. The *New York Times* carried an account of the ceremonies on the front page, and most other major newspapers gave the affair some space. Part of the program was broadcast, and representatives of the Fox, Pathé, Paramount, and Universal motion picture companies were present. If popular support was to be assured, it was important to tell the public about the work. The occasional outbursts of sarcasm or opposition were overwhelmed by popular approval.

Florence Davies, art critic for the *Detroit News*, bitterly assailed the project. She admitted that "hacking up the mountains . . . may be news," but thought it was poor art. "The mountain . . . is a kind of earth sculpture of its own and loses its intrinsic majesty and dignity when man uses it as a billboard," she said. There was nothing wrong with spoiling a natural hillside if it was not done in the name of art and sculpture. She thought mountain-carving was "inspired by a type of sentimentality which springs from a kind of mental elephantiasis." Such figures might be "astonishing, stupendous, or spectacular," she wrote, but they had nothing to do with art.

One editor, after considering Stone Mountain and Mount Rushmore, asserted that such movements could lead to serious results. "Every village," he said, "will be looking for some defenseless hill out of which some tombstone chiseler may be hired to make a statue of . . . the Honorable Silas Slick, who got more free seeds and postoffices for his constituents than any other congressman. . . . Instead of lifting our eyes to the soft, restful hills, whence cometh our help, shall we instead contemplate the hard features of Henry Hokum, president of the First National Bank and donor of the town library? Unless this movement is nipped in the bud it will come to that." Such were the critics' views.

President Franklin D. Roosevelt dedicates the Jefferson face. Governor Tom Berry of South Dakota stands at the left. Borglum is pointing to the memorial.

Although not scheduled to speak at the Jefferson dedication in 1936, Franklin Roosevelt was so moved by what he saw that he grabbed the network microphones as his son Franklin, Jr. assisted.

Borglum directs work on the Lincoln face. The various stages of carving are apparent: vertical drill marks in the upper left corner, horizontal drill marks in and around the eye and on the temple, and the finished quality of the stone on the outer rim of the nose, produced by "bumping."

The unveiling of Lincoln, September 17, 1937. The protruding pupils cast the shadows which make the eyes appear alive.

The Lincoln face: Cracks in the granite presented many engineering problems.

CHAPTER TEN

Dimes and Dollars

ASIDE from Borglum, the man on whom the commission placed greatest reliance for progress at Mount Rushmore was John A. Boland, who as chairman of the executive committee was chief administrative officer. His job was to help raise money and, of equal importance, to see that it was properly and judiciously spent. He had the task of dealing firsthand with the sculptor, a job in personal relations which would have exhausted and defeated a less determined and capable man. Until he was purged in 1938 when Borglum reorganized the commission, Boland made a remarkable contribution to the progress of the monument.

Born of a hard-working pioneer Scotch-Irish family in 1884, Boland had spent his entire life in the Black Hills. As a boy, he roamed over the hills around Keystone and more than once scaled rugged Rushmore peak. His father, Abram C. Boland, had arrived in the region from Ontario during the lusty gold-rush days and had established the first feed store in Rapid City in 1880.

Young Boland entered the South Dakota State School of Mines in 1899 and finished the preparatory course two years later. After working in his father's feed and flour store in Keystone, he spent a few months in the gold mines and bought out his father early in 1903. It was an inopportune time to undertake a new enterprise. Within six months most of the mines in the region closed down, creating unemployment and forcing Boland to liquidate. The liberal credit he had extended to unemployed miners left him $1500 in debt. This was paid off by working in the gold mines. In the fall of 1904 he enrolled in the Lincoln (Nebraska) Business College, and after completing the nine-month course, he became a bookkeeper for a contracting firm. In 1906 he returned to Keystone, the site of his first business venture, and bought a grocery store. He operated this successfully until 1917 when he purchased a sizeable interest in the

133

Rapid City Implement Company in partnership with I. M. Humphrey. Later he became president and chief stockholder of this establishment and ultimately full owner.

Sensible, practical, calm, and industrious, Boland achieved business and civic leadership in his community. Contrary to the biblical maxim, he enjoyed the respect and confidence of those who knew him best. He held many positions of local honor and was elected to the state senate in 1928. He was a small, thin, bald, energetic man who radiated efficiency and had a marked ability to master details. There was no lost motion in his activities; every move counted. Hard work, wise investments, and skillful management had brought him more than average affluence. Disdain for those who did not share his quality of financial responsibility and honesty was a revealing trait of his character. Discussing an employee of the Mount Rushmore project, he once wrote, "The worst fault he had was that he did not pay his bills."

Few men could make a dollar go farther than Boland, who was generous but not profligate. He worked his money just as hard as he did himself. A man of quick decision, he readily assumed and discharged responsibility. There was a certain positivism about him which precluded compromise when principle was involved. In many respects he was a typical middle-class American, living in an ordinary western town, gaining repute locally but not becoming widely known outside the Black Hills. With friends like Humphrey, Bellamy, Warren, and others, he actively solicited funds for Mount Rushmore after 1927, the year he served as president of the Rapid City Commercial Club. Senator Norbeck had come to depend upon him and had insisted that he be appointed to the commission.

As in the case of other Rapid City business leaders, Boland's first interest in Mount Rushmore was commercial. While he could not sell farm machinery to tourists, his business sense and civic-mindedness told him that anything that was good for the community would indirectly benefit him. The art and spirit behind the memorial brought him no particular message or meaning. But by 1929, when the face of George Washington began to peer from the cold, shapeless granite, Borglum's work struck a deep chord in Boland. His determination that nothing should interfere with the monument's completion resulted in a feeling of practical responsibility for the work. When garnishment proceedings in the Tucker case tied up the commission's meager funds, he advanced more than $1,600 to meet expenses. Characteristically he declared, "I want everyone to know that the Mount Rushmore National Memorial Commission owes no person or firm anything."

Boland, who was highly pleased with his appointment to the commission, told Norbeck that he considered it a greater honor than being governor of South Dakota. He soon learned, however, that his task was to carry the work from one financial crisis to another, each mounting in fury and threatening the project's very existence. His was not an enviable position. When money was available he must see that it was wisely spent, often arousing the wrath of Borglum who had his own ideas about expenditures on the mountain. If funds were unavailable, it was Boland who bore the bitterness of unpaid creditors, including the sculptor, and who had the responsibility of holding things together until the treasury was replenished.

The excitement accompanying the unveiling of the Washington face could not conceal the dark financial outlook for the rest of 1930. On July 3 Boland reported that only $17,374 was available to pay obligations of $18,812. "Unless prompt arrangements are made for additional funds," he told the commissioners, "it is necessary to consider discontinuing operations at a very early date." Since the commission still had no overall plans for raising money, work was closed down on July 26.

This was a deep disappointment to all concerned since such remarkable progress had been made on the monument during the preceding months. At this time it was necessary to appoint William S. Tallman superintendent to replace J. C. Denison, who had resigned. Tallman, an artist of some ability, had been associated with Borglum for several years. He had worked at Mount Rushmore in the technical capacity of "pointer" and had demonstrated great efficiency in all phases of the work. For more than four years he cooperated with Borglum successfully, which was more than any other superintendent could do, with the cooperation of Lincoln, the sculptor's son. Borglum also hired Hugo Villa to assist him in carrying out his artistic designs. Villa had helped Borglum on other commissions over a period of fourteen years.

When Borglum learned that funds were nearly exhausted and that work had stopped, he donated $1,500 and bought five memberships in the Mount Rushmore National Memorial Society to help continue operations. His love for the memorial and his careless generosity would permit no other course. Work was resumed on August 15 and continued until November 6.

The financial outlook was so desperate that during October a drive to obtain money was made among South Dakota school children. The idea originated with Thomas Q. Beesley, vice president of the McCutcheon-Gerson Service of Chicago. Grade-school children were asked to contribute ten cents each, those in junior high school, fifteen cents, and high school and college students, twenty-five cents. It was believed that if children in South Dakota took the lead, similar campaigns might be launched successfully in Illinois, Virginia, and New York.

The governor designated October 20 as "Mount Rushmore Week," during which time a concentrated effort was made to solicit funds. Borglum toured the state to stir up public sentiment and made many radio talks and personal appearances. Schools that contributed were given a rotogravure certificate showing their participation. There was some grumbling and opposition to this campaign among the state's citizenry. Doane Robinson was criticized by many people who thought he was responsible for the plan. In any event, another valiant effort to meet the financial problem ended in dismal failure. After expenses were paid, only $1,707.80 was realized. But Boland consoled himself by saying, "We brought the story of Rushmore to all of the school children and teachers of the State."*

It was in an atmosphere of gloom and discouragement that the commission met for its annual session in Chicago on November 19. Only Borglum's generous contribution and funds provided by the Mount Rushmore National Memorial Society had kept the work from being discontinued in midsummer. One major financial success had been the payment of several thousand dollars in old debts, including $10,619 to Borglum and $3,375 to other creditors of the Mount Harney Memorial Association. But unpaid accounts still amounted to $19,129, and current obligations exceeded the commission's available cash by $195. About $7,000 was still due Borglum from the old Mount Harney Association.

*The author of this narrative contributed his dime through the Dale Center School in Jerauld County.

A method of providing money for the next season's work was the major item of business. Federal funds were lying idle in Washington waiting to be matched. Of the $160,000 appropriated, only $77,260 had been used owing to the lack of private funds. No constructive plans, however, were forthcoming. The commission seemed to be facing an insoluble problem since the deepening depression made it virtually impossible to solicit money for such a purpose. Most people thought that mountain-carving was one luxury the country could forego. Finally, Rosenwald moved that each commissioner buy additional memberships in the Mount Rushmore Memorial Society with the understanding that they be paid for by April 1, 1931. This would make some money available at the beginning of the work season. The eight members present subscribed seventy-three memberships, providing a total of $7,300 before matching. These donations by Cullinan, Spoonts, and Rosenwald raised their individual contributions to $2,500 or more.

Borglum was miffed because the commission turned down his proposal to hire the John Price Jones Corporation, a professional fund-raising organization, to solicit money for the memorial. He recommended that a drive be opened in Illinois during January 1931, to end on Lincoln's birthday. Funds could be raised for the Lincoln figure, he said, if a concentrated campaign was carried on by a professional agency. The commissioners refused to approve this plan because the corporation would work only for a fixed fee. The fact that the campaign would not be attempted on a commission basis indicated a certain lack of confidence on the part of the John Price Jones officials. Members of the commission considered it a poor time to make a drive. As Williamson said, "We might find ourselves out of pocket for a lot of fees without adequate returns." Even if they were available, commission funds could not be legally used for such expenses, which meant that individual members would have to advance the corporation fee. The commissioners had no desire to be responsible and agreed that if they spent their personal money, they would spend it directly on the mountain.

Borglum was openly critical and wrote sharply to Cullinan, saying that it was "inconceivable" that the commission had not developed some plan to match the money available in Washington. "It seems equally hard to believe," he said, "that they should allow me to carry the burdens." After consulting Cullinan, Borglum concluded that Cullinan expected the executive committee to solicit sufficient money somehow. The sculptor argued that it was not Boland's responsibility to raise the money. If Boland had to do it, however, Borglum said he would lend a hand. He added that in his judgment Boland had done more for the monument than anyone except Senator Norbeck.

The commission did authorize Borglum to publish another brochure, hoping that the previous year's experience might be duplicated. Borglum planned to carry more advertising in this Jefferson brochure and hoped to realize a net amount of $30,000. With federal aid, this would provide a total of $60,000.

But this was all speculation. Only the promises of direct support by the commissioners offered any immediate hope. On February 1, 1931, the treasurer reported a balance of $10.65. The only income for the preceding month was $2.00 from the sale of Washington brochures. How ludicrous could the situation become?

It was under these circumstances that Cullinan called a special meeting of the commission for March 17. Only five members and Borglum were present. Since there was no quorum, the session was informal. After considerable discussion Sargent agreed to give an additional $5,000, and Borglum promised a similar amount. With the subscriptions of other commissioners, enough money would now be available to start operations later in the spring. The commission's only resource seemed to be the bank accounts of its members and the restricted funds of the federal government. After great effort Boland was able to collect more than $18,000, mostly from the commissioners. By matching this and adding some miscellaneous receipts, $43,280 was provided for the 1931 season.

The commission was greatly strengthened in the spring by Hoover's appointment of Senator Norbeck. He had been helping as much as possible, but now he was in a position to lend official influence. Norbeck's present financial condition did not permit him to make any significant contributions, but his aid in other respects was invaluable.

The idea of personally financing the memorial did not set well with some of the commissioners. The absence of a quorum at the 1931 meetings reflected their lack of interest. One member wrote frankly that he could not contribute further and would gladly resign. "I did not understand when I went on the Commission that the members would be expected personally to provide the funds," he wrote.

Borglum arrived in the Black Hills from his winter home in San Antonio on April 23 and outlined his plans for the current season. The figure of Washington, he said, must be perfected so that in 1932 Mount Rushmore could participate in the celebration of the two-hundredth anniversary of Washington's birth. He intended to carve down to the waist, finishing the coat lapels and other aspects of the figure. Operations were quickly resumed, and workmen slightly remodeled and redecorated the studio, built paths and walks, and improved sanitary facilities for the convenience and comfort of tourists. Work on the faces began on June 5 and continued uninterrupted until October 1.

After plotting the work he wanted done, Borglum left early in June for Poznan, Poland, to attend the unveiling of his statue of Woodrow Wilson. Critics of the Rushmore project warned Europeans that with Borglum on the continent they had better place the Alps under lock and key! Just before leaving New York Borglum showed much of his old optimism when he wrote, "About money for Jefferson—I've got all the big dem's on the carpet and they will I'm sure raise me $35,000 for Jefferson." But again the sculptor's faith in financial accomplishment exceeded his works. At about the same time the commission was considering hiring President G. W. Nash of Yankton College to solicit funds, but nothing came of the plan. It was also suggested that an appeal be made to the South Dakota Legislature for an appropriation, with the idea that lawmakers of Illinois, New York, and Virginia would then be approached. Boland, who was a member of the legislature, deemed this unwise in light of the state's appropriations for highways to the memorial.

During Borglum's absence Superintendent Tallman and Hugo Villa made remarkable progress. Two men were stationed on Washington's face to continue the rough modeling, and eight drillers were busy on Jefferson. By the end of the summer more features were beginning to take form, and some stone north of the Washington figure was blown away preparatory to roughing out the Lincoln head.

It was a hard summer for Boland. The money came in slowly and only after he exerted great pressure on the other commissioners. Some of those outside South Dakota seemed willing to permit a moratorium on the carving, but Boland stubbornly refused to allow it. He feared that it would be difficult, if not impossible, to resume operations once they were shut down. "I think it is only fair to tell you that the man responsible for progress at Mount Rushmore this summer is John Boland," wrote Francis Case to a number of state editors. "How he keeps the till filled enough to pay the workmen, God knows, I don't." Doane Robinson explained to his readers through a column in the *Sioux Falls Daily Argus Leader* that Boland had stretched the "small revenues . . . to keep the wheels greased." He believed that "with one less resourceful and tenacious at the helm" Rushmore might not have weathered "the bad spell."

When Borglum returned to the mountain on August 26, he was surprised and pleased with the rapid progress. He praised Boland for "his understanding of the problems . . . and his ability to meet them" and said that Tallman and Villa "seemed in a common conspiracy . . . to make a big showing." Boland proudly reported, "We are accomplishing as much for one dollar this year as we did for three dollars in the summer of 1929." Tallman's and Villa's efficient operations were responsible for a part of this gain, but equally important was the fact that the workmen were becoming better trained for their particular and unusual work. Experience was the only satisfactory teacher. It took time to become an expert with a pneumatic drill and dynamite on the side of a six thousand–foot mountain, or to follow intelligently the instructions of Borglum and his assistants.

The harmony that prevailed during Borglum's absence was shattered soon after his return. Within two weeks he fired Villa following a controversy over wages and sculptural design. Practically everything Borglum did was attended by controversy, and Mount Rushmore was no exception. The breaking point came when the sculptor paid Villa less than he expected. But the fundamental difficulty was the clash of artistic temperaments and ideas. Villa wrote to the governor of South Dakota charging that Mount Rushmore could never be completed unless Borglum made a model which would fit the topography of the stone. He said that there was not enough rock to carve a Jefferson head according to the existing model, that the stone did not conform to the model, and that money was being wasted on a figure which could not be completed in its present location. Villa further declared that the project suffered from Borglum's long and frequent absences and his failure to give proper instructions. Villa was not alone in believing that there was not sufficient granite to carve a good head of Jefferson on the present site. Some of the ordinary workmen, who were on the mountain daily, agreed.

As might have been expected, Borglum reacted violently to these criticisms of his work. He said the charges were only "evil tongued gossip" and that plenty of stone was available. Indignantly he told Boland, "I've never been criticized in my life by competent people, either here or abroad, never."

Borglum lacked the ability to get along with his employees, just as with professional artists and others. His workers testified that he was completely unpredictable and that one never knew whether he would be greeted with praise or criticism. One workman commented, "Nobody could get along with the 'Old Man,' " as Borglum was called in his absence. This was an exaggerated but fundamentally correct statement. The best way to achieve harmony with the sculptor was to avoid him as much as possible. It was fatal to disagree with him. An employee who spent many years on the mountain remarked, "If the Old Man said it was going to rain and the sun was shining, I said, 'It sure looks like rain.' " Merle Peterson, one of Borglum's carvers, established a record of being hired and fired eight times during the fourteen years he worked at Mount Rushmore. The men found, however, that after they adjusted themselves to Borglum's temperament, they got along fairly well.

Despite his irascible nature, Borglum's employees came to admire him although most of them had little regard for him as an engineer, particularly in the use of dynamite. They thought he was too cautious and conservative. His powder men were for the most part former miners who had had experience with explosives and who constantly urged heavier charges. In Borglum's absence more dynamite than he prescribed was frequently used without harm. Since the main responsibility rested upon Borglum, it is understandable that he exercised undue care. Mistakes were costly and might be very harmful. But the work at Rushmore could have been done more efficiently if he had turned the engineering phases over to a group of trained engineers. Not withstanding his self-acknowledgments, Borglum was not that type of artisan.

Workmen were also silently critical of the sculptor's frequent changes in plans. His inability to follow a part of the job through to completion seemed to them a loss of efficiency and a waste of money.

But Borglum built a loyal crew of workers, many of whom returned season after season and took pride in working on the great memorial. During the depression, one was considered fortunate to be employed at Mount Rushmore. In 1933, when thousands of South Dakotans were on relief rolls, drillers earned sixty-five cents an hour while trained carvers earned a dollar an hour. Even the less skilled workmen made relatively good wages. The main drawback was the uncertainty of the work period, which seldom lasted more than six or seven months a year, and usually less.

Everyone admitted that Borglum was careful with his men and, as far as possible, protected them in their dangerous work. Some workers were injured, and one ultimately died from breathing granite dust; but Borglum furnished masks and took every available precaution to protect his men from the dreaded silicosis.

Only two major accidents occurred. On the afternoon of August 20, 1936, a rainstorm blew in accompanied by heaven-splitting lightning and rolling thunder. As usual, the men kept working. About two-o'clock a tremendous crash of lightning struck the mountaintop, setting off dynamite caps and shocking three men. Both shoes were blown from the feet of one workman, but no permanent injury resulted. On another occasion, after the installation of an aerial tramway, which transported workmen to the carving surface, a sprocket chain broke while five men were in the carriage near the top of the mountain. The carriage rapidly began its five hundred–foot decline, but the new emergency brake held and only one worker, who jumped out, was seriously hurt.

During the fourteen years of carving, not a single workman was killed or permanently injured on the job. This was a record of which Borglum could be and was justly proud.

Before Borglum departed for Europe, he had been planning the Jefferson number of the Mount Rushmore brochure. In his absence he asked Francis Case, editor of the *Custer Chronicle*, to assist him. Case had long been a strong booster of the project. Shortly before he climbed the one-way trail in 1925 to help dedicate the creviced mountain, he and his brother Leland had purchased the *Hot Springs Star*. He quickly changed the editorial policy of the former owners, Mr. and Mrs. Johnson, who had bitterly opposed the Rushmore project. Later he moved to Custer.

By 1930 Case fully realized the importance of completing the memorial. He wrote editiorials and personal letters to fellow editors, trying to stir up greater interest in the work. "South Dakota is, as yet, not even dimly aware of the tremendous thing Mount Rushmore National Memorial is," he wrote in 1931. "FOR ALL TIME TO COME," he continued, "South Dakota will be getting dividends. . . . Every tourist who comes to South Dakota now asks about Rushmore and most of them see it." He had caught Doane Robinson's vision.

While Borglum was gone, Case edited the Jefferson brochure and mailed out some thirty thousand copies. Following the pattern set in the Washington number, the booklet carried articles on the project and pictures of the actual carving. Borglum's discussion of the philosophy behind colossal sculpture was the most significant section of the issue. The brochure gave valuable publicity, but by November it had netted only a meager $1,500, which was turned over to the commission.

Upon returning from Europe to his mountain studio, Borglum again began working on his models. The Lincoln figure was placed farther to the right, that is, to the north, in order to free more of the Washington head. Most people agreed that he was improving the general design, though it was still far from satisfactory. The three figures appeared crowded, and Jefferson and Lincoln seemed to be leaning against Washington. Norbeck complained that Lincoln was out of place resting against anyone else. Roosevelt had not yet been worked into the pattern. The portraits did not do justice to Borglum's great ability, and they failed to satisfy him. He was admittedly experimenting, working and reworking his designs to make them fit the available rock and still be of high artistic quality. By 1931 nothing was fixed, not even the exact position of the Washington figure, although it appeared to be near completion.

During 1931, 26,449 visitors registered at Borglum's studio between June and September. This was the first year that the commission attempted to count the tourists. Since it was believed that only about one-fifth of them registered, Boland concluded that approximately 111,000 people were then viewing the memorial annually. It was rapidly becoming the state's greatest tourist attraction, and only poor roads and depression-flattened purses kept many more people from observing and enjoying Borglum's experiment in colossal sculpture. Few people any longer agreed with the *Chicago Tribune* columnist who had written:

O Gutzon Borglum, have a heart
Spare just one mountain top
Leave one, I beg, just one at least
That you won't chop and chop.
You cruise around with dynamite
And drills and tools and gears;
And carve up some grand mountain
That has stood ten thousand years.
A mountain fills me full of awe
I only gaze—and gulp
But to you, Gutzon, a mountain is—
Just something more to sculp.
I love to see the mountain tops,
In silent grandeur rise;
But you are never satisfied
Till you give them ears and eyes.
The mountains that I once adored
You've changed them, one by one;
To Roosevelt, Adams, Lee and Grant,
And, of course, George Washington.
No longer can I feel alone
As a mountain trail I plod;
The great stone faces all around
Make me think I'm in a mob.

I shriek for solitude and turn—
And run and run and run
At last an unspoiled peak I see,
Oh, Gosh! it's Jefferson.
I'd rather see a mountain
Just as it's always been
Than after it's been all dolled up
With whiskers and nose and chin.
And so, I beg, spare just one peak
Though you hack up all the rest;
I know, Gutzon, you're wonderful
But I like nature best.*

*Used by permission.

CHAPTER ELEVEN

"Nothing Succeeds Like Results"

THE Mount Rushmore National Memorial, which had only limited local interest at the time of its inception, was gradually winning national attention. Six years had seen the development and refinement of an idea, a dream, into a project designed to strike the patriotic chord of every American heart. A vision which had conquered Borglum's imagination and driven him to the Black Hills at the expense of more lucrative commissions elsewhere was slowly spreading to the country at large.

But it was the snail-like pace at which his concept gripped people's minds that embittered Gutzon Borglum. Why did not people see what he saw or feel what he felt? A few hundred thousand dollars was standing between him and the completion of a great shrine to American institutions. It seemed incredible to him that a nation of such wealth and power could be so insensible to his wonderful plan. Where was American idealism? Did materialism so dominate the average mind that men could not see or feel great emotional, spiritual, or aesthetic values? Whatever the effect of the mountain on others, it attracted Borglum irresistibly. Like an ancient slave, he was chained to his task and the rock of Rushmore was riveted to his neck.

Borglum found it difficult to tolerate indifference to his monumental work, and he freely criticized anyone whom he considered an obstructionist. It was not in his makeup to accept frustration and disappointment gracefully or to work steadily and patiently on a difficult problem. His cup of bitterness was full and was soon to overflow.

There was not enough money to begin operations at the mountain in the spring of 1932, and it appeared that the whole project might have to be closed down. Borglum was angry. On March 7 he wrote long letters to Cullinan and President Hoover, accusing the commission of indifference and failure, and urging Hoover to call its members to Washington "so as to enable a fresh start to be made and some life and coordination . . . put into the organization." However, Hoover refused to intervene, holding to his policy of delegating authority and then standing aside. The president probably thought, too, that this was a matter of little consequence compared to his economic depression problems. To Cullinan, Borglum declared that it was an "unpardonable and unforgivable disgrace to shut down the work precluding participation in the Washington Bicentennial celebration." He concluded by saying, "I am utterly sick of the do-nothing policy that we have allowed for three years."

Borglum's sharp attack was too much for the harassed Cullinan. About a month later he submitted his resignation to Hoover, explaining that private business demanded his full time. Undoubtedly the sculptor's constant nagging had forced his decision. Cullinan had donated $2,500 to the project, but this was much less than Borglum had expected when he recommended his appointment to the commission. According to Borglum, Cullinan had promised an estimated $100,000, or enough for the Jefferson figure. Fred W. Sargent, a man of many community and business interests and president of the Chicago and North Western Railway, was then elected chairman.

The sculptor's complaints had no cash value, and unconcern continued. Members of the commission refused to make further substantial donations, wealthy people elsewhere would not contribute, and every other money-raising scheme proposed and tried had failed. Financial resources for Mount Rushmore were as dried and parched as the South Dakota plains. During the winter of 1932–1933, a gift of $2,500 from Walter Hayes of Washington, D.C., was virtually the only income. Even with this and other contributions, which were matched by federal funds, there was not enough to resume carving. Boland, who abhorred debt, applied the available cash on the obligations of the Mount Harney Association. He was able to pay off $7,876, which left a balance of around $11,000.

About February 1, 1932, a plan was developed to solicit dollar contributions by mail. George G. Behrens of Washington, who was in charge of the campaign, sent out thousands of form letters asking for one dollar. Donors were given a certificate signed by Cullinan and Borglum. But this effort, like its predecessors, was a complete failure. Boland advanced $700 for printing and stationery, but Behrens collected only $538.

Since there was no activity at Mount Rushmore, Borglum turned to other commissions, devoting much of his time to a statue of William Jennings Bryan. During the spring he also made a trip to Atlanta to discuss the resumption of work at Stone Mountain. He even took time for another round of interviews with such wealthy prospects as Owen D. Young, John J. Raskob, George Eastman, and Bernard Baruch. Baruch, he said, refused to help because Wilson had not been included in the Mount Rushmore design. His "old connections" all failed him; efforts to raise money for the Black Hills project were fruitless.

It was Senator Norbeck who finally rescued the monument from complete abandonment. On July 23, when tourists were visiting the almost deserted sculpture and wondering if Rushmore was destined to be another Stone Mountain, he wrote to C. M. Day of a plan to get money from the unemployment relief fund. "I am optimistic," he said. Congress was then considering a $300,000,000 federal emergency relief bill, and Norbeck hoped to get a sizeable slice of South Dakota's allotment for mountain-carving. He had previously discussed his plan with Williamson and had asked him to draft an innocent-looking amendment permitting part of South Dakota's share to be used at the mountain. Widespread unemployment in the Black Hills region and the great amount of handwork necessary around the memorial gave "some justification" for the scheme, Williamson believed. He added, "It is a safe bet that he [Norbeck] will not disclose the real purpose of the amendment."

The bill passed in late July, and South Dakota was awarded $150,000 by the Reconstruction Finance Corporation. To be sure, this was technically a loan, but nonetheless, the money was at hand. By early August Norbeck and Williamson were in Pierre trying to persuade Governor Green to release $50,000 to the Mount Rushmore Commission for work on and around the memorial. There was still time to get in two or three months of carving if the governor acted at once.

But Green refused to act. The small area obviously did not present a pleasant political situation—and the governor was running for re-election. Norbeck rankled at Green's delay. After several conferences in Pierre, he wrote Green a sharp letter saying that work on the mountain was being held up by the governor's refusal to turn over the funds. "A month and a half of good weather has now been lost," he wrote in September, "and opportunity for a National Memorial has also been lost." Norbeck told Boland that it had been necessary to "get rough" in this matter, and the state's defeated politicians who had crossed Norbeck knew that he could be rough. Secretary of the Interior Ray Lyman Wilbur, who was then in South Dakota, also urged Green to earmark part of this money for Mount Rushmore.

Finally, on September 22, Governor Green released $50,000 to Boland, who four days later ordered work resumed at the mountain. For the next several weeks about twenty men were employed on the faces, and about fifty worked at landscaping, building roads and paths, enlarging the parking space, and otherwise improving tourist facilities. Opposition developed, particularly in the eastern part of the state, to spending relief money at the memorial. The idea of using these funds to buy materials such as explosives and to pay Borglum aroused sharp criticism. But Boland promised the South Dakota State Relief Committee that none of the money would be used except to employ the needy.

While this restricted the use of the money, the grounds around the base of Mount Rushmore did need to be improved. The commission had previously hesitated to expend much of its meager fund in the area around Borglum's studio, the central observation point for tourists. Consequently, facilities were inadequate for the growing number of visitors, which reached moe than one hundred thousand in 1932. Drilling and blasting were also resumed by unemployed workmen who were properly qualified. The only difficulty was that Borglum's honorarium from these operations had to be found elsewhere since he could not be paid from relief funds.

Even with the relief money, so little was accomplished in 1932 that Williamson was hard put to prepare his fourth annual report to Congress. He called on Borglum, whose fertile mind never lacked for something to say, but the report contained little more than a general discussion of mountain sculpture and a financial statement.

With one federal windfall in hand, the question arose whether it could be matched by other government money. Again Norbeck carried the day and obtained a ruling permitting the relief funds to be matched from the regular Rushmore appropriations. This added another $50,000 to the treasury. Boland was now able to report more than $95,000 to carry on work in 1933. The commission's bank balance had never been in such a healthy condition, and prospects for rapid progress appeared bright.

Norbeck's action had come at a crucial time. For almost a year prior to the receipt of the relief money, practically no work had been done on the memorial. No subscriptions were in prospect, and Borglum had temporarily left the mountain for other work. Some of the wealthiest members of the commission had resigned. There is reason to believe that without the senator's timely assistance, the project would have dragged along and finally died, a victim of indifference and depression. Thus 1933 was an important turning point in the history of Mount Rushmore. Norbeck had always argued that the best publicity for the project was to complete one figure after the other as quickly as possible. "Nothing succeeds like results," he repeatedly told Borglum.

With money to finance work at full capacity, Borglum ordered operations started earlier than usual. Beginning on March 24, 1933, work continued steadily until cold weather forced a shutdown on December 10. During that period splendid progress was made in spite of the sculptor's lengthy absences. Ivan Houser assisted Borglum on the studio models, and L. Del Bianco, a skilled carver, was employed. Bianco was one of the most competent men ever to work on the mountain. Tons of rock were removed from the left side of Washington's wig, from the top of his left shoulder, which had to be cut back, and from his chest. By the end of the season one lapel of his coat was clearly visible and the other was beginning to take shape. Much refinement was done on the face.

Borglum's opportunity to display artistic talent came in the finishing, and until his death he never considered his colossal portraits perfectly sculptured. Within two or three inches of the completed face, mountain sculpture was largely a matter of engineering—the removal of surplus stone. But as the last rock was removed, Borglum personally studied the effect of light and shadows, which, after all, brought out the artistic excellence. Under direct light an eye might appear quite unnatural, cold, and lifeless—only a gap in the mountain; but proper shadows gave it life and vitality. The pupils in Lincoln's eyes are jutting pieces of granite about twenty-two inches long. At close range they do not look like pupils, but when viewed from Borglum's studio, the shadows make them appear human and natural.

During the finishing Borglum showed his zeal and desire for perfection. He would view the faces through powerful glasses from atop Iron Mountain about four miles away, as well as from other distant points. Then viewing the work from his studio and swinging over the face itself, he noted the changes and corrections which would improve the work. His purpose, he said, was to bring to it the criticism that applies to any piece of sculpture in the street or city park. After determining that more rock must be removed at some point in order to give the best and most accurate effect, he would ascend the mountain and mark the spot with paint. In some instances, he would call a trained assistant from work on the figure to sketch changes which he desired. Those who thought that Mount Rushmore was only a mechanical enlargement of studio models were mistaken. If Borglum's models, which today stand in the Sculptor's Studio at Mount Rushmore, were enlarged to the size of the mountain faces, many differences could be seen. Borglum carved his colossal sculpture just as he would a studio bust, making many changes and seeking accurate expression by using natural light and shadows to their fullest advantage.

Perhaps the most notable development in 1933 was the abandoning of the first Jefferson figure for a site north of Washington, where Borglum originally planned to carve it. The rock there was so imperfect, however, that he found it necessary to drill and blast deeper and deeper into the granite wall to find good stone. By the time Borglum located suitable rock, he had penetrated about ninety feet from the original surface. During the summer of 1934 dynamite blasted away the Jefferson mask which had fitted snugly to the right side of Washington. At least $10,000 in terms of labor and materials went rumbling down with the crumbled and broken granite. The uncertainties of mountain-carving were great.

Removing the first Jefferson head and setting the second one deep into the mountain freed the Washington figure from surrounding stone and brought it out in full relief. Furthermore, it increased Washington's predominance in the sculptural group and permitted the late afternoon sun to pass behind the Washington head and light up the faces of Jefferson and Lincoln.

In the fall of 1932 Borglum announced another change in design which would place the entablature and inscription on the west wall, or reverse side of the mountain, completely hiding it from the faces.

On this matter he was back where he started in 1926. Nothing more was done about preparing an inscription. Norbeck had suggested in April 1932 that the commission postpone consideration for another year. He did not want to publicize this phase of the project again for fear of irritating Coolidge's friends in Congress who might otherwise help with appropriations.

There was a general local feeling that Borglum wasted time and money on the monument by not following fixed plans and designs. The destruction of the first Jefferson face and the changing of the inscription site seemed to confirm this opinion. However, when he announced in October 1933 that he intended to "turn" the head of Washington, citizens openly voiced their disapproval. Borglum flayed the local populace for attempting to judge his work or plans and for having little understanding of the difficult problems. "Rapid City has never understood Mount Rushmore, the intent of it, the soul of it, the vast effect it will exercise upon the city's future," he said. Borglum explained that he was not actually going to move the head, but rather to carve the shoulders so as to make it appear that the head was turned.

He stated time and time again that it was "practically impossible to prepare and complete a fixed or final model which could be followed. . . . The design of this colossal work is subject to constant changes as the uncovering of the stone progresses." By 1933 Borglum's studio model of Washington was 24 feet tall and scaled to 240 feet on the mountain. He intended to complete the figures down to the waist. By that time he had changed his models seven times to make them conform to Rushmore rock.

More than $8,000 was spent in 1933 on walks, landscaping, and other work around the studio. This work employed men on relief and complied with Reconstruction Finance Corporation regulations. Some of the commissioners were critical of these expenditures, but Boland insisted that they were necessary in order to keep faith with the state and federal governments. During the year all debts were liquidated, including those to Borglum. When he obtained the $10,000 federal matching funds in November 1933, Boland finished paying Borglum his overdue honorarium as well as his loan of $5,000 which had gone to Tucker. All of Borglum's balance was figured at 6 percent interest. Thus $11,864 was paid to him during the fiscal year ending October 31, 1933. This represented full payment of his fee and back debts, including $2,145 in interest.

In spite of the depression and the dust-bowl conditions in western South Dakota during 1933, tourist traffic significantly increased. In 1932 about 108,000 visitors viewed the memorial, and the next year more than 135,000 made their way to see Borglum's gigantic sculpture. People came from every state in the Union and from twenty-four foreign countries, some of them as distant as Russia and South Africa.

The monument was becoming better known throughout the United States, and improved roads were a major factor in the growing number of tourists. By summer the State Highway Department had finished grading and graveling a road between Rapid City and Mount Rushmore. The memorial could also be approached from the southeast over Senator Norbeck's incomparable Iron Mountain Road, now graveled and well maintained. Motorists who had the pleasure and excitement of making that trip experienced an unforgettable tour.

For several years Norbeck had been one of the leading advocates of scenic and artistic roads. He had pioneered in laying out beautiful highways framed with natural scenery for the benefit of tourists. At Mount Rushmore was an opportunity to continue this project. He planned a highway beginning near the Game Lodge where Coolidge had stayed during his visit and approaching Mount Rushmore from its most effective and imposing side. The road would pass through a remarkably beautiful mountain region and would present to the tourist the virgin beauty of the Harney National Forest. During the late 1920s Norbeck walked and rode over Iron Mountain some twenty times, working out an artistic route which would best introduce travelers to the memorial. His ideas often contradicted commonly accepted engineering principles, but his policies generally prevailed. There would have been no Iron Mountain Road, he later said, "if I had listened to the diploma boys [engineers]." Luckily, he was aided by such men as Scovel Johnson and Owen Mann who had some appreciation of his objectives.

By 1931 he had selected the location of the Iron Mountain Road, and the State Highway Department was following his plans. In landscaping and design it had few equals in the United States. The most spectacular feature of the road was the framing or telescoping of Mount Rushmore through three different tunnels several miles away. Superbly designed, the highway wound over pigtail bridges and through virgin forests, presenting one naturally framed picture after

another. This represented his second triumph in building picturesque highways. Just ten years before, the Needles highway had been
completed according to plans outlined by Norbeck. Borglum was
lyrical in his praise of the senator's work. The Iron Mountain Road,
he declared, promised to be an integral part of the memorial. He had
never seen anything about Norbeck's highways that he would change,
Borglum wrote on a later occasion.

Not only was the year 1933 important in the memorial's history
from the standpoint of actual progress and accessibility, but it was in
that year that the first major change in administration occurred. A
presidential order of June 10 placed Mount Rushmore under the
jurisdiction of the National Park Service in the Department of the
Interior. The position and responsibility of the commission, however, was unchanged. Secretary Ickes wrote, "We do not construe this
provision as in any way affecting the present organization of the
Mount Rushmore National Commission." The new order simply
provided that all federal funds, budgets, and requisitions must pass
through the National Park Service for "administrative examination."
The service did not interfere beyond checking finances and did not
even immediately change the general bookkeeping and accounting
practices. So the commission still enjoyed the relative freedom of an
independent agency.

National Park Service officials really showed little interest in, or
knowledge of, their new administrative charge. Norbeck called on
Director Arno B. Cammerer in October and personally explained the
work to him. He found Cammerer, who had served as secretary of
the Fine Arts Commission for several years, sympathetic to all art
projects; but, according to Norbeck, he was like other "eastern
artists" who thought that the "beautiful mountains" should not be
mutilated. It was somewhat disappointing, the senator said, to find
that Cammerer "had heard more about Stone Mountain than about
Rushmore." He seemed confident, however, that the top officials in
the Park Service would be helpful. One of these was A. E. Demaray,
whom Norbeck characterized as "a very ambitious young man, a
worker and a clear thinker."

From his interview with Cammerer, Norbeck concluded that the
National Park Service had no intention of taking over the duties of
the commission. He admitted, however, that the Interior
Department's "supervisory power" might possibly come into conflict

with commission policies. Knowing that Borglum would resent any effective federal control, Norbeck hesitated to tell him of the change in administration. He told Boland to explain the situation to the sculptor "at some opportune time."

As early as 1929 consideration was given to making a national park or monument of the area immediately surrounding Mount Rushmore. Probably after conferring with Borglum, Cullinan suggested this to his friend, Secretary of the Interior Ray Lyman Wilbur. Borglum recommended to the commission that the park be called the "Mount Rushmore National Memorial Park" and that it be so proclaimed by the president. His purpose was to guarantee the integrity and preserve the beauty of the region. Complete control of the land was desired in order to prevent hot-dog stands and the like from cluttering the entrances to the memorial. Senator Norbeck, Scovel Johnson, and Forest Supervisor J. F. Conner had originally worked out a plan with Borglum and had recommended that an area of seventeen square miles be set aside around the mountain and held inviolate for park purposes.

Norbeck had previously arranged with the United States Forest Service that no public campground would be established in the area without the approval of the Custer State Park Board of which he was the dominant member. Neither were special-use permits for home-building to be issued without the consent of the district forester and the park board. Since the memorial was in the Custer State Game Sanctuary, a part of the Harney National Forest, it was assumed that these restrictions gave adequate protection.

When Cullinan asked Wilbur for special administrative regulations or legislation to guard the immediate area around Mount Rushmore, the matter was referred to the Department of Agriculture and the Forest Service. A. S. Peck, district forester at Denver, explained that the region was already protected by regular Forest Service rules and that the act setting up the game sanctuary had withdrawn the land from any form of entry. Timber was being cut on a scientific basis, he said, but the natural beauty was not being destroyed. He agreed that perhaps one thousand acres closely surrounding the monument might be "kept strictly inviolate," but he did not think it was necessary to create a park or national monument.

Director Horace Albright, speaking for the National Park Service, also opposed creating a national monument, but for a different reason. National monuments had been created, he said, "because of some outstanding historical or scientific characteristic, and under the policy that has grown up with the National Park Service deliberate inclusion of elaborate works of man has been strenuously opposed." He could not reconcile this policy with the work at Mount Rushmore, "for obviously the most outstanding feature of the area will be a great man-carved monument. Neither the historical nor the scientific, the prerequisites of national monument establishment, are represented."

In 1931 Norbeck pushed a bill through the Senate, part of which provided for setting aside a Mount Rushmore reservation of 1,420 acres. But the measure died in the House Public Lands Committee. However, the senator himself did not at first favor a national park around Rushmore and expected the Custer State Park Board to maintain jurisdiction. He told Albright that it "should remain as it is, a part of the national forest and state game sanctuary, and should be maintained by the State as required by law." As a close friend and advisor of the National Park Service, he was well aware that mountain-carving was the very antithesis of the policies of that service.

Opposition to changing nature's handiwork was illustrated by the situation at Mount Whitney. As the story was told by Albright, the mountain for many years was thought to be 14,501 feet high. However, an exact measurement from sea level showed that it rose only a fraction over 14,496. An altitude measurement of slightly less than 14,500 feet was most unpleasant to the superintendent of Sequoia National Park. He asked permission to bunch rocks on the peak in such a way that four feet would be added, but the Park Service promptly and vigorously refused his request.

In spite of what Albright had said regarding National Park Service policy, he anticipated that Mount Rushmore might someday come under the jurisdiction of the Department of the Interior. He wrote an office memorandum in 1930 saying, "I think you better make up a little file on Mount Rushmore and the work that is being done out there under congressional sanction. I anticipate that in time it will be a national monument under our supervision. Secretary Wilbur is a good deal interested in it." Since the federal government was furnishing part of the money and the memorial was located on federal land, it seemed logical to assume that Mount Rushmore would eventually fall to the National Park Service. The president's order of June 10, 1933, was the first positive step in that direction.

CHAPTER TWELVE

Conflict and Crisis

FROM 1933 on, the Mount Rushmore project was under constant stress and strain because of sharp differences between Borglum and the commission, which was represented chiefly by John Boland. Although the average tourist saw no sign of it, this conflict actually threatened continuance of the work. The difficulties were well known all the way from the workmen on the mountain to President Franklin D. Roosevelt in the White House.

Everyone knew that it was hard to work with Borglum because of his extreme individualism, his egocentricity, and his refusal to cooperate with others. His determination to dominate and to be absolutely free from all restrictions could only result in strife and conflict unless commission members agreed to act as puppets while Borglum pulled the strings. The commissioners refused to do this, fearing that he would fritter away the meager funds and leave an uncompleted memorial.

In Borglum's mind, John Boland came to personify the collective impediments to his progress at Mount Rushmore. As resident commissioner and chief administrative officer, Boland had to deal closely and constantly with the sculptor. When anything went wrong, financially or otherwise, it was Boland who bore the brunt of Borglum's venomous attacks. Boland had a deep admiration and affection for Borglum and desired more than anything else to see the monument completed by him. But he recognized the sculptor's irresponsibility and impracticality in money matters, and he believed that he must protect the work from loose and extravagant fiscal control. When he assumed management of the project's finances, he saw difficulties ahead. "I know we can handle the Rushmore affairs in a businesslike manner," he wrote, "though I greatly fear that a man of Borglum's type is going to be very difficult for me to handle." This was an understatement. Borglum would not submit to control or handling by anyone. He never had. It was not in his nature to do so. No one expected him to be skilled in business practices or wise in economics. But the

Mount Rushmore promoters hoped that Borglum would willingly entrust business matters to men of experience. At the same time, however, Borglum had lived up to the popular conception of an artist, and South Dakotans expected him to be temperamental and difficult.

It would be hard to imagine two men more unlike than Borglum and Boland. Borglum's erratic, impatient, and impractical disposition contrasted sharply with Boland's methodical, efficient, and businesslike approach to problems. Frequent differences over expenditures and procedure were inevitable. When he had funds, Borglum was a free spender. He was not at all materialistic, and he seldom thought about money except when he found himself without it. He believed his work was so important that he should not be bothered about finances.

The stories of Borglum's generosity are legion. When the South Dakota Golden Jubilee booklet was being published in 1939, an embarrassing deficit developed. When Robert E. Driscoll explained this, Borglum asked, "Bob, how much do we need?" Driscoll replied that they lacked $368. "Here it is," Borglum said, as he wrote out a check for the amount. During the winter of 1931 when the Sioux Indians at the Pine Ridge Agency were literally starving to death, he started a campaign throughout the Black Hills to collect food and clothing for them and donated several cattle from his own ranch.

Mrs. Borglum assumed most of the family bookkeeping and banking duties, and the sculptor often did not know his financial condition. Thrift was no virtue to Borglum. He valued money only for what it helped him to accomplish. In spite of lucrative commissions throughout his career, he was incapable of building up and maintaining financial reserves commensurate with his earnings. His tastes were expensive and he lived well, sometimes extravagantly, judging by ordinary standards. For example, he claimed that the Mount Harney Association owed him about $5,900 for traveling expenses in connection with the early Mount Rushmore work. Items of $200 a day at the Blackstone Hotel in Chicago and other leading hostelries were not uncommon in his accounts. These claims were presented to the association with the nonchalance of one to whom expense meant nothing. Of course, some of his money went back into his work.

In summarizing his economic philosophy, Borglum once told Norbeck that every man should spend a certain portion of his funds to make himself happier. He recalled a time when he was a lonely boy away from home with only a quarter to his name. He bought ten cents worth of candy to cheer himself up and then spent ten cents for food. He approved of that policy, he said.

Scottish in ancestry and conservative by habit, Boland rebelled at any kind of waste or inefficiency. When a dollar was spent, he wanted a dollar returned in goods or services. He was precise and exact in his own affairs, and he insisted that Mount Rushmore business be operated by similar standards. The differences which ultimately developed between Boland and Borglum arose from their conflicting philosophies of life and opposing views on the place of the commission in the work. Borglum wanted support and approval of his actions without interference or restraint. Boland agreed with Norbeck that the commission must be something more than a rubber stamp for the sculptor. Furthermore, Boland demanded that government regulations be strictly adhered to, while Borglum ignored them if he thought they interfered with his work. He felt no such restrictions should exist for him.

The best illustration of his contempt for what he considered bureaucratic rules and regulations is found in connection with the construction in 1939 of his second studio. The project was then being supervised by the National Park Service, and building plans had to meet the approval of Park Service architects. Six copies of blueprints for the new building had been sent to Borglum, but he disliked them and called in C. C. Gideon, a longtime resident of the Hills, to draw up a new set of plans. Gideon demurred, explaining that the National Park Service would not be apt to approve anything he did. But Borglum was insistent, and Gideon complied. Borglum liked the plans and asked him to make blueprints. Again Gideon hesitated but acceded to appease the sculptor. When Gideon brought in his blueprints, Borglum studied them, made a few hasty changes, and said they were just what he wanted. Reaching for the six copies of the Park Service blueprints, he crumpled them and threw them in the wastepaper basket. Then turning to his construction assistant, Lloyd (Lively) Virtue, he shouted, "Lively, I make ͏ ͏ ͏ ͏ ͏ ͏ ͏ ͏ ͏ ͏ ͏ ͏ ͏ ͏ Such was the man with whom Boland had to deal.

There were minor differences between Boland and the sculptor from the time work began, but in the early days of the project Borglum was generally complimentary. He once said to Norbeck that he knew of no better man than Boland for chairman of the executive committee. There must be something wrong with anyone who could not get along with Boland, he added. But this attitude was short-lived. Borglum's disposition was closely geared to his financial status. Much of the time after arriving in South Dakota he was short of cash, and this made him especially cantankerous. His lack of money was due to several factors. He was notoriously careless with his personal finances, but this was only part of the difficulty. The commissions he received at Mount Rushmore were much smaller than he had originally anticipated. He had undertaken the work on the assumption that some $75,000 would be spent annually. Allowing for certain payments on which he did not receive a commission, he could reasonably expect his 25 percent honorarium to total $15,000 or more a year. As it was, he received $7,008, $1,090, and $11,864 respectively during the fiscal years of 1931, 1932, and 1933.

Progress at the mountain and Borglum's bank balance were directly connected. The more money spent at Mount Rushmore, the faster the work advanced and the greater was his income. Consequently, when carving proceeded at a snail's pace only a few months a year and with limited personnel, Borglum chafed not only because his great memorial was being completed so slowly, but because his personal financial troubles were increased. This was a double source of irritation.

To make matters worse, Borglum had spent several thousand dollars buying and stocking a ranch so that he could be near his work. He blamed the commission for forcing him to make this outlay, arguing that Boland's petty policies had driven Tucker away. Without Tucker, he said, it was necessary for him to give the work closer personal attention. Moreover, the commission was unable to pay his advances and honorarium in full during the first few years. But even when Borglum received more than $10,000 a year, as he did in 1933, he still could not meet his obligations. Unable to adjust his expenditures to his income, he was threatened with lawsuits, and he suffered the embarrassment of having to assign future commissions at Mount Rushmore to demanding creditors.

Under these circumstances, Borglum was obliged to borrow additional money. As he had neglected or ignored his debts, his credit was very poor around Rapid City. He often asked Boland to intercede at banks and business houses, and at times requested advances on his commission on the ground that he had loaned money to the commission and it should return the favor. Boland refused to make illegal prior payments from official funds. However, he frequently interceded successfully with local bankers.

Boland probably knew better than anyone else what effect a shortage of cash had on the sculptor. Often he handled the matter personally; his bank statements reveal loan after loan to Borglum between 1933 and 1936. Although this was accommodating, it was nevertheless humiliating and embarrassing to Borglum, and he bitterly resented the circumstances which made it necessary. He didn't want to be bothered with the more mundane aspects of life. Thus the relation between Boland and Borglum cannot be properly understood without considering financial matters.

Even more important, however, were Borglum's feelings that Boland interfered with his activities at the mountain. He charged that every obstacle was thrown in his way and that Boland's caution and pettiness retarded his work. "The kind of work I am doing for the nation can never be completed and the standard maintained by the niggardly methods prevailing," he complained. Borglum insisted on freedom to hire and fire workmen at will, to raise and lower wages as he desired, and to order materials and equipment to suit his fancy. In his judgment, Boland's job as chairman of the executive committee was merely to approve the sculptor's decisions and policies.

Basically the conflict was over financial control of the project and all that implied. Boland took the view, strongly supported by Norbeck, that the executive committee needed to handle all business matters in order to get the greatest possible return from every dollar spent. This would have the advantage, too, of leaving Borglum completely free to concentrate on the artistic features of the project. But Borglum wanted to determine how and where the money was expended. He saw nothing improper in his own handling of the business affairs of a group which employed him on a commission basis. Boland resisted every attempt of the sculptor to encroach on the financial administration, and this naturally aroused Borglum's ill will

and use of equipment. He urged the commission to install its own power plant when the original engine failed, to purchase at least one additional compressor, and to add more drills. From the beginning he had also insisted that an aerial tramway be provided to transport his men from the base to the top of the mountain. It was a stiff climb up the rambling wooden stairway from the boarding house to the work-ing area, and the trip took about half an hour. Borglum declared that the workmen should be spared this tiring ordeal each morning. All these demands were reasonable enough in themselves, but the sculp-tor refused to recognize the financial situation. If adequate funds had been provided, it would indeed have been foolish to operate at any-thing short of full efficiency. In such a case, providing more power, installing additional drills, and hiring more skilled carvers and work-men would have been matter-of-course.

Boland, however, refused to increase the capital outlay by several thousand dollars to satisfy these demands, pointing out that money was not available to operate the existing machinery for more than a few months a year. To buy more equipment without funds to run it would be poor business. It was more economical to use the available machinery and have the extra money for longer working seasons and heavier payrolls. Boland explained the problem by saying, "The addi-tional cost of machinery for the increase in power would materially cut down the total man hours of drilling and carving . . . and thereby result in less productive work and efficient expenditures." This was a sensible and practical view.

No partial solution to the worker problem would satisfy Borglum. When Boland leased an additional compressor from the Keystone Consolidated Company at a dollar a day, making possible the opera-tion of fourteen to sixteen drills, Borglum was furious. He charged that Boland was more interested in giving business to local dealers than in seeing progress on the memorial.

Borglum could not or would not understand the realities of busi-ness. He only knew that progress was slow, that he did not have all the power, equipment, and labor he needed, and that Boland refused to permit greater expenditures until there was assurance of a larger operating budget. Boland looked at these problems from the view-point of a successful businessman, while Borglum saw them through the eyes of an impatient artist.

Typical of Borglum's outlook was his statement to Norbeck in October 1933 that by doubling the number of carvers and drillers, he could finish the Washington and Jefferson figures in 1934. Assuming that this was theoretically possible, which it was not, only about $24,000 remained in the treasury for the next year, and there was little prospect of obtaining more. That amount would not keep his current crew of drillers busy for more than two or three months, which fact indicated the foolishness of insisting on more drills and skilled workmen while the treasury was in such a weak condition. Furthermore, neither Boland nor Norbeck had much confidence in Borglum's judgment, should he be permitted to buy more equipment. Although he took great pride in referring to himself as a "Sculptor-Engineer" and signed most of his letters in that fashion, his engineering talents were strictly limited. In the early days of the project he designed and purchased a large bumper for finishing the faces at a cost of more than $3,500. However, it proved to be impractical and was cast aside near Mount Rushmore to rust and ruin.

On another occasion Borglum arranged for the purchase of two used submarine engines through the United States Treasury Department at only $100 each. The commission would not pay the freight until a mechanic had examined them. When Norbeck checked with the Navy Department, he found that the engines were in poor condition and that repairs could not be made. Borglum was deeply irked and reacted in his usual inconsistent manner. On August 16, 1934, he wrote to Commissioner Sargent that he must have the engines. Two days later he expressed grave doubts about their usefulness.

Relations between Boland and the sculptor became more critical after the National Park Service began to participate in the administration of the work. Such an independent government agency as the commission had enjoyed a great deal of freedom, adhering only to very general regulations regarding employment, purchasing, and similar functions. Under these circumstances, an impulsive increase in salary or dismissal of an employee by Borglum could be overlooked. While Boland might not agree, he generally made the adjustment in his office and thought nothing of it. But after 1933, and more particularly after early 1935, Boland found himself responsible to a department of the federal government that required him to follow regulations. In keeping with this concept, he demanded that federal rules be followed. But federal rules meant little to Borglum, who was willing to let Boland worry about explaining any violations to the government. Boland could not impress on him the importance of following federal regulations or show him that refusal to obey them might endanger the work.

During heated controversies, Borglum relied on his literary talent to scalp his adversaries. Face-to-face conferences with him were generally most cordial. After Borglum and the commission had discussed certain problems and had seemingly reached a mutually satisfactory solution, the sculptor would often return to his home or studio and write long, bitter letters overflowing with charges and recriminations. A typical Borglum philippic was that of May 7, 1934, in which he accused Boland of trying to use the memorial for political purposes, depositing Mount Rushmore money in the First National Bank of Rapid City for personal gain, general unfriendliness, and destructive interference. He frequently distributed such letters widely, and he sent a copy of this one to George Philip of Rapid City, a close friend of both Boland and Borglum.

Philip replied that he feared disaster for the project if the two men continued to misunderstand one another. Whether Borglum admitted it or not, Philip said, "one of the complexities of this work is the financial burden . . . and that falls on Boland in large measure." "It is not easy," he continued, "to get money from financially minded people and [report] to a financially minded Commission. He also has to cooperate with one of the greatest artists the world has produced, and harmonize the two." On another occasion Borglum was making rash charges to Philip, who was a very calm and unruffled man. After listening briefly, Philip laughed and said, "Hell, Borglum, you know that isn't so." Borglum paused, thought a moment and then replied, "I wish more people would laugh at me."

Borglum undoubtedly worked under severe handicaps and unsatisfactory conditions at Rushmore, and many of his complaints were valid. But he would not admit that the irritating circumstances were not the fault of Boland or the commission.

It should be emphasized that the disagreements between Boland and Borglum, while fundamental, were only occasional until 1935, when they became almost constant. Borglum was so changeable that he might be damning the chairman of the executive committee one week and singing his praises the next. There was no telling the charges he might level in a rash moment or the extent of his glowing praise when more self-possessed. Late in 1933, for example, he wrote Norbeck a blistering attack on Boland and his policies. Less than three days later he referred to Boland as sympathetic, honest, helpful, and capable.

Boland, though he deeply resented the unfair accusations, treated Borglum with the understanding and patience of an indulgent parent for a precocious child. The failure of the Stone Mountain promoters to do this had helped ruin that project. Boland's replies to Borglum were aggravatingly calm and restrained. He refused to enter into literary fisticuffs with a man who had thirty years' successful experience in that art. Moreover, it would have only made bad matters worse. His sharpest retort was that Borglum made "silly and untrue" statements about him.

There were times when Boland's actions would have tried the patience of a less easily aroused artist than Borglum. When Boland ordered the beginning of a season's work or urged that carving be done on a particular figure, the sculptor justly felt that Boland was poaching on his preserve. There may have been good reason for such suggestions, and they were within Boland's authority, but they showed a lack of propriety and gave Borglum an excuse to charge interference. Doubtless, however, Borglum would have invented other causes for complaint without these.

On one occasion the executive committee postponed buying four chairs and a table that Borglum wanted for his studio. Whether or not these were needed was beside the point. A small expenditure to satisfy this request might have been wise, even if it was poor business. Boland had an almost miserly attitude toward the treasury, and although most of the commissioners supported him, some of them felt that he was picayunish and over-cautious.

A feeling existed that an occasional uneconomical purchase of a few hundred dollars—perhaps even one of questionable legality— would have gone a long way toward soothing the sculptor. But to a man who had solicited dimes and quarters from school children to help keep the project alive, a "few hundred dollars" to appease a temperamental artist was no small expenditure.

Boland held that if the commission were to loosen its tight financial rein on Borglum, he would become unmanageable. The Stone Mountain debacle gave some credence to this view. After 1925 when more money became available, it was less imperative that every dollar be spent efficiently. But in the early days when funds were scarce, it was necessary that a good showing be made in order to elicit interest and obtain further contributions. No one questioned Boland's accounts, which were correct in every respect. But his financial conservatism sometimes added fuel to an already roaring flame.

Once the quarrels reached the stage of constant bickering, the contrasting natures of the two men prevented any kind of lasting reconciliation. Boland was businesslike and thoroughly rational, while Borglum's extreme sensitivity made it difficult for him to take a rational view of any problem. It might be said the Boland typified the hard-working, stable, draft horse, and Borglum the nervous, high-strung, excitable thoroughbred. There were good and legitimate reasons for the interference of Boland and the federal government at Rushmore, but the artist did not consider himself amenable to the rules and practices which govern others.

The first major crisis in personal relations occurred in September 1933. Norbeck, Boland, Williamson, and Borglum met at the studio for what the senator called a "showdown." Norbeck did most of the talking and later admitted that he lost his temper. He flayed Borglum for trying to assume business duties for which he was unfit. In language he might have used on an inefficient well-drilling crew, he attacked the sculptor for attempting to take over Boland's responsibilities and warned him to tend strictly to the artistic features of the work. He complained about the lack of progress at the monument and declared that it would take twenty years to complete at the present rate. Finally, Norbeck demanded that the bickering between the sculptor and the executive committee cease immediately.

This meeting placed a severe strain upon a friendship of some eight years. Borglum was deeply hurt by Norbeck's tongue-lashing. For once he did not relieve his feelings in a bitter letter but wrote calmly a few days later explaining his problems and giving his side of the controversy with Boland. Norbeck then apologized but held to his accusations. Borglum would not permit him to apologize: "I don't blame you," he said. "I do blame others" (meaning Boland). Disappointment, he added, came only because Norbeck sided with those incapable of understanding the memorial and its problems.

Borglum accepted criticism from Norbeck which he probably would not have taken from any other person, partly because he realized that Norbeck had been the real promoter of his grand opportunity. By securing federal funds the senator had recently kept the work from being closed down—perhaps permanently—and it seemed that all future money must also come from Congress. In that event, Norbeck would be needed. In his calmer moments Borglum realized this.

Considering Borglum's actions at Stone Mountain, one naturally wonders why he did not leave the project in a huff, damning everything and everyone connected with it. A number of reasons have been suggested for his staying on and suffering what he considered interference and indignities. A second Stone Mountain experience would undoubtedly have affected his reputation adversely. He admitted that protection of his professional standing was an important consideration. But that is only part of the reason.

It has been charged that a main consideration was the income he received at Rushmore—that he delayed the work in order to increase his honorarium. This is untrue. He could have earned larger fees elsewhere, and he held other commissions to supplement his income while he worked at Mount Rushmore.

Borglum stayed primarily because the monument had become a part of his very being. It was one thing Borglum admitted was bigger than himself. He would not deviate from his central purpose in life: the completion of the monument. And he would not tolerate anything or anyone he thought was obstructing progress. His spirit and courage were admirable if his judgment was poor. It was incomprehensible to him that Boland, Norbeck, and others could share his obsession, even in a small way, and still be concerned with paying bills, meeting government requirements, and handling other ordinary matters. He could not see that great achievements such as this were possible only through amiable cooperation and harmony. Possibly Borglum's cantankerousness was not without value. He kept people around him so stirred up that they worked all the harder.

Part of Borglum's attitude resulted from his jealous protectiveness of the project. He developed a possessiveness, a conviction that it was *his* and that no one else should have any credit for the great work. Norbeck chided him for this attitude, declaring that a "big man should appreciate the fact that the big credit is the only important credit. . . . Isn't it sufficient to be known as the world's greatest sculptor without also craving the hand clapping of those who live in the Styx?" Norbeck found it difficult to criticize Borglum because of his fondness for him. But there were times when nothing else would thrust him back into the world of reality.

The whole problem of personal relations was most unfortunate. No one knows how much progress would have been made had active cooperation prevailed among the principal sponsors of the Rushmore memorial.

CHAPTER THIRTEEN

Indulgent Uncle Sam

ONLY some $16,000 remained on hand when operations ceased early in December 1933. The commission would need several thousand dollars to resume work in the spring of 1934. Unfortunately, conditions were no more favorable for raising money than they had been during the previous two or three years. Consequently, the commission decided to ask the Public Works Administration for $50,000. Norbeck had explored this angle and had even presented it to the president. At a meeting of the commission in November 1933, no source of finance had been suggested other than the federal government.

As usual Borglum was impatient with delay, and he went to Washington in March 1934, hoping to facilitate quick action. He saw Secretary Ickes but received no encouragement from him. In fact, Ickes opposed the whole Mount Rushmore project. He once said that he never wanted to see the Black Hills after Borglum had begun carving there. To him it smacked too much of carving one's initials in the bark of a beautiful tree. Finding no sympathy there, Borglum laid his problem before President Roosevelt while attending a White House dinner on March 22. The president, he said, was greatly interested. At about the same time, he sent Mrs. Roosevelt two motion pictures of Mount Rushmore.

The sculptor wanted Norbeck to introduce a bill which would eliminate the necessity of matching federal money and would include an additional appropriation of $280,000. This would provide about $48,000—enough Borglum thought, to finish the memorial. Norbeck canvassed his colleagues and concluded that it would be impossible to pass a bill carrying such a large appropriation. He may have been too conservative, but his judgment of congressional temper was generally accurate. He believed that additional groundwork needed to be laid in Congress and that it would be wiser to seek money for one year at a time. Norbeck was sure that sufficient funds could be obtained once the monument became better known. "When we get two figures on the mountain instead of one incomplete figure, it will inspire a lot more confidence," he told Borglum. Meanwhile, the Public Works Administration refused to help. H. M. Waite, deputy administrator, explained to Norbeck that as long as matchable funds were available in the United States treasury for Mount Rushmore, a relief grant could not legally be made. Norbeck was now thoroughly discouraged, and Borglum was fretting. The Senator told Chairman Sargent, "I think the only thing that can be done at Washington, and there is little chance of that, is to get the law changed so we can get the remainder of the federal funds without matching." About $105,000 remained of the original authorization. This much might finish the Washington and Jefferson figures.

Norbeck, ill and lacking much of his old vigor, introduced a measure on May 3 designed to make available the unexpended appropriation of $49,626 without matching, plus another $55,000 which was part of the authorization but was not yet appropriated. Passage of the bill would mean more than $49,000 for 1934 and $55,000 that would presumably be appropriated the next year. He tried to camouflage his legislation by pointing out that an amendment to the basic act was needed because of Coolidge's death. Someone else had to be designated to write the inscription.

The first legislative hurdle was obtaining the approval of Director of the Budget Lewis W. Douglas. Norbeck, Boland, and Borglum called at Douglas's office and found the director friendly but firm. If the bill was approved, Douglas asked, how would the money be spent and what would be accomplished? These were embarrassing questions. It was almost impossible to impress strangers with the fact that the vagaries of mountain sculpture could wreck the most carefully drawn budgets. Furthermore, they knew that it was difficult to keep Borglum on any specific schedule of work and that his plans were mostly in his mind and subject to frequent change. But Douglas would not favor the measure until he received a written statement of how the funds would be spent. Consequently, Norbeck and Boland wrote a letter, which was also signed by Borglum, outlining a program of operations and promising to follow it.

In 1934, they said, work would be devoted to completing the Jefferson figure and putting the "finishing touches" on Washington.

This could be done with $60,000. During the following season Lincoln's face would be blocked out and completed, if possible. Any remaining work on Lincoln would be finished in 1936, as well as work on the entablature or the Roosevelt figure. "The commission is firmly of the opinion," the letter concluded, "that this work should be completed in the fall of 1937." It was also explained that a plan was being developed to raise private funds for carving in 1936 since by that time, if Norbeck's bill passed, the original authorization of $250,000 would be exhausted.

Norbeck had to promise verbally that the Mount Rushmore promoters would not ask for more federal help—at least, not until they had raised $105,000 from private sources. With these commitments Douglas approved the bill. It is interesting to speculate on whether or not the friends of the Rushmore project seriously intended to solicit additional private contributions. In light of past experiences, one would conclude that promises to match any federal funds later were merely expediential.

When the measure passed the Senate on May 31, Norbeck implied that the government was doing nothing more than advancing its share of the cost, thereby giving the commission "a little more time" to "raise additional funds." He was not one to quibble over methods if his objective could be achieved, and it was certainly necessary to indicate that further individual donations would be obtained. Within less than a year, however, all pretense of raising private funds was abandoned. During the summer of 1934 Norbeck mentioned soliciting $25,000 from the Homestake Mining Company, but he was really whistling in the dark to keep up his courage. Borglum's statement that the president and the rest of official Washington would see the project through obviously indicates that he, too, was looking solely to the federal government.

The Senate had passed the measure as a courtesy to Norbeck, but the situation in the House was dangerous. Kent Keller of Illinois, chairman of the Committee on the Library and an old federal and business associate of Norbeck's, was in charge of the bill. He was a large, somewhat pompous, distinguished-looking man, who appeared important but had relatively little influence in Congress. He played a significant role in the story only because he was chairman of the committee which handled Rushmore legislation in the House.

On June 15 the bill was slated for passage in the House without opposition or objection, but Keller could not obtain recognition. "There was not a chance in a million to get the legislation," he informed Norbeck. Meanwhile, Congressman Theodore Werner, a Rapid City Democrat who had replaced Williamson the previous year, was working vigorously. Werner knew that the bill could be brought up and passed only with support of the House leaders. Thus he laid the matter before Speaker Rainey and other influential members. Keller's jealousy hampered any close working relationship between himself and Werner.

Norbeck, who was watching the situation closely, finally called on Congresswoman Isabella Greenway of Arizona. She and Borglum were close friends, and he had carved a statue of her husband. When Keller gave up, Norbeck sent a page to Mrs. Greenway with the message, "The chairman cannot get the bill up. I think you can." Werner and Mrs. Greenway then prevailed upon Speaker Rainey to consider the measure. It passed so quickly that there was hardly time to object. There were no speeches, no explanation. All of that had been taken care of earlier. "Without Werner," Norbeck wrote, "we could not have gotten the legislation."

The first tangible results of Borglum's publicity campaigns began to bear fruit during this legislative crisis. In February the Hearst newspaper chain promoted a contest for a six hundred–word inscription to be carved on Mount Rushmore. The work had not received so much favorable advertising since the controversy over Coolidge's proposed history. Norbeck believed that this publicity helped get his bill through the Senate. Readers were led to believe that the inscription judged best by a committee of leading citizens headed by President Roosevelt would be used by Borglum. This was improbable since the law had named Coolidge the author, and this law had not been amended since the former president's death. Later in 1934 this provision was changed by Norbeck's bill, and the commission was given authority to determine who should compose the inscription. In any event, about eight hundred thousand entries or "histories" were submitted, and prizes were awarded in the various classes. While nothing came of the contest, it kept the memorial before the public and, in the long run, was of great value.

Delay in obtaining funds caused the loss of two months of good working weather in spring 1934. Operations were finally resumed on

June 15. Never had personal relations among the sponsors of the memorial been less satisfactory. Inability to start the work earlier had added to Borglum's grievances and further aroused his ire. Upon receipt of an especially abusive letter, Boland said, "My first thought was to resign and be relieved of all of this unnecessary trouble." However, he was as stubborn as Borglum was unreasonable, and he finally decided to "remain on the job until removed by the commission or the President."

So serious did the relationship between Borglum and Boland become that the sculptor ordered Superintendent Tallman not to give information to Boland. Norbeck explained the situation to Commissioner Spoonts, a close friend of Borglum, and expressed the fear that "unless we can exercise firmness with much patience and wisdom . . . we might have something approaching [the] Stone Mountain blowup." Boland, who was outwardly calm and self-possessed, constantly had to fight the urge to explode. His statement expressing hope that Borglum would spend two-thirds of the summer at Stone Mountain and the other third in Washington leaves no doubt about his feeling.

In 1934 Borglum's almost constant criticism of the local administration grew more intense and bitter. He accused Boland of protecting the railroad interests in the state legislature, thereby gaining Commissioner Sargent's support. He charged both Norbeck and Boland with using the Rushmore project for political advantage. But his main attacks were against interference, which in effect meant that he resented his inability to control the business aspects of the memorial. Patiently Norbeck tried to explain the situation but finally lost his temper and wrote, "You are so deficient in business judgment as to be almost blind." He concluded, "I know I am writing something now that you do not comprehend any more than a businessman comprehends your art." He later told Borglum, "Your letter file will get us all in trouble—so full of charges and complaints. This file is now a public record." He added, "If Congress should investigate, it might conclude "that the commission is made up of a bunch of crooks or that the artist is a nut—or both."

A crisis was reached on June 25 when the executive committee passed a resolution refusing to assume liability "for any bill or obligations contracted for materials, supplies, labor, or otherwise, unless such materials, supplies, and labor have first been requisitioned from and approved by the Executive Committee." Moreover, no labor was to be employed until Borglum had submitted a plan of operations to the committee for advance approval.

The justification for hamstringing Borglum was that all expenditures had to conform to promises made to Director of the Budget Douglas. Boland tried to convince the sculptor that it would also avoid the possibility of Borglum's "being accused of raising wages or employing unnecessary men for the purpose of increasing his honorarium." Borglum, however, was not misled, and he recognized the resolution for what it was—an attempt to deny him all business responsibilities. He viewed the resolution as an unwarranted obstruction and a petty meddling with *his work*, as he so often reminded the commission.

Borglum was also ordered to spend no more funds on the entablature except for minor details. The sculptor justly felt that the commission was now interfering with his art and design. He was not satisfied with the explanation that all money should be spent on the faces in order to make a good showing for the general public and Congress. The executive committee attempted to remove some of the sting by voting to employ Borglum's son Lincoln on an hourly basis. Lincoln had worked on the project previously without pay. He was not a recognized artist although his natural talent and close association with his father had given him some preparation for his work. Within a short time he became chief pointer and ultimately superintendent. Sufficient artistic ability to follow Borglum's instructions accurately and complete loyalty to his father were his chief assets.

But this did not appease the irate sculptor. "The resolutions," he told Boland, "will destroy the Mount Rushmore Memorial." Borglum even refused to attend a dinner party given by Sargent for members of the commission. In declining he said that the attitude and spirit of the meeting had shocked and distressed him. Sargent replied that he regretted Borglum's attitude because "we all regard you so highly and so affectionally that I am sure we want to do everything within our power to make your work pleasant and to make it the outstanding success of the ages." Even Cullinan, who generally took Borglum's part, was "surprised and distressed" by the sculptor's charges. His advice was to "swallow your castor oil, and carry on."

Norbeck threatened to resign from the commission. He probably hoped that this would have a sobering effect on Borglum. But on the contrary, "I think it pleased him," he remarked. Borglum saw that he could never get rid of Boland without also eliminating Norbeck.

Borglum's irritation reached the point where he was appealing for help to people who knew little or nothing about the work. To his friend Herman Oliphant, general counsel in the United States Treasury Department, he wrote many letters of complaint and suggestion. Oliphant was slightly acquainted with Mount Rushmore for he had spent two weeks there with Borglum in 1934. But this was not the case with Edward Bruce, who was appointed to the commission in 1936. He wrote that he was quite ignorant of his new duties. If a commission must exist, Borglum hoped to fill it with personal friends and others who would not restrain him in any way.

Looking to the future, the sculptor urged the passage of a bill which would abolish the old commission and set up a new five-man group. He suggested Oliphant for chairman, with Norbeck, Mrs. Greenway, Spoonts, and Sargent for the other members. These selections, he explained, would save everyone worthwhile on the old commission and would soften the blow of the change. Then he recommended an executive officer who was not a native of the Black Hills to handle the bookkeeping, purchases, disbursements, and other administrative tasks. Borglum wanted a salaried employee at the mountain to whom he could dictate.

Borglum also advocated the inclusion in the bill of a $500,000 appropriation, estimating that this amount, together with the $55,000 already authorized, would finance the rest of the work, including the museum (generally called the Hall of Records). Furthermore, he said, a reservation two miles square should be set aside around the monument, and after the memorial was completed, the president should provide for its administration. Until something of this kind was done, he announced his refusal to deal personally with the ne'er-do-wells around Rapid City.

Despite bickering and lack of harmony, work on the memorial progressed splendidly although it did not fulfill the predictions of Borglum or the cairrairlune of Norbeck. About thirty men among them thirteen drillers. Most of the workmen were employed on the Jefferson head, and from four to six worked on Washington's collar. By the end of the season in early December 1934, the lapels of Washington's coat were nearly finished and his left shoulder and arm had been partly freed from the encasing granite.

Work on the new Jefferson figure had caused Borglum many problems. He recounted his troubles as follows: "Probably a third of the time spent on the Jefferson head has been spent in refitting it or relocating it within the mountain itself, so that the nose, in particular, would not have a crack running through it. I have no intention of leaving a head on that mountain that in the course of five hundred or five thousand years will be without a nose.

"Jefferson's nose at the right-hand nostril has one of these cracks. When I started or rather located Jefferson's head the crack ran across the end of it. I reset the head five degrees to the north, set it back four feet, then tilted the head about eighteen inches. Finally the crack just escaped the right-hand nostril; it still cuts down across the right eye, past the nose and upper lip and through the middle of the chin. In that location, it is perfectly harmless because it is supported by all the mountain back of it, and can be easily seamed against moisture." (A mixture of white lead and granite dust was used to seal such cracks.)

Problems of this nature played havoc with time schedules and budgets. They also explain why it was artistically unwise to finish one figure before proceeding to another as some had advocated. It was impossible to determine in advance where a face would finally fit. Therefore, it seemed better to locate all the faces before finishing any one of them. Otherwise, a head might be completed in such a way that it would not blend properly with the others. Borglum, who was aware of all this, bore much unjust criticism from engineers and others who did not understand the overall sculptural design. The absence of trained stoneworkers also may have retarded the finishing work. Few people realized Borglum's tremendous responsibility and the agony he suffered during his struggle to mold the unyielding mountain into a colossal and everlasting monument to American greatness.

As had been true at the end of nearly every working season, the commission was practically without funds when operations closed down in December 1934. The most encouraging aspect of the budget for that year had been the large proportion of money spent for construction payrolls. In 1931 and 1933 only 27 and 22 percent of the expenditures went for this purpose. In 1934 construction payrolls increased to 48 percent of the total, indicating that more men were being employed directly on the mountain. Installation of the plant, retirement of old debts, and efficiency of operation were making this possible. Remarkable progress seemed certain if additional funds became available.

There was still $55,000 of the original authorization unappropriated. If this money could be obtained, work might proceed during 1935. For the first time the Interior Department included a request for Mount Rushmore in its regular appropriation bill, and A. E. Demaray, associate director of the National Park Service,* appeared before the house subcommittee on appropriations to justify the expenditure. Hearings were held on January 28, 1935. Committee members present were Chairman Edward T. Taylor of Colorado, Marion A. Zioncheck of Washington, and Jed Johnson of Oklahoma, Democrats, and Richard B. Wigglesworth of Massachusetts, Republican. The general attitude of the committee was critical. Only Zioncheck had seen the memorial, and he seemed slightly more sympathetic, telling his colleagues that Mount Rushmore was a "very impressive thing." It is significant that most of the people who saw the monument became its friends, and it was for this reason that Borglum constantly planned dedications and celebrations at the mountain and invited distinguished national leaders to visit the project.

During the questioning, Demaray evaded embarrassing inquiries about future requests for help from Congress. Wigglesworth expressed the committee's attitude when he said, "You will probably come back and look to us for more money, will you not?" Demaray would not commit himself. Assuming that the figures could be completed for $100,000 each, Taylor thought that the memorial was "pretty expensive." It was obvious that the National Park Service officials were not enjoying their tussle on behalf of Mount Rushmore. E. K. Burlew attempted to justify the Park Service's request by saying, "We have just gotten this by executive order, and we have no jurisdiction over it. They just threw it into our appropriation."

Despite the unfriendly attitude of the House committee and the weak case offered by the National Park Service, the $55,000 item remained in the Interior Department appropriation bill and became law on May 9. Accompanying this appropriation was stricter administration of the project by the Park Service. L. M. F. W. Wanson, disbursing agent at Yellowstone National Park, arrived in Rapid City to instruct Boland in financial procedures acceptable to the Interior Department. Boland was pleased with this increased interest for he

---

*A. E. Demaray became director of the National Park Service in 1951.

felt that once the National Park Service became genuinely concerned about Mount Rushmore, it would help secure additional money from Congress. No longer pretending that further private contributions could be obtained, he realized that from now on reliance must be placed upon the federal government. Boland also hoped that close supervision by the Interior Department would impress upon Borglum the fact that the project was a federal responsibility and that he must abide by regulations.

Although the National Park Service demonstrated greater interest in the monument during 1935, it showed no inclination to campaign for funds. That was still up to the commission. Since federal appropriations offered the only hope, much of the financial burden came to rest on Norbeck. During the spring he decided to introduce a bill authorizing $200,000 to continue the memorial. An improved attitude in Congress increased his chances of success. "Rushmore is becoming an institution instead of a joke," he wrote. "It is no longer in the Stone Mountain class."

His task was not easy, however, because Borglum was in Washington working on his own financial plan. Since he was sure that the Interior Department would not help him, Borglum got his friends in the Treasury Department to draw up a bill abolishing the commission, asking for an appropriation of $355,000, and placing the administrative control in their hands. According to Norbeck, when Borglum saw there was no chance to pass his measure, he naively suggested borrowing from the United States Treasury. Satirically Norbeck told Boland, "I will sign the note—you won't mind!" Replying in the same vein, Boland advised him not to sign for anything less than $400,000.

Borglum's attempt to bypass the commission, and perhaps even to muddy the legislative waters, thoroughly irked Norbeck. In a letter to Boland he said that he could not accomplish anything because Borglum had been "fussing around," and he sharply told the sculptor, "I will not even start until you quit, for you will not harmonize your plans with the views of anybody else. You will not even confer with me before drafting a bill and filing reports which are conflicting and will materially hinder me in getting money."

Borglum's activity in Washington had a dual effect, one helpful, the other harmful. He unquestionably built up general support in Congress, and he had many good friends on Capitol Hill.

His publicity on the memorial was beginning to pay dividends. "It is not the uphill work that we had before to get anywhere," Norbeck declared. Borglum had won Senator Barkley's support for the project, and the Kentucky senator advised Norbeck that he would "feel awfully bad if Borglum is not permitted to finish this undertaking." But the fact remained that none of the sculptor's friends outside South Dakota were willing, or had the time and influence, to push Rushmore legislation through Congress. It is one thing to favor the work in an impersonal manner and something entirely different to get an appropriation.

Borglum continued to make it difficult for Norbeck by issuing statements, reports, and estimates which were generally wrong and almost always conflicting. His own inconsistencies did not bother Borglum, but since his statements were often checked by the Budget Bureau or members of Congress, they caused Norbeck no end of embarrassment. The senator frequently chided Borglum for having told Andrew Mellon back in 1927 that $500,000 would not be needed from the federal government. Of course, the nature of the work naturally made it difficult to estimate costs accurately, but the files reveal that Borglum was consistently inaccurate by large margins. His estimates were usually the product of guesswork. His assertion in 1935 that $355,000 would finish the memorial illustrates his gross error in judgment. Approximately $580,000 was spent after he expressed that opinion, yet the figures were still incomplete, and practically nothing had been done on the Hall of Records or the entablature. A year earlier he had made a much closer guess on the total cost in his letter to Oliphant.

Seeing that he must rely on Norbeck, Borglum asked him to dinner so that they could discuss Rushmore matters. "I would enjoy the dinner," read the senator's frank reply, "and I certainly would have enjoyed a conference with you in making up some plans for Rushmore, but when you decided you would not have a conference with me prior to making plans, filing reports, and drafting legislation, I just gave up." He continued, "Let us have dinner but let us talk about something on which we can agree. We can not agree on Rushmore. Your conflicting reports are now on file and would embarrass me greatly should I undertake any legislation." Norbeck actually did intend to seek a new appropriation, but he wanted to impress Borglum with the importance of keeping his hands off legislative matters.

Part of Borglum's aggravating conduct was again the result of his personal financial troubles: he was about to lose his ranch through foreclosure. Should that happen, he told Norbeck, he would never again set foot in South Dakota. However, through the helpful cooperation of Williamson and Boland, this loss was averted.

Before introducing the Rushmore bill, Norbeck sought clearance at the White House. Without the support of the president and the director of the budget, there was little hope of getting the $200,000. " I saw the big Chief this morning," he wrote on June 28, "and his attitude is entirely satisfactory." After conferring with his budget director, Roosevelt wrote Norbeck, "In our conversation the other day regarding the Mount Rushmore National Memorial, your description of the progress of work . . . and of its inspirational value to our people in the years to come convinces me of the need for legislation to authorize an additional appropriation of $200,000 for the completion of this project."

In order to allay Democratic opposition, Bulow and Norbeck jointly introduced the Senate bill, and Representative Werner handled it in the House. As had been true in the past, Norbeck quieted opposition in the Senate by personal conferences, but House members were less easily calmed. The repeated calls on the federal treasury to bail out Mount Rushmore were arousing increased antagonism. The House Committee on the Library reported the bill favorably but only with the understanding that the commission finish the memorial with the $200,000, "as the Committee feels that further appropriation at some future date . . . would be entirely out of order."

When Werner's bill came up for passage, he stated the situation frankly. "The question of appropriating additional funds," he said, "simply resolves itself into whether we are going to leave this memorial unfinished or whether we are going to complete it." Representative Tabor, well known for his interest in economy, thought Congress should pay more attention to protecting the treasury. He thought South Dakota should be satisfied with what had been accomplished. A memorial with the likeness of Washington and Jefferson, he argued, "would make a very good park all by itself." Any community having such a monument, he continued, "should not ask for $200,000 more."

T. L. Moritz of Pennsylvania staunchly insisted that it was unwise to spend more on Mount Rushmore during depression times. "You cannot eat art," he complained. "We are not interested in art. . . . Right now we should concentrate on the necessities of life." Representative Robert F. Rich, commonly known as "Where-is-the money-coming-from" Rich, thought it would be better to appropriate funds for South Dakota farmers.

Congressmen White and Roy O. Woodruff, the latter a personal friend of Borglum's, struck telling blows for the measure. White said the country should utilize Borglum's "matchless genius" while it was available. Woodruff explained that Congress had appropriated about ten billion dollars "for God knows what," and that $200,000 more was of little importance. He received hearty applause when he concluded: "In view of the ridiculous purpose for which billions are being spent . . . and in view of the worthy purpose for which this $200,000 is proposed, I hope the House will overwhelmingly approve the bill."

But before the House would pass the measure, it was amended to include the words "execution and completion" of Mount Rushmore. Norbeck knew that $200,000 would not finish the work, and wrote later that at least $250,000 would be required. His estimate, while closer than Borglum's, was several hundred thousand dollars short. Boland showed the best business judgment when he predicted that $750,000 would be necessary. But Norbeck was famous for compromise, and he operated on the principle that half a loaf is better than none. So he accepted the $200,000 and remained silent about how far it would go toward completing the memorial. The House finally approved the bill on August 24. Once the authorization was provided, Norbeck succeeded in getting $100,000 appropriated, $20,000 of which was made immediately available. This set up a budget of more than $70,000 for the 1935 season and assured money for 1936 and 1937 as well.

An important factor in Norbeck's success in this instance was the general attitude of the New Deal toward expenditures. The philosophy of spending the country out of a depression contrasted sharply with the program of government economy of the 1930s. Roosevelt's interest, stirred by Borglum and Norbeck, was significant. Because of the president's attraction to unique and unusual projects, it is not surprising that he took more than a casual interest in the colossal sculpture. Moreover, a distant relative would ultimately grace the mountainside if the monument was completed.

Whatever the causes, Norbeck achieved success and made it possible for the work to proceed. He had not for years been so enthusiastic over future prospects. Referring to the unpleasantness between Borglum and the commission, he wrote, "The $200,000 . . . will stimulate me sufficiently so I will be able to overlook much of our trouble."

CHAPTER FOURTEEN

"The Figure of Washington Is—"

WITH another financial gap thus bridged, work on the mountain proceeded rapidly between June and November 1935. About fifty persons were employed, and more than $73,000 was spent, the largest annual disbursement up to that time. Although thousands of tons of rock were removed, progress was not easily discernible to the average visitor. Jefferson's face looked complete, but his chin was on solid rock and appeared to be resting on Washington's shoulder. The sides of the face and collar had not been finished, nor had the granite between the two figures been removed.

Little was done on the Washington figure except on the collar and chest. Borglum declared that he would not undertake additional refinement of the faces until he could hire trained assistants. The Lincoln figure, merely roughed out at this time, was barely recognizable. More than 197,000 people from every state in the Union and from twenty-two foreign countries saw the memorial in this stage. During August, at the height of the tourist season, an average of about 3,300 tourists visited the monument daily. Accompanied by a guide, quite a number of the more ambitious and daring climbed to the mountaintop, a hard but exciting trip. Because it was somewhat hazardous, the National Park Service later forbade this excursion.

When the work season closed, Borglum told newsmen that he hoped to put the "finishing touches" on the three figures in 1936 and perhaps do something on Roosevelt. To accomplish this, he said, he would require double his present working force. The passage of Norbeck's bill authorizing an additional $200,000 made the chances of employing more men and buying additional equipment the best in years.

Borglum showed increased determination to remove any influence of the Mount Rushmore Commission. Somebody or something had to be substituted for Boland's administration. The National Park Service had provided a special disbursing officer responsible to the Interior Department, but Boland still held the real authority. Borglum criticized nearly everyone connected with the project, and a heavy flow of communication reached the president and other officials in Washington. One of his letters to Roosevelt, written at a time of strain and frustration, was so full of ridiculous charges that his friends advised that he not mail it. Insufficient power, lack of a hoist for his men, failure of the commission to hire skilled carvers, and general interference were complaints repeated with growing regularity. To these he gradually added new accusations. He claimed that the commission owed him about $14,000, although an audit of the books at the close of 1935 had shown only $1,703 due the sculptor.

When he was in financial need, Borglum was likely to insist that he be paid something extra for taking over Tucker's responsibilities. A new contract, adding 5 percent for "work and construction" would be a fair payment, he said. Boland's refusal to approve such a contract on the ground that Tucker's work was being done by others was one of the major sources of friction. In any event, Borglum's irritation grew to the point where he was accusing Boland of financial irregularities.

The sculptor constantly complained that the commission refused to hire skilled carvers or finishers. Such skilled workers were necessary. But, as Norbeck explained, when finishers were employed at high wages, Borglum often placed them on work which cheaper laborers could perform. And when Borglum shifted skilled carvers to ordinary drilling, their higher wages were resented by other employees doing the same work. "More finishers," Norbeck said, "would have been employed if they had been confined to their jobs. Our trouble is due to a poor system only."

Chairman Sargent, a man of great patience, became thoroughly disgusted. "I should gladly resign from the chairmanship . . . and . . . intend to do so . . . because I do not like the unpleasantness incident to the entire situation; and especially the critical letters that I receive." He was willing for the Treasury Department to assume control if that suited the sculptor, but in that event the entire commission should resign. Sargent explained this to the National Park Service, but Director Cammerer made it clear that he was not eager to assume jurisdiction over Mount Rushmore.

One way to eliminate the commission and its control was to badger the members into retirement and replace them with hand-picked friends. The weakness of this approach was that Boland and Norbeck could not be intimidated. Consequently, Borglum saw that only by some fundamental administrative reorganization could he gain control. He informed Sargent that he was determined to direct the operations at Mount Rushmore without interference by those whom he considered ignorant and selfish. How reminiscent this was of his statements that he planned to *control* the work at Stone Mountain *without interference.*

When Borglum began charging Boland with financial irregularities, Norbeck advised the National Park Service to investigate. He confided to his friend Demaray that nothing was wrong, but that a survey by a government official might be helpful. Demaray directed Edward D. Freeland, superintendent at Wind Cave National Park, to look into matters at Mount Rushmore. After consulting both Boland and Borglum, Freeland concluded that lack of power was "undoubtedly the cause of much delay in the work." He added that efficiency was not up to National Park Service standards, but there was no mishandling of funds.

Increased tension between Boland and Borglum was reflected in the resignation of William S. Tallman. His principal sin, according to Borglum, was friendship with Boland. In his letter of resignation Tallman asserted, "As Mr. Borglum maintains the feeling he has toward the Commission as a whole and toward certain of its . . . members, it is very difficult to work with him. . . . He accused me," Tallman continued, "of being so friendly with Mr. John A. Boland, whom he believes to be working against him, that he cannot trust me."

Borglum stated frankly to Freeland that he wanted someone representing the Interior Department to replace Tallman, someone who would handle purchases, payrolls, timekeeping, and other administrative duties, and someone who would take orders from the sculptor. These conditions put a severe strain on Boland and other members of the Commission. "What could be done?" "I couldn't sleep nights," Boland confessed. "Borglum was driving me crazy." He finally concluded that a solution to his problem might be found in greater administrative control by the National Park Service. Putting his affairs in order, he took the train for Washington in February 1936 to plead for assistance.

When Boland approached Demaray, he was referred to John L. Nagle, superintendent of memorials, an experienced and highly qualified engineer in the Park Service. Boland explained his troubles. Having recently experienced some differences with Borglum over locating his Bryan statue in Washington, Nagle was reluctant to assume any administrative responsibility at Mount Rushmore. His first advice was to return home and carry on. But Boland persisted, and after four conferences Nagle finally agreed to send a National Park Service engineer to Mount Rushmore during the working season. Somewhat hesitantly, Demaray approved this arrangement. "We will put the Park Service man here," he said, pointing one way, "and Borglum will be there." He told Boland, "You will be in between." This was not an enviable position.

Promise of National Park Service aid pleased Boland and also met with Borglum's hearty approval. He had been advocating the active participation of some governmental department for nearly two years, preferably the Treasury, where he had several personal friends. But the Interior was better than none. At about the same time, he was telling his troubles to Harry Slattery, administrative assistant to Secretary Ickes. Borglum wrote Slattery late in February, after Boland's visit to Washington, that a small group of "leftover politicians" in the Black Hills were causing most of his trouble. Norbeck, he wrote on another occasion, would trade his mother for a vote. Repeating most of his old charges with even more venom, he stated that he would actively campaign for the Democrats in the forthcoming presidential election. Mount Rushmore, provided by a Democratic administration, was being controlled by a little coterie of Republicans including Norbeck and Boland. This, he added, was not conducive to further federal appropriations. He maintained that Secretary Ickes should appoint someone to assume local control, a person free from "the clique and cabal of Rapid City that corrupts what it can control and kills what it cannot control."

Somewhat aghast at this communication, Slattery asked Demaray to draft an answer for him. Had Borglum known how letters circulate among department officials, he would have been furious. Demaray explained that the National Park Service had already decided to take more active part in the work. "This is agreeable to all members of the Commission." he said. He pointed out that sending an experienced engineer to Mount Rushmore would leave Borglum free to handle "purely artistic phases of the project." Recognizing the probable outcome of this action, Demaray concluded, "This inevitably will begin clashes between the Park Service engineer and the sculptor, and undoubtedly we shall need the support of the Department if Mr. Borglum is to be kept in line and progress made toward the completion of the memorial." Upon the basis of this memorandum, Slattery informed Borglum of the service's intentions. Borglum wired, "With right man your plan perfect." Thinking it was Slattery's idea, he later wrote, "God bless you."

Meanwhile, Congress had occasion to take another look at the project. Early in December 1935 the National Park Service asked lawmakers to appropriate $150,000 of the $200,000 previously authorized. Norbeck's observation that members of the subcommittee "gave Mr. Demaray quite a time of it," was an understatement. The principal questions centered around the length of time Congress was expected to appropriate money for Mount Rushmore, the amount needed to complete it, the reason for failure to match federal funds, the percentage Borglum received, and the inaccessibility of the monument.

Addressing Demaray, Representative Taylor opened the hearing by asking, "The main thing that we would like to hear from you is, when is this thing going to stop? What is the status of the work? . . ."

MR. DEMARAY: The figure of Washington is—

MR. ZIONCHECK: About to be completed?

MR. DEMARAY: About to be completed.

MR. TAYLOR: Last year that was "completed," was it not? . . .

MR. DEMARAY: I think that there is still some additional work to be done on it.

MR. TAYLOR: It seems to me that it was "completed" last year when we had this hearing . . .

MR. DEMARAY: There are degrees to completion, apparently . . .

Then sharp-witted congressmen referred to past statements which indicated that Washington and Jefferson would be finished in 1934. It was now late in 1935, and the figures were still incomplete. "Does any limitation into matter? Taylor asked impatiently. "This is getting very serious," Zioncheck added. As the questions became more embarrassing, Demaray sought refuge by explaining that "we are merely an agency supervising the expenditures of this money, as long as Congress continues to authorize it."

With the cost per figure running at least double the original estimate, the question was half-humorously raised, were there mountains in the vicinity "for four of five more presidents?" Demaray replied, "*Well, I hope not!*" He had spent a day at Mount Rushmore during the preceding summer and considered it "very heroic work." But when he was asked for the motive behind the project or just what it was meant to portray, he answered, "I do not know." Under these circumstances, he could hardly work enthusiastically for further appropriations. Representative Zioncheck concluded the discussions by stating that "the whole thing would not be so bad if George Washington knew that these hills existed before he died."

The entire subcommittee was reluctant to provide more money, but an appropriation of $100,000 was finally secured in late June 1936, and work was resumed on July 7. Congress, however, inserted a definite restriction in the bill forbidding the carving of any figures not yet begun. This reflected a lack of confidence in Borglum's judgment when he was given a completely free hand, but a more influential factor was the agitation of certain women's groups for the carving of a likeness of Susan B. Anthony on Mount Rushmore. As early as 1935 Congresswomen Mary T. Norton and Caroline O'Day, Mrs. Franklin D. Roosevelt, and others had urged Borglum to add another figure representative of American womanhood. The strongest proponent of the idea was Mrs. Rose Arnold Powell, leader of the Susan B. Anthony Forum in Washington.

Borglum never seriously considered these requests. He later told Representative Francis Case to ignore the movement. He explained that there was insufficient stone on Rushmore for another head and that an entirely new design would have to be made. But in June 1936 Congressman Keller and Senator Capper introduced bills to amend the basic Rushmore act by adding the name of Susan B. Anthony. While few except Mrs. Powell took these measures very seriously, the House appropriations committee made sure that none of the money for Mount Rushmore would be spent on additional figures.

Several weeks before work began in 1936, Nagle called in Julian C. Spotts to inform him of his assignment at Mount Rushmore as resident engineer for the National Park Service. Spotts was a University of Missouri graduate and had been in government service about ten years. He was a tall, partly bald, pleasant-looking man, whose sharp gray eyes twinkled as he spoke. Friendly, accommodating, and well-trained in his profession, he had served as first principal designer and resident engineer for the Arlington Memorial Bridge. He had visited most of the large granite quarries in the United States to study methods of quarry and to inspect granite for government purchases. But he was without adequate briefing or instructions and admittedly unfamiliar with the project as he headed toward the Black Hills.

His first impression of South Dakota was anything but favorable. As he traveled across the state in July, the temperature soared to 106 degrees, and a terrific wind whipped the fine, grimy dust into his car and trailer. Upon arrival at Rushmore, Spotts soon learned that the wisdom of Solomon was needed to keep things on an even keel. When it appeared that he might exert some authority for the National Park Service, Borglum resentfully asked, "Have you ever carved a mountain?" Spotts admitted his inexperience in this field, after which Borglum told the engineer that he knew nothing about "projects such as this" and intimated that ordinary engineering principles could not be applied. Compared to this stormy reception, Spotts's trip through the dust storm seemed pleasant in retrospect. He may have thought that the project needed something more than an engineer.

Spotts immediately turned to the problem of power about which Borglum had complained so often. He concluded that from an engineering standpoint, the project had been operated inefficiently and had grown up "without any definite plan." He found that electric current was insufficient to run the three compressors at full capacity when demands for power in Keystone were heavy. Under these conditions, not more than fifteen jackhammers could be operated at once. To correct this situation, he made more economical use of the available compressed air by stopping leaks. This alone permitted the use of four more drills. Then the commission bought a portable compressor, making possible the use of twenty-two jackhammers simultaneously.

He next worked toward installing an aerial tramway to transport workmen to the faces, another improvement Borglum had been demanding since the work began. Other technical improvements were made which helped to increase efficiency.

One might suppose that this performance would please Borglum, for Spotts had relieved him of many administrative problems, improved the plant, and left him free for his artistic work. But on the contrary, within six weeks after his arrival the National Park Service engineer was being damned in the sculptor's most effective manner.

The first trouble arose over general Park Service regulations, particularly those regarding employment. Spotts agreed that Borglum should determine who was to be hired, but he wanted to check on qualifications and experience before men were actually placed on the payroll. "I wish to assure you," he wrote Borglum, "that it is not the policy of the National Park Service to place employees under your supervision who do not meet with your approval." But Borglum acted as he had in the past. When Spotts insisted on compliance with Interior Department regulations, Borglum became arrogant. "There are occasions," he told Spotts, "where we can not wait upon or delay to meet preconceived regulations." He advised Nagle, "I will yield just as much as I can—even to what I consider foolish regulations . . . [but] don't let hindering red-tape interfere too much—and, as the surgeon deep in the cares of surgery, I'm likely to forget Bureau rules."

Borglum continued to complain about the lack of trained carvers, but when Spotts and Boland authorized him to bring in three skilled workmen from the East, he failed to obtain them. Thus local men were hired and others were promoted to the carver class on Borglum's orders. One of the reasons for Borglum's insistence on importing what he called "skilled carvers" was to convince the commission that Mount Rushmore was an exalted work of art. Actually, most of the work on the mountain was of an engineering rather than artistic nature.

By late August the situation had virtually reached an impasse. Of course, this was not an unusual condition. Borglum wailed to his Washington friends that he could do nothing at Mount Rushmore without consulting a "brainless jelly bean," and he frankly admitted that he had ignored government regulations. He contemptuously referred to Spotts as that "two by four" engineer and wondered if President Roosevelt could transfer the project to some other department.

Relations finally became so strained that when Spotts went to discuss the power problem with Borglum on August 20, the sculptor would not invite him into his office. Although the offices of the two men were within a hundred yards of each other, they did most of their business by correspondence. Characteristically, Borglum gave out cries of interference. "It is difficult to find this unique work becoming the victim of petty bureaucratic entanglements," he complained.

Although Spotts vastly improved the technical arrangements, Borglum insisted that he knew nothing about conditions at Mount Rushmore. "I have forgotten more about this than most men can learn in the time I have given to it," he wrote. In looking over this letter, Nagle red-penciled in the margin, "Could he have forgotten too much?" The mild manner and friendly smile of Spotts was not to be confused with weakness. When necessary he was firm with Borglum and insisted that as long as he was on the job, federal regulations would be followed.

The Interior Department was irritated by Borglum's refusal and failure to draw up an outline of operations and by the haphazard manner which had characterized the work program. E. K. Burlew explained that when the department took over, "no accurate maps . . . of the working plant and other working conditions at the mountain were available; no estimate of the power supply and power requirements, or the capacity and efficiency and state of repair of the pipe lines conveying compressed air . . . had been prepared; no personnel roster had been drawn up showing present and future needs for the various classifications of supervisors and workmen; and no comprehensive reports of the progress already made either on the preparation of the models or on the stone carving operations had been sent in." Burlew made it clear that the Interior Department expected Borglum to supply this data "so effective control of the work will be feasible." The very word "control" was enough to antagonize the sculptor.

While Borglum and Spotts sparred over administrative problems, plans were being made to put things in readiness for President Roosevelt's visit. As early as February 1936, and especially since July, Borglum and others had been urging Roosevelt to see Mount Rushmore during his tour of the nation's Dust Bowl. With the President on hand to dedicate the Jefferson figure, Borglum promised to make this the most elaborate celebration ever held at the mountain. Roosevelt finally agreed to visit the memorial, and he was in top form as he prepared to leave Washington. "Then Sunday," he informed Secretary McIntyre, "I leave you to have some place to go, and I was wondering whether . . . I could spend the day at Mount Rushmore and go to church, if they have one and if they have not got a church out there, suggest to Tom Berry [cowboy governor of South Dakota] that he get a Methodist preacher and hold an outdoor service for the whole party."

The presidential party arrived in Rapid City Saturday evening, August 29. The next morning Roosevelt attended the Episcopal church, relieving Governor Berry of the duty of sponsoring an old-fashioned revival meeting. It was early in the afternoon before Paul Bellamy, who had first shown Borglum the magnificent scenery around Harney Peak, drove the president toward Mount Rushmore. Borglum, waiting at the mountain, was boiling mad. He had explained to Roosevelt that it was essential to hold the dedication about noon, before the shadows covered Jefferson's face. He even threatened "to go ahead with the dedication and let the President go to —, and had he not been the President of these United States, I suppose he would have done just that," Williamson wrote.

But when Roosevelt arrived about 2:30 p.m., Borglum gave no sign of his irritation. Jefferson's sixty-foot face was covered by a huge flag, dynamite had been placed in the drill holes, and everything was in readiness. At the proper moment, Borglum set off the blasts to demonstrate how rock was removed, unveiled the head, and hoisted a flag. Turning to Roosevelt, he said, "I want you, Mr. President to dedicate this memorial as a shrine to democracy; to call upon the people of the earth for one hundred thousand years to come to read the thought and to see what manner of men struggled here to establish self-determination of government in the western world."

Although Roosevelt had not planned to speak, he responded brilliantly. Borglum and Norbeck had told him about the project, and Bellamy had added to his knowledge on their way to Rushmore. "I had had no conception until about ten minutes ago," he said, "not only of its magnitude but of its ... permanent importance." Continuing, the president said that Mount Rushmore could be an inspiration for democratic government in the United States and throughout the world. He expressed a hope that Americans of his generation would pass on the blessings and privileges of freedom, as represented by the sculptured figures, to future Americans. The crowd of three thousand, predominantly Republicans, cheered enthusiastically. Depression-ridden and dust-blown South Dakotans were encouraged by the chief executive's presence. They knew, too, that since the monument must be completed with federal funds, presidential support was of great importance.

After the ceremony, Borglum and Roosevelt chatted informally. The president asked, "Where are you going to put Teddy?" The sculptor explained that the president's cousin would be between the head of Jefferson and that of Lincoln which was just taking form. "I have it all planned out in my studio," he said, as he invited Roosevelt to see his models. But the president replied, "I will come back some day to look this over more fully."

Now that another figure was dedicated, though far from finished, Roosevelt returned to the grim problems of drouth relief, and Borglum went back to the mountain. He was encouraged but not satisfied. There was still too much interference, he said, and not enough support.

In order to work out a satisfactory relationship between the National Park Service and the sculptor, John Nagle decided to visit the project in person. Arriving on September 13, he went over the face of the mountain with Borglum and learned something of the difficulties involved in colossal sculpture. Borglum told Nagle that with an additional $100,000, he could complete the four figures as then modeled. His lack of familiarity with the work did not prevent Nagle from recognizing Borglum's estimate as extremely optimistic, and Spotts asserted that it was greatly exaggerated. Nagle soon learned not to take Borglum's estimates seriously.

Following a thorough inspection, he reported to his superiors in Washington that Borglum was well qualified and zealous in handling the carving. He added that local authorities had not always helped as they should in overcoming difficulties. In summarizing the situation he said, "If he [Borglum] can be convinced, as I think he can, that it is in the best interests of the project that he relinquish administrative supervision and purely technical operations, and confine himself to the preparation of models and execution of the carving work, then many of the difficulties encountered in the past would disappear."

Nagle had some definite ideas about the way the work should be handled. Every effort should be made, he said, to complete the Lincoln and Roosevelt figures to the same degree as those of Washington and Jefferson. He thought that most of the finishing and trimming should be delayed until all of the forms were recognizable. Acknowledging that it would always be necessary to distribute workmen over the entire sculpture, he recommended that work should be concentrated on one or two figures at a time. He did not think carving should begin on the inscription until the faces were nearly completed, or until Borglum had prepared an overall plan.

Boland, to whom Nagle wrote, did not agree that all finishing touches should be delayed, but he did agree that no work on the inscription should begin until "the figures have been practically completed." He declared, "It is the desire and intent of the commission to complete the four heroic figures to the exclusion of all other items and to leave the inscription, museum [Hall of Records], and incidental details to the fortunes of the future."

Minor differences between Nagle and Boland did not overshadow their fundamental agreement on problems at Mount Rushmore. Probably with a feeling of relief Boland wrote to Norbeck, "He understands Borglum and I think he can handle him better than any person who has attempted to do so in the Rushmore work."

But Nagle was not to be denied a file of famous Borglum letters similar to those which filled the desks of Norbeck, Boland, Williamson, Sargent, Spotts, and others. By November the sculptor was voicing his troubles in detail, lambasting Boland, Norbeck, and the Rapid City Chamber of Commerce, and insisting that the monument remain in the National Park Service. "I've no disagreement with Spotts," he concluded, "except when his departmental red tape trips up our efficiency." Nagle patiently attempted to convince Borglum that aesthetic and artistic work was not necessarily hindered or thwarted by "administrative regulations, sometimes referred to as red tape." Art and administrative procedures, he said, are not incompatible or irreconcilable.

But despite these occasional clashes, Nagle, like almost everyone else, was fond of Borglum. Being entertained at the Borglum ranch was an unforgettable experience for this government engineer. One time Nagle and his host were lounging on the huge buffalo robes in the sculptor's spacious living room, idly talking. Suddenly Borglum said, "Nagle, you are a married man, aren't you?" When Nagle replied that he was, Borglum jumped up, selected a small piece of sculpture, scratched his name on it, and directed him to take it to Mrs. Nagle. Lovable, generous and unpredictable, Borglum often made it easy to overlook past or current difficulties.

As the work progressed amid new controversies, Senator Norbeck lay on a sickbed at Valhalla, a few miles from Mount Rushmore. For several years his tongue and jaw had been diseased, and the condition had now become increasingly malignant. He had attended the Jefferson dedication with his neck wrapped, and as he sat in the front row on a special platform, he looked only a shadow of his former self. Yet his ill health had not lessened the differences between him and the sculptor over Rushmore matters.

After Roosevelt's visit Borglum became incorrigible. As Williamson wrote Norbeck, "His ego has grown until one wonders that one head can hold it all." The former Congressman added that he had long since stopped answering Borglum's tirades and that someone must "take him in hand." Norbeck, being a United States Senator, could "do so without his blowing up completely. If any of the rest of us were to do so he would explode." It seemed that by informal agreement, Norbeck had been designated the thankless task of taking Borglum "in hand."

For only a little longer did Norbeck have to bear the brunt of the sculptor's attacks. His files would soon be closed. On December 20, 1936, at his Redfield home, he quietly died of heart failure. Mount Rushmore had lost one of its most devoted and helpful patrons. He had fought and won financial battles when the project had had few friends, and more than once he had saved Borglum's dream from ruin. The principal crises had been weathered, and it was Norbeck who had steered the troubled project through the shoals of abandonment. Mount Rushmore was now a federal project, and with the senator's past help, it seemed sure to be completed.

The personal relationship between Borglum and Norbeck ended on a sad note. But a happy postscript was written on March 1, 1951, when a bronze bust of Peter Norbeck was placed in the state capitol at Pierre. It was the work of Gutzon Borglum.

CHAPTER FIFTEEN

The Unveiling of Lincoln

"**Y**OU will be interested to know that stone for all the figures to be carved has finally been located; and the models in the studio again remodeled for the ninth time to meet stone conditions. I believe this is the last time now." Thus Borglum described his sculptural labors at Mount Rushmore in the summer of 1936. The work had been enlarged and spread over a greater area, requiring, according to Borglum, "the removal of more than three times the amount of granite that was originally estimated."

For the first time Borglum could talk with some certainty about the final artistic form. His most recent problem had been the proper placement of the Roosevelt figure. The only logical location was between Lincoln and Jefferson, but it had been doubted for a time that enough suitable rock existed there. It was not until the granite had been penetrated some 80 feet from the original surface that reliable stone was found. Only about 30 feet of rock remained behind the Roosevelt face, and for a while Borglum thought it might be necessary to leave this area blank. To the casual observer, the eastern face of Mount Rushmore appears solid, but a small canyon 40 to 50 feet wide begins just north of the Lincoln figure and runs southwest behind the heads for about 350 feet.

There was great progress during 1936 although the working season was confined to four months as a result of the late appropriations. About fifty workers were again employed, including eight carvers and eleven drillers. Drillers went some depth on the heads of Washington and Jefferson, and on Lincoln's brow, nose and eyes. Much excess stone was removed from Washington's chest and the areas beneath Jefferson's chin and between Lincoln's face and Washington's shoulder. Tons of granite were blasted away preparatory to beginning the Roosevelt face. Near the end of the season workmen were within five feet of the point of the nose. Practically no finishing work had been done below the necks of any of the figures, but much rock had been removed. The lapels of Washington's coat and his shoulder were carved only in the rough.

Despite Borglum's controversies with National Park Service officials and his constant charges of interference and red tape, he admitted that 1936 was the most profitable season "ever spent on the sculpture from the standpoint of efficiency and the least wasteful as regards lost time." He reported his intention of finishing the Lincoln face to the same degree as the Washington and Jefferson faces by the end of the year. He optimistically predicted that, in spite of insufficient trained help and inadequate power, the four figures would probably be completed by 1938 and the entablature a year later.

A total of $402,659 had been spent on the memorial by June 30, 1936. Of this amount, the old Mount Harney Memorial Association had contributed $54,670; the commission, $99,209, including $50,000 in relief funds; and the federal government, $250,000. A small balance remained in the treasury. Borglum's honorarium totaled $72,347, or about 18 percent of the entire cost. Those who accused the sculptor of receiving excessive fees judged him unfairly. He made sizeable financial sacrifices at Mount Rushmore. Only his outside commissions helped him to achieve something near his accustomed standard of living. Yet there was a widespread belief that Borglum was getting an unduly large share of the money spent at Mount Rushmore. Criticism was heard both locally and in Congress. In the annual report for 1935 the sculptor's fee was listed as a separate item. The next year it was included in the total for salaries and wages. No one could learn how much he received without access to the official records. The annual reports for 1938 and 1939, however, again listed his honorarium separately. But by that time money was more plentiful.

During the year, more than $7,000 was spent for new equipment, and Spotts had put the physical plant in good working order. A greater percentage of future appropriations could now be spent directly on the mountain for payrolls and supplies. The buildings at the base of Mount Rushmore included the studio, a hoist house, a blacksmith shop, a compressor plant, a restaurant, a bunkhouse, and a custodian's residence. Above the faces were a workshop, a dynamite storage room, a lunchroom, shelters for winchmen, and a room for the castings made from models in the studio. These temporary structures were moved about as the work dictated. Both Borglum and the National Park Service officials were eager to improve the grounds surrounding the studio. Although Borglum had not drawn up any plans, he intended that this area should become an integral part of the memorial. A beginning was made when Spotts ordered the grounds cleaned up, buildings repaired, the interior of the studio painted, and other improvements which increased the attractiveness of the area.

The people who came to view Borglum's heroic sculpture built up stories in legend and fact that would fill a volume in themselves. The average tourist was amazingly ignorant of the project. In 1931 Horace Albright accompanied Senator Norbeck to the mountain where they found a car parked in a restricted space. Senator Norbeck asked the people to move their car, but only aroused the driver's wrath. She refused to budge until after considerable argument she was persuaded to park her automobile elsewhere. Unhappy about the entire affair, she looked stormily at Norbeck, then at the sculpture, and then burst out, "Well, we'll leave. That doesn't look like Woodrow Wilson anyway."

When the famous war correspondent Ernie Pyle visited the monument in 1936, he was startled to see the large amount of machinery and equipment. His idea of mountain-carving had been that Borglum arose each morning, took his hammer and chisel, ascended the peak, and began to carve.

Although almost everyone could easily recognize Washington, the Jefferson face caused some confusion. "That is a very poor portrait of Martha," one onlooker exclaimed. This was not an uncommon mistake, partly due to Jefferson's youthful appearance and hair style. Furthermore, of the four presidents his portrait was probably the least familiar.

One of the most interesting Rushmore stories was related by Robert J. Dean in his book *Living Granite*. Dean was driving Borglum to Mount Rushmore one morning over the Iron Mountain Road. As they approached the western point on Iron Mountain, some four miles from Rushmore, they saw a man renting a small telescope to tourists who wanted to view the memorial from a distance. Borglum asked Dean to stop, "I want to talk to this fellow," he said. Dean continued the story in *Living Granite* as follows:

"How's business?" Borglum inquired. "Good", the man said laconically. "What do the people say when they look at the mountain?" Borglum asked. The man looked at him quizzically. "You're Mr. Borglum, the sculptor aren't you?" he asked, and when Borglum nodded, he went on cautiously, "Well, some say one thing and some say another." "Of course," Borglum agreed pleasantly. "But what do they say most often?" "I guess I'd better not say any more," the man answered, and his lips closed in a firm thin line.

"You'd really do me a great favor if you'd tell me," Borglum assured him, but the man seemed suddenly unaware of our presence, and stood looking down the road hopefully for a car which might contain a customer. At this Borglum's gigantic curiosity exploded. "Go ahead man, damn it!" he cried. The man looked up at him with raised eyebrows. "You're sure you won't get mad?" he said. "No, No!" Borglum said. "I can take the worst you've got."

"Well," the man said hesitantly. "I guess since you've asked it as a favor, I owe it to you to tell you. If it wasn't for you I wouldn't be in business. Most folks want to know how much concrete it took."

We both roared with laughter, and Borglum asked, "And what do you tell them?" "I tell them I don't rightly know," the man said earnestly. "How much did it take?"

On another occasion, a well-meaning but ill-informed woman was acting as a self-appointed lecturer for a group of friends. She made several comments as they marveled at the size and location of the heads and crowned her statements by saying, "Girls, just imagine the job of taking those faces down and storing them in the studio during the winter."

The importance and majesty of Borglum's work was lost on the majority of visitors. One teenage girl glibly declared, "Oh, isn't it ducky." Others thought that it was a waste of time and money and that Borglum was just chiseling the rock—and perhaps the public. Some, to be sure, caught something of the meaning Borglum intended. But the principal interest was the magnitude of the undertaking rather than its significance. "Heroic," "colossal," "impressive," "striking" were the terms most commonly applied to the work.

When John Nagle left Mount Rushmore in September, he had the firm conviction that a sequence of carving should be developed and strictly adhered to after agreement between Borglum and the commission. Consequently, the National Park Service drew up a program of operations to become effective when work started in 1937. This plan called for intense roughing-out work on the Lincoln and Roosevelt heads to proceed simultaneously with the finishing of the Washington and Jefferson figures. The sculptor was then instructed to rough-finish the bodies of Washington and Lincoln, since they were most evident to tourists, before turning to Jefferson and Roosevelt. Finally, the Lincoln and Roosevelt faces were to be fine-finished. The effect of this plan would be to complete Washington, Lincoln, Jefferson, and Roosevelt in that order. Nothing was to be done on the entablature until the faces were finished and Borglum had prepared a model. Landscaping of the area would be undertaken last.

Borglum resented any attempt to tell him how to proceed with the carving. Understandably, he felt that this was his business. No small part of the trouble the Park Service and Boland had with Borglum came from an effort to dictate procedure at Mount Rushmore. The service saw its actions as bringing administrative order out of chaos, but Borglum saw it as interference and bureaucratic strangulation. Was God a creative artist, he once asked, or a bureau engineer?

Work could not advance far in 1937 unless more money was obtained. There was only about $34,000 on hand, but $100,000 of Norbeck's $200,000 authorization was yet unappropriated. The commission left the responsibility of raising funds to the National Park Service, and the request became a part of the regular Interior Department appropriation bill. Much of the burden, however, rested on Representative Francis Case of Custer, who had defeated Werner in 1936. This was Case's first term in Congress, and he found his colleagues indifferent or opposed to appropriating any more money for Mount Rushmore. Case, who had been personally interested in the memorial for more than ten years, intended to overcome this attitude. Furthermore, many of his constituents would judge his ability in terms of his success or failure to obtain funds to complete the monument.

However, the freshman congressman was not optimistic. Members of the appropriations subcommittee were "pretty skeptical," he said, especially in light of President Roosevelt's request for economy. "They apparently thought this was one item they could eliminate or greatly reduce," he wrote.

On March 16, A. E. Demaray again appeared before the subcommittee in support of the Park Service's request for $100,000. The item carried the restriction that no money could be spent on any figure not started by June 1936. How much would it cost? When would the monument be completed? These were the chief questions posed by the subcommittee. When Demaray attempted to show pictures and explain the work's progress, Congressman O'Neal interposed, "I am more interested . . . in the financial set-up of this monument." When pressed on the matter of cost, Demaray frankly admitted that the memorial could not be completed without a new authorization. In other words, the $100,000 being requested would not finish the figures. Then O'Neal asked, "How much more is the estimate . . . required by your department to complete the work?" Demaray replied, "That is quite a difficult question to answer." When O'Neal pressed his inquiry further, Demaray admitted that a direct answer "would seem reasonable," but said that the Park Service had only one year's experience by which to judge, "and with the very temperamental sculptor in charge of the work, not knowing what he may change, or may not change, it is quite a difficult thing for us to give an accurate estimate."

Unable to obtain any commitment on cost or time of completion, Representative Kirkpatrick asked if the commission had ever considered leaving the memorial unfinished. "I do not think the commission has ever for one moment given up the thought of completing it, but they will have to bring their case back to Washington and ask Congress to authorize additional funds." There was no attempt to hide the fact that the federal government was saddled with all financial responsibilities connected with the memorial. Representative Rich gloomily predicted that the taxpayers would have $1,500,000 invested in the monument before it was finished.

Demaray did not relish this third major bout with the economy-minded congressmen, and he sought refuge several times in the fact that, after all, the National Park Service had only recently participated in the actual administration of Mount Rushmore. In any event, he was determined not to make statements or commitments that might be embarrassing later.

His unfortunate reference to Borglum as a "very temperamental sculptor" aroused a veritable hornet's nest. Never had this rather inconspicuous government career man received so much publicity. The Associated Press in Rapid City immediately asked Borglum for a reply.

John Boland was deeply chagrined at the developments. He feared that Borglum might issue a blistering attack that would antagonize the National Park Service, and he knew that service help was absolutely necessary to complete the memorial. He called Phil Potter of the *Rapid City Daily Journal*, and the two agreed that Boland should scrutinize any statement by Borglum before it was published. This accounts for the sculptor's rather moderate reply—moderate, at least, for him.

Borglum was sorry, he said, that "so fair a man as Mr. Demaray should hide his own inability to answer questions only mechanically-minded men would ask and use the shield of 'temperamental' against an artist in his own defense for not being able to explain what neither he nor his congressional listeners could understand." He continued, "If America wants a product of art, if America wants an interpretation of Washington's character, of Jefferson's intelligence, of Lincoln's vision and soul, of Theodore Roosevelt's force and modernness—then she must trust to the judgment, insight and understanding of an artist." Jabbing at the layman's lack of knowledge, he concluded, "The formal rendering of the philosophy of our government into a granite on a mountain peak is no boy's job, nor road contractor's job and is not, must not, and cannot be the victim of engineer's rule and compass."

This episode only tended to increase Borglum's dislike for the supervisory powers of the National Park Service. Demaray should have weighed his language more carefully.

It was obvious that Demaray had not satisfied members of the sub-committee, so Congressman Case appeared about a month later armed with pictures and Rushmore booklets. Having concluded that his colleagues had no real idea of the Rushmore project, he intended to educate them. Without waiting to be questioned, Case explained why it was so difficult to estimate the time and cost necessary to complete the memorial. "This is an unconventional type of work," he said, "and you cannot compare it with ordinary construction." As he was describing the monument's tremendous size, he was interrupted by Congressman Scrugham who wanted to know if the memorial could be completed with the current authorization. "I think probably we will have to have a further authorization, but . . . I think that the major part of the cost is past now," Case replied.

When committee members insisted on knowing something about the total expense, Case said that he, Senator Bulow, and Demaray could work out an estimate and submit it for consideration. The

Congressmen were definitely irked by the lack of specific facts and figures on the monument's completion. Representative O'Neal impatiently declared, "No one has any definite information on this proposition."

To meet this objection, Case, Bulow, Demaray, and Nagle drew up an estimate on April 22 and submitted it to the subcommittee. They concluded that $287,000 must be yet appropriated to finish the project, or $187,000 more than had been authorized. Of this amount, $175,000 was allotted to complete the carving, and the remainder was earmarked for landscaping, steps and trails, water, light, and other tourist facilities. It was agreed to eliminate the inscription from the plan because it would be "extremely costly" and would add no "particular dignity to the monument." Furthermore, it could not be indited by Coolidge as originally intended. Nothing was included for the Hall of Records, a part of the project which had become very dear to Borglum. It was recommended that the existing studio ultimately be remodeled for a museum.

Case admitted that this group had no authority to make such a proposition, but he deemed it a necessary move in order to secure further appropriations. Borglum and the commission should have worked out an overall plan of expenditures, but the tense relations between the sculptor and Boland had made this impossible. And Borglum was not in the habit of developing reliable plans in advance.

Congress reluctantly appropriated $50,000 for the fiscal year of 1938, but Representative Jed Johnson left no doubt about his attitude toward future money for mountain-carving. The House in the Committee of the Whole, he warned, "gives notice now that it expects the Commission . . . to stay within the authorized limits of the act of Congress."

While national lawmakers considered additional appropriations, Borglum camped in Washington to obtain a new contract for his services at Mount Rushmore. Early in the year he had gone to Paris to participate in the dedication of his statue of Thomas Paine. Now back in the United States, he worked among his congressional friends, attempting to stir up interest in his Rushmore sculpture. Explaining why he would not be at the mountain when operations began, he wired Boland, "Long-standing irregularities failure to support properly memorial work has created confusion misunderstanding in Congress. I must remain to properly explain if work is not to be completely stopped." Borglum was in an unusually critical mood because of contract problems.

The original agreement had set his maximum commission at $87,500, and by April 1937, all but $1,768 had been paid. If Borglum was to receive his normal compensation for the following season, a new contract must be negotiated. Norbeck's bill authorizing $200,000 in 1935 also permitted the secretary of the interior to employ artists and other personnel for the project. Dissatisfied with his commissions, Borglum now saw the possibility of obtaining a more favorable stipend. He had an agreement drawn up calling for a 30 percent honorarium. However, as previously mentioned, Boland would not sign the new agreement on behalf of the commission. The National Park Service also refused to approve it because the old contract had not been fulfilled and because Borglum had inserted provisions not customary in government contracts. Director Cammerer recommended to Secretary Ickes that the best interest of the government would be served by continuing under the old arrangement.

This infuriated Borglum and contributed to his bitterness toward Boland and the Park Service. He held that he deserved a 30 percent commission plus a lump sum for out-of-pocket expense which he claimed had never been repaid. At one time he placed that figure at $80,000! Borglum argued that he deserved an extra 5 percent for assuming Tucker's work. The old contract, he told Slattery, was "dishonest and drawn in bad faith."

Boland, on the other hand, opposed a new agreement which would increase the honorarium. The more Borglum received, he insisted, the less remained for other payrolls. He wanted to pay the sculptor a fixed fee or salary based on the time spent on Mount Rushmore. He believed $10,000 annually was somewhat excessive. Boland's correspondence reveals that he wanted to pay Borglum on the basis of accomplishment rather than ability as a creative artist. He even discussed the possibility of a daily or monthly wage, an unhappy suggestion since Borglum was not a stonemason and such financial arrangements were not customary among sculptors. But Boland had become thoroughly impatient. Paying on a "percentage basis . . . has been very disagreeable to me," he declared. The unpleasantness had arisen through charges, both in and out of Congress, that Borglum's fee was too large; that the sculptor was inclined to raise wages and spend unnecessary money in order to increase his income; and, finally, that "Mr. Borglum keeps no records [and] is always of the opinion that his fee should be more than as computed by this office." In any event, Boland was sick of the arrangement.

National Park Service officials believed that Borglum must be paid on the percentage basis, but thought that 20 percent was adequate. Nagle stated that Spotts had relieved the sculptor of his technical responsibilities and that the original $87,500 had adequately paid Borglum for his idea and conception. Cammerer and Demaray agreed, but insisted that it was a matter for the commission to settle.

During July and August, the commission met with Nagle, Borglum, and Borglum's attorney, John G. Harlan of Washington, and, after considerable controversy, agreed to a new contract. During the negotiations, it became clear that Boland was leading the fight to limit Borglum's honorarium. Both Williamson and Sargent thought that the sculptor had earned 30 percent. Sargent argued that Borglum "is doing . . . what I think is going to be one of the greatest things of its kind in all history up to this time," and insisted that it was unfair to limit him to 25 percent. "Laying aside all of the eccentricities of Mr. Borglum and looking at his genius and the encouragement it would give him if he were treated more liberally, should not the government give him more than 25 per cent?" he asked.

But Boland was adamant. He asserted that Spotts was doing the work for which Borglum requested additional compensation. "Mr. Borglum should not receive any more than 25 per cent and you could not justify any more," he concluded. Partly because of Boland's opposition, but chiefly because they feared the secretary of the interior would not approve a more liberal contract, they agreed on a 25 percent honorarium.

In most other respects the new agreement was similar to the old one. Work was specifically confined to the four figures, and any changes had to be approved by the commission and the secretary of the interior. Nothing was said about the Hall of Records or the grand stairway, and the inscription already had been eliminated by agreement among Case, Demaray, Bulow, and members of the appropriations subcommittee. It appeared to Borglum that there was a conspiracy to keep him from completing his grand design, which included the inscription, a museum or Hall of Records hewn out of the solid rock back of the faces, and a stairway leading to the great hall, a design surpassing anything undertaken by the ancients.

The new contract was to run until June 30, 1939, when it was hoped the project would be finished. It could then be renewed annually by mutual consent. To become effective the agreement must be approved by the secretary of the interior. This approval was delayed until November 12, temporarily denying Borglum any compensation for his summer's work. It was not until 1938 that legal difficulties were overcome and he received his overdue commission. This contributed further to his ill feeling although the commission and the National Park Service both worked diligently to facilitate payment. Borglum felt, too, that Boland and the service had connived to deny him a more favorable contract. His bitterness grew.

Work at the mountain moved ahead despite personal problems. Borglum was absent more than half the time in 1937, but Spotts was on hand, and Lincoln Borglum efficiently supervised the actual carving. When the sculptor was present, conditions were often in an uproar. On September 9, after a sharp conflict with Borglum over his peremptory dismissal of an employee, Spotts's assistant wrote, "Another day of hell with Gutzon Borglum." On one occasion Borglum called Spotts a liar, and, though the engineer tried to be diplomatic, he said, "I fear that my patience is exhausted and sooner or later I will tell him to go to hell." Thus reads the daily record.

Most of the effort was directed toward finishing the Lincoln face and roughing out that of Roosevelt. Practically nothing was done on Washington or Jefferson. Three faces were easily recognizable although much remained to be done. More than 265,000 visitors saw the monument during the summer.

The commission and the National Park Service had urged Borglum to make a noticeable showing during the 1937 season. Progress should be "easily estimated by the layman," Nagle wrote. Only obvious signs of progress carried any weight with congressional committees and encouraged further appropriations. And the results were becoming evident. Case reported Congressman Leavy of Washington as saying that some of his constituents thought Mount Rushmore was the "most outstanding thing they saw on the trip across the country." Case added, "That did not hurt us a bit."

The Lincoln head was dedicated on September 17, in commemoration of the 150th anniversary of the adoption of the Constitution. A major artistic question confronting Borglum was whether to carve Lincoln with or without a beard. Norbeck, who had always been greatly impressed with Borglum's large, beardless head of Lincoln in the Capitol rotunda in Washington, had urged him to carve a clean-shaven face. It was only after great soul-searching that the sculptor finally decided to include the beard.

The dedication ceremonies followed the general pattern of previous celebrations. More than five thousand people were present. Senator Edward R. Burke of Nebraska, the principal speaker, described the virtues of Lincoln and pledged support to the Constitution. But the sculptor held the center of the stage. When Borglum appeared, he instantly had the crowd at his command. Beginning on an emotional note, he called the roll of sponsors now departed, among them Coolidge, Norbeck, and Cullinan. "They are with the Gods!" he dramatically exclaimed. "We must keep their faith! We will carry on!" He paused. Not a murmur was heard as taps sounded from atop Washington's head. Then he continued: ". . . It is my privilege and now my bounden duty as the creator of this memorial as its sculptor to emphasize the cultural necessity to make of this colossal undertaking something more than the 'biggest' in the world, that is, to make it a great work of art—a work of art as great for us and our time as the subject merits, and our ability permits, determined, with just pride, that it shall rank with the great records of awakened Egypt, Greece and Rome.

". . . No excuse—lack of funds, the common lack of understanding, ever present in unusual undertakings—will suffice to forgive or protect us against eternal censure civilization will bury us under, if we produce simply a monstrously big thing! Where greatness is promised, history and civilization never forgive its absence—or those responsible for its failure.

". . . Further—I want to emphasize to you—Americans—no forms, mechanical, architectural, or of builder-engineer craft, that dominate and destroy the very soul of most of our art efforts in America, are ever applicable in a pure work of art or can put soul into this mass of granite. There are no books, guides, or mathematical formula[e] that will recreate the character of Lincoln, of Jefferson, of Washington or Roosevelt, or model here into the facial forms the energy, the soul of all, or even one of these men in this mass of stone.

". . . The world at large assumes we are creating in this memorial an immortal work of fine art, that ranks with the best of Greece, Egypt or Rome. In my conception, in my purpose, the subject matter selected as related to our civilization, expressing the story of our human and political accomplishments, this is true, but as a work of art, as a masterpiece of great sculpture, we have been able to little more than indicate its fine possibilities, not [having] been aided or permitted such aids as to assure its being a great work of art.

". . . What we have accomplished in this cracked cliff, as a purely mechanical feat, is little short of phenomenal. To even dare to do this work at all lifted it forever into the realm of great pioneer and cultural adventure. In its execution—without proper tools, without adequate power, without funds, without any trained assistants, it is an accomplishment without parallel in this or the old world. . . . We have literally driven a super-clipper into the stratosphere of noblest human aspirations, on a crust and a gallon of gas and that in spite of a resisting unbelieving world. . . .

". . . This work, to be a credit to the men who founded civilization, must proceed much further; it must be carried on with a fresh and a new sense of its greatness and the need of perfecting this message from the soul of America to posterity."

After a few other remarks, Borglum ordered a dynamite blast. A cloud of gray granite dust rose lazily as the flag slipped from Lincoln's face.

CHAPTER SIXTEEN

The Flush of Victory

"WE have reached an impasse in the work. . . . I must have *friendly* representatives of the Government who are not interfering with *my* part of the work in a manner that is destructive to it . . . " With these words Borglum informed President Roosevelt that a change of administration at Mount Rushmore was imperative. He repeated his old charges of interference and damned practically everyone connected with the project from Rapid City to Washington, D.C.

Unhappy personal relations had, indeed, created a precarious situation. Borglum refused to report at the mountain or to order work to begin in the spring of 1938. Boland wired him, "Commission unaware any right sculptor had under contract to refuse to work and the Commission hereby requests the Sculptor report for duty." Borglum replied that he had not yet been paid for the previous season's work and would not begin operations until he had received his honorarium.* He again sharply criticized Boland and Spotts.

A few days later, however, Lincoln Borglum arrived in Rapid City with instructions from his father to commence on May 9. Borglum was at the Metropolitan Club in Washington. He intended to camp near Capitol Hill until legislation was passed giving him complete control of the project. Mount Rushmore might never be finished under current conditions, he told friends. "I shall stay here," he wrote. "I must."

The relationship between the sculptor and the National Park Service representatives and members of the commission had grown steadily worse since work was shut down in the fall of 1937. Borglum had repeated his charges of interference so often that he believed

---

*On March 19, 1938, the comptroller general ruled that Borglum could be paid for his work in the year 1937 when no contract was in force. The sculptor then received $10,594.

them himself, although most of his accusations were either false or greatly exaggerated. He criticized the commission for anything it did, then accused it of doing nothing.

Borglum's animosity, first directed at Spotts, soon spread to Nagle and other officials in the National Park Service. He declared that he had "drawn a Frankenstein" in getting service collaboration. He wrote to Case expressing opposition to any supervision or control by officials of the Park Service.

One of his long, biting attacks, in which he criticized nearly everyone connected with the project, reached the president at Warm Springs on March 23. Roosevelt interrupted his vacation to send a memorandum to Secretaries Morganthau and Ickes saying, "I wish you would talk over this problem of Mount Rushmore . . . and let me have a solution and some form of reply to Gutzon Borglum."

Ickes did not mince words. The real problem, he replied, was that the sculptor "objects to any type of supervision." Practically everyone who had attempted to cooperate with Borglum agreed. Borglum had asked presidential support of legislation abolishing the old commission, but on Ickes's advice Roosevelt temporarily refused this support.

As the sculptor's charges grew more rash, even Secretary Ickes showed some concern. After receiving a copy of Borglum's letter of May 9 to Roosevelt, Ickes personally initialed a memorandum for Director Cammerer of the National Park Service. "Mr. Borglum complained to me," he said, "that some representative of the Park Service even tried to tell him how to do his carving. Of course there should be no interference with his work beyond such necessary supervision as is required under the laws and regulations. There are some charges made in this letter which need to be answered in detail."

Borglum's statement that someone attempted to tell him *how* to carve at Rushmore was an old one and utterly ridiculous. It was true, however, that both the National Park Service and the commission had suggested procedure as to *when* and *where* to carve, something entirely different, but nonetheless repugnant to Borglum. As a matter of fact, the executive committee met in April 1938 before work commenced and instructed Borglum to follow a specific plan of operations. This called for concentrated work on the Roosevelt face, certain finishing touches on Washington, and the completion of Lincoln's chin. The directive was designed to "realize the best and more nearly completed appearance of the figures from the top of the head to and including the chin and throat . . . that is possible . . . with available funds." Borglum interpreted this as "destructive interference" and arrived at the conclusion that he was being told *how* to carve the figures.

Director Cammerer asked Demaray to study the matter. He instructed John Nagle to make an independent investigation at Mount Rushmore without consulting Spotts. Nagle even went about Rapid City inquiring into the character of John Boland. After a thorough study, Nagle reported that Borglum's charges were baseless. In fact, it seemed that Spotts was quite reluctant to make necessary suggestions. He found everyone friendly to Borglum. As for Boland, he was "an excellent man personally, a useful citizen, a successful business man, and a thoroughly loyal supporter of the Mount Rushmore project." Rapid City citizens believed that the monument would not have been so far advanced without the efforts of Boland, and Nagle concurred. With Spotts's help and direction, he had said earlier, the work was being carried on quite efficiently, compared to "the emotional and day-to-day policy which had been previously maintained." His reports were sent to Ickes.

Nevertheless, the Park Service was continually called on to defend itself against the sculptor's charges. It was difficult for rational men to understand how Borglum could say that the work had never progressed so well, as he did at the close of 1936, and almost simultaneously accuse the National Park Service of harmful meddling.

By the middle of 1938 a file had been set up in the Park Service offices labeled "Mount Rushmore Borglum Controversy." After studying it, Secretary Ickes's assistant, E. K. Burlew, wrote, "I must say that I hope after this construction session is over, National Park Service will have no further function with construction of this work." His wish was granted, at least for a short while.

So the controversy raged. "Mount Rushmore has been a headache from the time we have had anything to do with it," said Demaray. Commission members could have said the same thing. Contributions of time and money, while helping the project, had brought them damnation rather than praise, criticism rather than gratitude. Borglum was a tough antagonist, a fighter. Those who crossed him seldom escaped without the scars of battle, and the commissioners and service officials were no exception. By this time most of them had had enough.

Upon receipt of a letter filled with jibes and barbs, Chairman Sargent sent his resignation to President Roosevelt. Ralph Budd also quit, and the South Dakota members were about ready to drop out. Even Boland wondered "if it's worth the while of the other members . . . to continue the struggle." Yet Boland did not regret his actions and expressed the conviction that he had cooperated with Borglum to the best of his ability.

Most of the commissioners favored turning the project over to the National Park Service. Dual administration created many problems which might have been solved more readily with centralized control. L. B. Hanna was sorry to see members of the commission resigning, but he expressed confidence that Park Service officials could better "fight out matters with Mr. Borglum." In spite of Borglum's bitterness toward individual commissioners, their correspondence reveals nothing but patience and good will toward him. Hanna praised Borglum's artistic ability and hoped that he would continue until the work was completed.

Meanwhile, Borglum was working among friends in Washington, seeking a solution to his problems through new legislation. He wanted to free his project from service administration and from any supervision by the old commission. He believed a new body should be formed which would be completely independent and subject to his wishes. For the first time in the history of the project, Borglum made a fairly accurate estimate of the ultimate cost of the memorial. He said a new authorization of $600,000 was needed to finish the faces, the Hall of Records, the inscription, and the stairway.

During the spring he conferred with Senator Key Pittman, a friend of many years, Kent Keller, and other lawmakers. He also obtained support from men outside Congress, including Russell Arundel, a Washington attorney. Borglum was not without influence in Washington. He knew many members of Congress personally, and most of them were acquainted with his sculpture which abounded in the capital city. No one could see his magnificent head of Lincoln in the rotunda of the Capitol without appreciating his great ability.

Unaware of the real conditions at Mount Rushmore, many congressmen and senators accepted Borglum's interpretation of his difficulties at face value. He was always persuasive and convincing. Pittman and Keller agreed to lead the fight for new legislation, and both intervened with President Roosevelt. The senator wrote the president that he considered Mount Rushmore the "most wonderful work ever undertaken" and recommended a complete reorganization. On April 28 Keller introduced a bill which met with Borglum's wishes. House bill number 10462 provided for an independent ten-man commission of which Borglum would be a member and clothed it with authority to complete the monument in accordance with the sculptor's "designs and models." The commission was empowered to employ artists and other workmen without regard to civil service regulations. A $300,000 authorization was included. Borglum agreed to this smaller figure when Keller advised him the $600,000 could not be obtained in one authorization. Other significant parts of the measure permitted the commission to designate a reservation around Mount Rushmore of not more than four thousand or less than two thousand acres. No charge could ever be made to view the memorial.

Hearings took place on May 5 before the Committee on the Library. It was not so much a hearing, in the sense of trying to determine the facts from witnesses on both sides, as it was a forum in which the sculptor could air his grievances. Keller, who was chairman, parroted nearly every accusation made by Borglum, generally in stronger language.

This was the first time Borglum had appeared before a congressional committee on Rushmore matters. He had not been invited previously because of the opposition of South Dakota congressmen and senators, particularly Norbeck. Fearing that Borglum would make inaccurate statements and estimates which might later embarrass those seeking funds, Norbeck had done everything possible to keep Borglum out of congressional committee rooms. But Borglum was to have his day.

His main complaints included the lack of trained assistants, insufficient power, delay in securing materials, and interference by Spotts and Boland. "Ridiculous as it is," he said, "I have worked through all these years without any trained assistants, without any carvers. I have been compelled to take the forgotten men in the mining camps acquainted with rough drilling for mines, and train them as best I could. . . . This itself has been the cause of a great deal of delay and unwise waste of funds."

Congressmen Treadway and Lambertson both thought it was unnecessary to create a new commission. "It seems to me,"

Lambertson asserted, "that the National Park Service . . . should take care of it." But Borglum reacted sharply against this suggestion and related in detail his differences with Spotts. Then Treadway interposed, "And the first thing that happened was that you quarreled with him." Borglum denied this and said it was a matter of "judgment and good faith." Then the congressman wanted to know why any commission was necessary. "Since you have not gotten along very well with the other selections why do you want ten associates?" Borglum replied that he was not concerned with the number. But Treadway persisted and asked, "If there is not some reason . . . in connection with your desire to practically control the whole proposition . . . why have a commission?" Borglum insisted that he had no desire to control it. Yet when it was suggested that the old commission be abolished and the National Park Service be allowed to continue its work, Keller vigorously asserted that "the Department of the Interior does not know anything about carving mountains."

One might assume from Keller's statement that a new commission would possess that ability. This, of course, was ridiculous, and Keller knew that Borglum intended to have a commission that would simply rubber-stamp his desires. That, together with the securing of additional funds, was the whole purpose of the legislation.

Demaray was present to defend the National Park Service. He pointed out the problems arising from dual administration by the commission and the service and declared that, alone, his organization could have been more successful both administratively and in its relations with Borglum. This may have sounded good to congressional ears, but his correspondence does not confirm it. Meanwhile, Keller kept repeating that the National Park Service "does not know a thing about carving mountains." When it was intimated that Spotts unjustly restricted Borglum, Demaray said somewhat positively, "I defy Mr. Borglum or anyone else to say that we have ever interfered with him." The sculptor was silent.

Congressman Case sat quietly during most of the hearing. His was not an enjoyable position. It was not pleasant to hear unfounded charges against Boland, one of his close friends. But being calm and levelheaded, he recognized that the important thing was to get enough money to finish the carving and to keep Borglum on the job. It was unanimously agreed among the Rushmore sponsors that no other artist could complete the memorial, and everyone wanted

Borglum to do it. Consequently, when Case spoke he weighed his words carefully. "You and I may sit in this committee room," he said, "far from the great memorial, and hear statements and counterstatements and soon our minds become centered upon personalities and controversies. . . . But I want to say most emphatically, that every doubt and every question will melt into nothingness if you will visit Mount Rushmore and see the memorial itself." Case felt that much could be achieved by directing attention to the monument and away from the incompatible personalities of Boland and Borglum.

Borglum was remarkably calm and restrained during the entire questioning. He did not refer to Boland by name and only became slightly aroused by the mention of Spotts. He had sensibly agreed not to let personal differences wreck the bill's chance of passage. Knowing his erratic friend, Senator Pittman had cautioned the sculptor to think carefully before writing or speaking about Rushmore matters.

Case asked Boland if he wanted to appear to defend the commission and its policies. Boland refused because he believed that if congressmen began questioning him under oath, his answers might destroy the memorial. It is easy to imagine what might have been the reaction of lawmakers to the revelation that Borglum had cast aside a $3,500 piece of machinery and had taken high-salaried drillers off the mountain to build a platform on which to seat dignitaries on the occasion of Roosevelt's visit to the memorial. Spotts had shuddered at the thought of an investigation. "In all considerable money has been wasted on this project," he wrote. "I do not mean dishonestly but rather unwisely."

Boland wrote a rather mild statement which Case inserted in the record. He denied that there had been any attempt to control employment or that the work had suffered from political influences. "I have endeavored to conduct only the purely business affairs of the Commission—a task delegated to me by the Commission—in a businesslike manner." Then he came to the crux of the problem. "Mr. Borglum is an artist and I am a businessman, therefore it is only natural that we should at times disagree regarding the business functions of the commission. Such differences, however, have never been serious and an amicable understanding has always been reached." This was a charitable statement.

"I do not wish to humiliate Mr. Borglum or injure his character by presenting facts to the committee which might do so," Boland wrote. "I only wish to defend my own character and ability from the charges which have been made by him." Earlier he had written, "There was a great deal that I could have said in my answer . . . but . . . I was charitable as possible with Mr. Borglum as I wanted to be helpful to Rushmore."

In the House of Representatives the outlook was dark for any Rushmore legislation. As objections were raised, Borglum's proposal of a ten-man commission was dropped for the previous twelve-member group. Congressmen saw the impropriety of appointing the sculptor to membership in a body which would employ him. In addition, an amendment was made which cut down the Rushmore reservation area to fifteen hundred acres.

It soon became clear that Keller did not have enough influence to stem the opposition. Therefore, it was up to Case. Several congressmen warned him that they planned to object when the bill was considered. This was a matter of great importance to Case. He not only had a deep personal feeling for the monument, but he felt that obtaining the money to complete it would be a feather in his political cap. And he was running for re-election.

When Keller failed, Case consulted the objectors and, one by one, finally quieted all of them except Treadway of Massachusetts. "He told me repeatedly, he simply had to object," Case declared. On June 6 the Rushmore measure was on the calender. Borglum sat in the gallery nervously watching as six other bills dealing with parks and monuments were defeated. Then, discouraged, he arose and left. He could not bear to see his measure meet the same fate. The Speaker called up the Rushmore bill. Case went to Treadway and sat down beside him in sheer desperation, "simply waiting for the execution." Surprised that no one else objected, Treadway asked some questions and indicated his intention to do so. But when he did not object in so many words, Case explained that Treadway's request was for an explanation. The Speaker banged his gavel and announced that the bill had passed. It was too late for the startled Treadway to block the measure.

Case left the House chamber to telephone Borglum the good news. Stunned, Borglum let the telephone receiver drop from his hand. He could not believe what he heard. After a few seconds, he regained his composure and expressed his deep amazement and appreciation. Thirty minutes earlier, he said, he had given up all hope of getting legislation. But now his hopes and enthusiasm were renewed. Rushmore would be completed. Pittman, a powerful administration leader, experienced little difficulty in getting the new Rushmore measure through the Senate the next day.

The anomaly of the entire legislative battle was the reliance Borglum had to place upon Case and other South Dakotans. Several months earlier he had gone to Washington, met with the president and prominent Democratic lawmakers, and paid little attention to Case and Senator Bulow. Yet in the end it was a South Dakotan, and a Republican at that, who saved the day for him. But he did not feel these coals of fire heaped upon his head.

Columnist Drew Pearson, who assumed that Borglum had won the battle single-handedly, did not miss the lively story. The "most amazing piece of lobbying of the entire . . . session was put across by turbulent Gutzon Borglum," he wrote.

Unhampered and unmolested, Borglum was now free to proceed as he pleased without any interference. In effect, the legislation gave him a hand-picked commission and an authorization of $300,000. In May Keller had asked members of the old commission to resign to save them the embarrassment of being legislated out of office. Boland said he was willing to quit at any time, but not on the basis of the unfounded charges. His resignation was accepted on July 15, and the purge was complete. The victory was Borglum's.

The ousting of Boland was absolutely necessary for continuing the work. He could do nothing to please Borglum, and he had come to personify delay and obstruction in the sculptor's mind. Since the two men could not agree, one of them had to go. Boland was expendable; Borglum was indispensible. The same might be said of the Park Service officials. Someone else could handle business matters, but no other man in the United States could finish the memorial as it should be finished. It was unfortunate that any offering must be sacrificed to the jealous gods, but Boland's dismissal was a small price to pay to get Mount Rushmore completed by Borglum. Boland knew this, but even so, he deeply resented the treatment accorded him.

Every controversy has two sides, and, as shown earlier, Boland was not entirely free from fault. There were times when he was conservative and obstructive. The commission erred in delegating so much authority to him and in failing to check closely on his policies. A more active and interested commission could have helped solve many of the problems. As it was, Boland became the dominant member, and little was done without his approval. On the other hand, he performed a valuable and lasting service in carefully guarding and wisely spending the meager funds. If Borglum had been unhampered during the depths of the Great Depression when funds were limited, he would probably have ruined the project by his lack of financial judgment. Boland's administration was steady and conservative, if somewhat arbitrary and uncompromising. After Borglum's death in 1941, Boland was unanimously elected president of the Mount Rushmore National Memorial Society by the trustees of that organization. He continued his interest in the memorial until his death in 1958, and he stands among the top contributors to its success.

CHAPTER SEVENTEEN

Alone at the Helm

ON Sunday, July 3, 1938, Borglum appeared at the mountain for the first time since the season's work had begun. When he arrived, Spotts left and the National Park Service washed its hands of the whole affair. During May and June, Lincoln Borglum had supervised the work. Although Boland had formally resigned in July, he continued to handle fiscal matters at the service's request until the new commission was organized on August 4. Borglum said that he would permit his old antagonist to gasp a little longer "like a trout in the sun."

Every Interior Department official, from the secretary to the staff of the Park Service, was pleased to bow out. The ill feeling between Senator Pittman, who was to become chairman of the new commission, and Secretary Ickes was well known, and the service officials wanted to rid themselves of conflicts with the sculptor. Moreover, mountain-carving was antithetical to service policy. John Nagle was about the only man in the service who showed any desire to fight the matter through.

Work was being carried on with money which had been secured by the Interior Department before the new commission was organized. Demaray had appeared before the subcommittee of the Committee on Appropriations the preceding January. Only $20,724 remained to begin operations in 1938 unless more funds could be obtained. Members of the subcommittee were still most concerned about the time and money necessary to complete the monument. In fact, when the Rushmore item first came up several congressmen said, "Oh, let's cut that thing out this time." But Representatives Leavy and Lambertson had visited Mount Rushmore in the fall of 1937 and had become friends of the project. "I went there with a definite prejudice against it and came away feeling very favorable to it," Leavy confessed to his colleagues.

Lawmakers for the first time questioned Demaray sharply about how much Borglum received for his services. And was any other member of the Borglum family on the payroll? they asked. Only the sculptor's son, Lincoln, was employed, Demaray replied. He was chief pointer and worked for $1.50 an hour. In 1935, 1936, and 1937, he had earned the meager sums of $988, $1,103, and $1,640 respectively. There was no objection to this.

Most members of the committee expressed opposition to undertaking any carving other than the faces. They thought it was unnecessary to carry out Borglum's plan to complete the full busts. "It seems to me," Lambertson said, "that the expenditures . . . for putting shoulders, buttons on the coats, and so forth, down the mountain would not be worth the money." Taylor declared, "What we will have to do will be to defeat the authorization for more money when it comes up."

Since this was the prevailing attitude, it is surprising that $50,000 was appropriated, and it is all the more remarkable that Case was able to get the Rushmore bill through Congress with an additional authorization of $300,000.

President Roosevelt had generally followed Borglum's recommendations in appointing the new commission. He selected Senators Pittman, Townsend, Norris, and Bulow; and Keller, Russell Arundel, L. B. Hanna, Williamson, Eugene McDonald, Herman Oliphant, Isabella Greenway, and Mrs. Spoonts. Five members of the old group were retained, of whom Williamson had been the most active. Roosevelt had refused to accept his resignation, and Borglum had always appreciated Williamson's efforts on behalf of the memorial, though he was skeptical of him because of his friendship with Boland.

The sculptor summoned the commission to meet at his Mount Rushmore studio on August 4. Several days earlier Oliphant, Pittman, Arundel, and Keller arrived in the Black Hills where they were entertained at Borglum's ranch. The sculptor was careful to keep them out of Rapid City and away from Williamson and Boland. These new commissioners must not be polluted!

The nonresident members and Borglum had developed a program beforehand, and the real purpose of the meeting was to ratify the informal decisions already reached. Williamson and Bulow were not supposed to carry any weight in the discussions. Pittman was elected chairman, and Arundel, secretary. Borglum wanted the United States Treasury Department to handle the financial administration;

therefore, Guy Allen, chief disbursing officer of the United States, was named treasurer.

When the matter of electing the executive committee arose, Senator Pittman said, "Can't we hear your preference for that committee, Mr. Borglum?" Most any other man would have retired, leaving this wholly to the commission. But not Borglum. After admitting that "I really have no business here," he went on to name his preferences. Williamson was not among them. Senator Bulow spoke up and asked if it were not advisable to elect someone familiar with the work. "How about Williamson?" he asked. "He has been on the commission for its whole life." Borglum threw up his hands in surprise. "I thought I named him," he said. "Didn't I mention him?" He looked flustered and embarrassed, and remarked, "It was an unintentional omission in my enthusiasm." Oliphant then gracefully withdrew and Williamson was named, together with Pittman, Keller, McDonald, and Arundel.

The commissioners delegated full authority to Borglum, which in effect made him general manager. He had complete power to hire and fire employees without regard to civil service regulations and to determine wages and salaries. Both the law and Borglum's contract specifically placed these responsibilities with the commission, but this provision was ignored. It was even suggested that the sculptor be made a member of the executive committee. Williamson protested vigorously, pointing out the impropriety, not to mention the illegality, of such action. Was the sculptor going to be on the committee that employed him and contract with himself, as well as manage everything? he asked. Those who had advocated this ludicrous situation appeared confused and embarrassed, and let the matter drop.

Williamson also argued forcefully against permitting Borglum to determine salaries, wages, and other expenditures independently. He reminded the commission that every increase in salary or purchase of equipment would raise the sculptor's honorarium. In other words, his administrative actions would affect his income. But Williamson was quickly and almost unduly overruled with the argument that only Borglum knew what should be paid in wages or spent for machinery and other equipment. It did not please Borglum for Williamson to insist that the law and contract be given some force.

The same evening Borglum gave a banquet for about fifty distinguished guests, including members of the commission, at the Alex

Johnson Hotel in Rapid City. It was, indeed, a victory dinner. Cocktails and hors d'oeuvres were served to the happy crowd before they gathered around a horseshoe-shaped table in the ballroom. Borglum, acting as master of ceremonies, was naturally the center of attention. Jubilant over the defeat of his opponents, he spoke on "Creative Impulses," a topic which permitted full play for his fertile imagination. Williamson made some remarks about the monument's significance, but it was Borglum's party and a situation in which the self-centered sculptor gloried.

Borglum now had virtually dictatorial powers to complete the memorial as he desired, subject only to budget limitations. He referred constantly to "my commission." Arrangements were quickly made with the United States Treasury Department to perform all accounting, disbursing, and procurement duties through the Treasury State Accounts Office at Watertown. George W. Storck was the accountant in charge, and Frank Skells was employed at the mountain to certify the payrolls.

Under these conditions matters at Mount Rushmore ran very smoothly. Part of this was due to the relatively large amount of money available after August 1938. Congress had appropriated $50,000 in June which, together with the balance on hand, made available more than $76,000. About $58,000 was actually spent between August and December. Only a few additional men were employed, but the larger expenditures greatly increased Borglum's honorarium. He was paid $16,233 between July 1 and December 31, and during August alone his percentage was more than $4,000.

Furthermore, since the commission had delegated all significant authority to Borglum, he no longer had anyone with whom to quarrel. Norbeck, Boland, and the National Park Service officials—those who had checked him closely—had been removed by death or administrative reorganization. There was no one connected with the project who dared to defer openly with Borglum or to criticize what he undertook. Yet he did not refrain from argument or impulsive outbursts. After receiving $2,201 in October, he complained to Storck that his honorarium had "been cut down and very much reduced from what it was even under the unpleasant conditions that the new commission was created to correct."

Storck explained in lengthy detail how he had computed each payment. Then Borglum, realizing the unfairness of his remarks, asserted that he might write frankly "about some things that are disturbing me *for the moment*. . . . I beg of you not to take me too seriously." Storck felt that many of Borglum's financial troubles could have been averted by "a financial advisor and confidant . . . during the past ten years."

For the most part, however, Borglum was very cooperative with the commission and officials of the Treasury Department regarding fiscal matters. He even volunteered to adjust expenditures, if necessary, to keep within budgetary limitations. This was a new spirit for him.

Borglum's disposition was greatly influenced by his advancing age (he was then seventy-one). His health was none too good, and he realized that the memorial must be completed quickly if it was to be finished in his lifetime. As he expressed it, *"The work on the Mountain is the only thing that is important."*

No longer hampered or restricted by any program of operations, Borglum could now proceed as he pleased. For several years he had wanted to work the full twelve months, despite the inclement winter weather. From an engineering standpoint this was impractical: when the temperature dropped below zero, the compressed-air lines often froze and reduced or cut off power. But Borglum, eager to finish the memorial, provided winter shelters for his drillers, and work continued throughout the winter of 1938–1939 with only one brief shutdown of three weeks. Borglum was pleased by the uninterrupted operations, and it must be concluded that one reason for the continuance of work was the resulting increase in the sculptor's honorarium. Some overhead expense was saved by employing men steadily, but the price was lost efficiency. Nevertheless, this uninterrupted period of work contributed to the progress of the memorial under the new administration.

All work other than that on the four figures had previously been held up by Boland and the Park Service officials, who insisted that all funds be spent to complete the faces. For years Borglum had planned to carve a Hall of Records, a stairway leading to it, and, of course, the inscription. The first Mount Rushmore act did not provide for a hall or stairway. Now freed from all restrictions, Borglum commenced in July 1938 to hew out the Hall of Records. By August he could report that this project was "progressing nicely."

Transplanting the idea from Stone Mountain, Borglum planned for a large room eighty by one hundred feet which would be drilled into the north wall of the small canyon behind the faces. His scheme also called for an eight hundred–foot granite stairway which would begin near his studio, rise gradually to meet the canyon mouth about one hundred feet north of Lincoln's head, and thence lead to the entrance of the great hall.

What was to be the purpose of this glorified cave? Borglum claimed that sculpture must be related to the civilization which produced it by historical and cultural data. Although his idea was vague and without specific plan, he outlined his general intentions to a startled newsman in August. Those who had doubted or scoffed at mountain-carving were to be overwhelmed by the sculptor's conception of his great hall:

> The 360 feet of wall space will be paneled and recessed to a depth of 30 inches. Into these recesses will be built in illuminated bronze and glass, cabinets into which will be placed the records of the West World accomplishments, the political effect of its philosophy of government, its adventure in science, art, literature, invention, medicine, harmony—typed upon aluminum sheets rolled and protected in tubes.
>
> These cabinets will be sealed and may be opened only by an act of Congress; they will extend 16 feet upward. On the wall above them, extending around the entire hall will be a bas-relief showing the adventure of humanity discovering and occupying the West World; it will be bronze, gold plated. There will be 25 large busts of great . . . men and women, together with one panel reserved for our own day—why and by whom the great Federal Memorial was conceived and built and the records of that work. . . .
>
> The facade of this great hall represents a perpendicular rise of 60 feet in height from the leveled dressed granite floor below; five steps lead to the entrance, 22 ½ feet in width, with great cast glass doors . . . These doors penetrate a panel 44 feet in height, surmounted by an eagle with the wings spread 38 feet, pylons on each side of the panel, 49 feet in height, rise like two great protecting barriers; upon these are carved two Colonial torches, the flames from which are more that 30 feet in length and in full relief. Cut into the panel under the edge are these words: "America's Onward March," and below, "The Hall of Records."

Such was the imaginative sculptor's dream for preserving the cultural achievements of his America. The Time Capsule to be buried in 1939, he said, would be a "trivial performance." He boasted, "It is my intention that this room shall be the most complete, carefully built and studied, elaborately finished archives in the world." To reach it, future generations would walk up an artistically designed stairway "15 feet wide, steps with an easy 5-inch rise, 18-inch tread and rests every 50 feet." He later wrote, "There is nothing like it in history but the steps leading in Athens to the Parthenon from the Acropolis."

At various times he suggested placing statues of Benjamin Franklin, John Hancock, Patrick Henry, Alexander Hamilton, and other leading Americans in the Hall of Records. He wrote to President Roosevelt, "I am determined Benjamin Franklin's statue shall be among the first and your own, which I am particularly anxious to do myself. . . . I will give Susan B. Anthony a place with the gods in the Great Hall," he said. "Her friends should be happy."

In addition to the busts, he intended to include modern inventions and other artifacts of nineteenth- and twentieth-century culture. Borglum's work was for all time to come. He would not have generations thousands of years hence ignorant of life in America in 1940.

His first plan for a single large room was soon abandoned for a more grandiose scheme. He considered the possibility of excavating a lower floor in the mountain's very heart, where five or six rooms might be located. More prosaic people probably considered this an idle dream, but Borglum was in dead earnest about it. Norbeck had been greatly interested in this aspect of the memorial. According to Borglum, one of his last requests was "Don't forget the museum and steps; and try to get money for a great gate."

A stairway would be of little use unless the museum was finished. However, two years before any work was done on the Hall of Records, Borglum, Boland, and Norbeck seriously discussed building the stairway, which would be based on plans drawn by Borglum in 1936. Norbeck and Boland wanted the Civilian Conservation Corps to build it, and the senator was certain that he could make the necessary arrangements in Washington. But Borglum opposed the idea, claiming that more skilled workmen were necessary. "It must be designed with taste and monumental dignity. It must be built in harmony with the big character of the work itself," he said. There is reason to believe that the sculptor refused to use CCC labor because he would receive no honorarium under those conditions. In any event, Borglum ruined his chances of getting the stairway when he refused to cooperate with Norbeck and the CCC.

During the 1938 season Borglum concentrated most of his carvers on the Roosevelt face. Some finishing was done on Washington's neck and the lapel of his coat. It was not until February 24, 1939, that Lincoln Borglum ordered work stopped because of budgetary problems. Borglum, Arundel, and George W. Storck were in Washington at the time seeking a $75,000 deficiency appropriation, plus $175,000 for the fiscal year 1940. Since $50,000 had been appropriated in June 1938, these requests exhausted the $300,000 authorization. Unless the work could be completed by July 1, 1940, a new authorization would have to be sought.

Borglum had always maintained that about $15,000 a month was necessary for maximum efficiency. On this basis, more than $175,000 a year was needed. Members of the House subcommittee on appropriations were asking the same old questions, perhaps with a little more impatience. "How much longer will it take to complete the work?" asked Congressman Fitzpatrick. Borglum replied that he could "get all the work done" within twelve to eighteen months. When pressed further about time and costs, Borglum declared that he had promised the commission, the president, "and I will promise you, if there is any more money needed I will go out with my hat to get the money." Fitzpatrick asserted that "the people of this country do not want you to do that. They want to find out when it will be completed."

After several congressmen had expressed displeasure about the slow rate of progress and the constant requests for more funds, Representative Joe Starnes asked, "Will this amount of money [$250,000] you are asking for complete it?" Borglum replied without hesitation, "I say so." Then the questioning continued:

MR. DIRKSEN: Is there any objection to inserting in the language of the bill the words "for the completion of"?

MR. BORGLUM: None at all.

MR. ARUNDEL: What would be the effect of that? Suppose we are—

MR. DIRKSEN: I know what the effect is; that is why I am asking that question . . .

MR. ARUNDEL: In the event that we found that we could not finish it, would such language bar us from securing funds from private sources to complete it?

MR. DIRKSEN: Not necessarily but it would put a complete stop
on further Federal funds.

MR. ARUNDEL: I understand that. That is quite a drastic step to
take, and I am surprised that Mr. Borglum would run the risk
of that.

MR. BORGLUM: I know how much stone each man can take out,
and I think we can do it.

If there had ever been any doubt about Borglum's financial
ineptness, it vanished with this performance. To state categorical-
ly that he could finish the memorial with an additional $250,000
was sheer foolishness. It was not necessary to make such a rash
promise to get the remainder of the authorization, and Borglum
had stated repeatedly—on one occasion, before a congressional
committee—that $600,000 was the minimum for completing the
project. Is it any wonder that Senator Norbeck did not want him
present when he approached Congress for funds? It would not
have been so bad had he been referring only to the faces. But he
told Dirksen that the Hall of Records and stairway could be finished with the same appropriation.

Borglum was also sharply quizzed about the inscription. Jed
Johnson considered it "absurd to talk about putting five hundred
words on the back of the mountain." Johnson had visited Rushmore
the previous summer and had left "very much impressed," but he
opposed any inscription. He grumbled that the appropriations committee had "done nothing except to pay the bills" and intimated that
its views deserved more consideration.

The amount of Borglum's honorarium likewise aroused members
of the subcommittee. Storck had included a $35,000 item in the
budget as the sculptor's fee for the 1939–1940 period. While this was
less than 14 percent of the $100,000 proposed expenditure, it seemed
a large amount to $10,000-a-year congressmen. Under sharp ques-
tioning, Borglum became utterly confused and said, "I have not
received $10,000 a year for ten years." He had actually been paid
$16,013 during the fiscal year of 1938 and more than $16,000 between
July and December 1938.

In spite of the unimpressive testimony of Borglum and the commission, Congress appropriated the $250,000, giving the sculptor money to finish out the current year and proceed at full capacity until July 1, 1940, when he promised to have the work completed. While the lawmakers committed themselves to finishing the project, they were eager to be rid of this annual headache. "We are trying to come to some definite conclusion so we can wind up the thing and do justice to everybody, and at the same time do justice to the work," Dirksen said.

Senator Pittman, chairman of the commission, testified later and helped to calm the doubts of House members. Though admitting that Borglum had done some work on "what might be called the Hall of Fame," he assured his listeners that first of all the commission wanted to complete the heads. Because of Borglum's age, he said, the commissioners were insistent that the faces be finished while Borglum was physically able. "Mr. Borglum," he continued, "has in mind other projects going on into infinity. The commission has in mind the completion of these figures." If the first and second commission and the National Park Service had not insisted that Borglum confine his operations to the figures, Mount Rushmore would not have been brought so near completion during his lifetime.

Despite Pittman's desire that work be done only on the faces, Borglum continued to drill in the Hall of Records. He spent about $16,000 on it before the commission persuaded him to halt operations in July 1939. By that time he had blasted a tunnel fourteen by twenty feet that ran some seventy-five feet into the solid mountain. For many years, because of insufficient funds and the National Park Service's coolness toward the project, nothing more was ever done on what Borglum had intended to be the most "elaborately finished archives in the world." After workmen left the mountain in 1941, mountain goats found excellent quarters in the $16,000 cave.

In 1939 more than three hundred thousand people visited the monument, three times the number of visitors in 1931. The three main roads leading to the memorial had been hard-surfaced in 1937, and South Dakota had spent more than $1,000,000 on highways built primarily to service Mount Rushmore. Within another decade the state estimated that it had spent about $2,000,000 on roads within a fifteen-mile radius of the monument.

The absence of proper tourist facilities was evident in the congestion and inconveniences about the mountain. Borglum particularly suffered as tourists jammed his studio to look at his models, purchase pictures and souvenirs, or perhaps see the sculptor at work. The atmosphere was anything but conducive to creative endeavor. In the summer of 1939 a new studio was started about 250 feet northeast of the original building. Borglum planned to move his office and models to the new location, leaving the old building for tourists and visitors. Other improvements undertaken during 1939 included two concrete water tanks, each with a capacity of about forty thousand gallons, and two modern comfort stations.

During the summer Borglum personally directed the finishing work on Washington and Jefferson, and continued to work on Roosevelt. Practically nothing was done on Lincoln in 1939. Borglum went over the Washington face many times, "refining and refining it." "Nobody knows the difference," he said, "except that they say it is more wonderful." Borglum's opportunity for artistic excellence came in the finishing work when he gave his figures their life and character. It was this final touch by Borglum which transformed the sculpture from colossal bulk without particular form to a portrait with "all the vigor and power that direct modeling" makes possible.

Men trained by Borglum did most of the refining. He had complained for years about the lack of trained carvers and had sharply criticized the old commission for not permitting him to hire such help. After gaining control in 1938, he immediately sought to employ trained assistants, but he could not find suitable men. Though he received sixteen applications, he found only one man who met his needs. "There are no mountain granite sculptors in America," he wrote. The responsibility was his alone. Failure to find men superior to those "cast-off miners" he had gleaned from the Keystone vicinity made his earlier charges against the commission sound somewhat hollow.

Theodore Roosevelt, the fourth and last figure to be completed, was dedicated on the night of July 2, just nine years after the Washington figure had been unveiled. The monument had been dedicated then as the Shrine of Democracy by J. S. Cullinan, and the intervening years had seen Borglum's dream brought near to completion. Now nearly done, the four faces looked out majestically from their 5,675-foot pedestal. About twelve thousand guests and admirers were present. Roosevelt had been a favorite with South Dakotans, and they turned out eagerly to see his portrait dedicated. Borglum had modeled the Roosevelt face from his small bust of the Rough Rider made in 1918.

The dedication was held in conjunction with South Dakota's fiftieth anniversary of statehood, and Borglum left nothing undone to celebrate the dual occasion. Although rain had fallen in the afternoon, by evening the sky had cleared, and a bright moon shone on the figures. Suddenly the faces were entirely lighted, first by rockets and aerial bombs, then by powerful searchlights. The spectators gasped in awe and delight. Sioux Indians in full native dress and such celebrities as William S. Hart of silent-picture fame added color and drama. It was a typical Borglum performance.

Harlan J. Bushfield, the state's conservative governor, delivered the main address. He lashed out against the general dependence upon government largess. Part of his speech seemed oddly out of place since he was helping to dedicate a project for which national lawmakers had appropriated $750,000. Neither did his remarks fit in with Roosevelt's character and philosophy. But it sounded good to his listeners, most of whom were philosophically in tune with nineteenth-century individualism, but who seemed willing to participate in the growing welfare state.

CHAPTER EIGHTEEN

"Viking Stock Overdoes"

G UTZON Borglum was happy. The greatest ambition of his life was nearing fulfillment. He was about to achieve his all-consuming desire to carve the world's most colossal sculpture. Although there was much refining and improvement yet to be done, what of it? The fiscal year 1940 was only beginning, and Congress had provided $175,000, the largest amount ever made available to the project in a single year. With more than $14,000 a month, Borglum could proceed under what he considered nearly ideal circumstances.

His own income was enough to buoy a man's spirits. During the calendar year 1939 he received $31,149. Harassing taxes, embarrassing mortgages, and other debts could be met at least in part. No one was around who personified the old regime. Now when Borglum spoke on Rushmore matters, whether business or artistic, he spoke as one having authority. No longer must he consult those he considered his inferiors. Is it any wonder that the sculptor rejoiced?

But Borglum's joy and the comparative tranquillity around the mountain were shattered in May 1939 when a presidential reorganization order returned the administration of Mount Rushmore to the Interior Department as of July 1. The commission which had jumped at Borglum's beck and call was stripped of all authority except for general provisions which instructed it to complete the memorial in accordance with Borglum's designs and designate a Mount Rushmore reservation. The National Park Service was given all other functions,

The order reverberated all the way from Rushmore to Washington. It was a logical administrative move since the Interior Department eventually would supervise the completed memorial. But Senator Pittman and Borglum were deeply agitated, Pittman because he disliked Secretary Ickes, and Borglum because he wanted no checks on his activities at the mountain.

While the change was still under consideration, Borglum object-ed heatedly. He wrote to Senator Pittman that he considered the National Park Service most intolerable. He charged that Nagle and Boland had nearly ruined the work, and he threatened to quit the project if Nagle was again put in a position of influence.

Borglum and Pittman both sought a reprieve at the White House and urged that the transfer be withheld. The senator wrote Roosevelt that it would be utterly impractical to let the Interior Department administer the great work at Mount Rushmore. Secretary E. M. Watson, writing a memorandum to his chief, said, "Senator Pittman is very excited over the transfer." But Pittman was calm compared to the sculptor. Appealing to the president, Borglum said that he could finish "the most stately jewel" if unsympathetic forces were not per-mitted to regain control.

On June 5, nearly a month before the transfer was to take place, Pittman, Borglum, and Demaray conferred with the president. The senator did most of the talking and was especially abusive of Demaray and the Park Service. As the atmosphere became strained under this attack, Roosevelt winked at the uncomfortable Demaray, putting him at ease and indicating his support of the service. The pleas of Pittman and Borglum were unavailing, and two days later the president instructed Demaray to "work out some simple plan" to coordinate the administration of Mount Rushmore. "The Treasury Procurement can, I think, continue the financial supervision," he said.

Roosevelt also withstood other efforts to get him to rescind the order. Ickes reported after a conference at the White House that "it will be necessary for the National Park Service to handle Mount Rushmore Memorial matters in the customary way and I hope that it may be done with a minimum of controversy with Mr. Borglum."

Thus after July 1, administration of the project was divided among three groups. Of these, the Interior Department had the most authority since it was responsible for general administrative supervi-sion including preparation of the budget and control over personnel. Accounting and disbursment were handled by the Treasury Department as in the previous year, and the commission retained some general responsibility.

Borglum was highly critical of members of the Interior Department, whom he considered responsible for the president's action. He even claimed that "no one knew less about it [the transfer] than Franklin Delano Roosevelt." The order "put me right back where I was," he said, "at the mercy of unsympathetic men who have no idea of how life can be given to blocks of granite." He maintained that National Park Service "agents" had no comprehension of his work, that Demaray was uninterested and Nagle ignorant. Borglum charged that service officials were "sore" about their previous "eviction" from the work.

There was at least one person in the Interior Department who did not relish administering Mount Rushmore. That man was Secretary Ickes. On August 29 he wrote President Roosevelt in his singular manner:

> When I have anything official to do in connection with Mr. Gutzon Borglum's enterprise at Mount Rushmore I always feel like equipping myself as a man does when he fusses with a beehive. Mr. Borglum has customarily made it so unpleasant for any one who assumes that he doesn't know all about accounting, Government procedure, landscape work, architecture, building craftsmanship, etc., etc., in addition to being an outstanding sculptor, that I groaned all night following the day when I learned that the Mount Rushmore National Memorial Commission had been sent here for administration. I am willing to take all of the wasp stings that may be coming my way, but I would like you to look over this confidential report from Mr. John L. Nagle, Superintendent of Memorials.

In July Demaray outlined a program of administration which he believed would constitute "minimum participation" by the National Park Service. The service, he wrote, must (1) approve all current expenditures and budgets, (2) control such personnel matters as appointments, separations, and promotions, and (3) maintain the right to make recommendations regarding contracts. He stated that the National Park Service would not retain an engineer at the mountain but would periodically check the work for efficiency.

Early in August John Nagle returned to Mount Rushmore to survey the situation. His visit must have been extremely distasteful to Borglum in light of the sculptor's recent blistering remarks about him. Nagle criticized much of the work around the monument, saying that the buildings, steps, and other construction had been poorly done. The worst feature, he said, was the absence of any general long-range plan for water, sewage, parking, and other tourist facilities. He reported that the commission had temporarily halted work on the Hall of Records and the new studio. Nagle agreed that nothing more should be done on the Hall until the faces were completed. Finishing the figures was paramount—other aspects of the plan could wait. This was the report Secretary Ickes wanted Roosevelt to study.

The following October a conference was held by Nagle, Arundel, Williamson, Bulow, and Demaray to discuss closer collaboration between the commission and the service. It was agreed to apply all currently available funds to the figures and to draw up a master plan of development before any further work was undertaken around the base of the mountain. The National Park Service demanded such a plan because it was the usual administrative procedure and because officials distrusted Borglum when he was left completely free. Nagle was particularly irked because the sculptor had wadded up and discarded service blueprints for the new studio building. Borglum, however, was in no mood to forsake any of his ideas. "I expect to follow that out," he said, "even if I have now to go to the public and raise the money necessary." But the service was in a position to make and enforce definite recommendations and decisions. While Borglum talked of raising money privately, he really knew the futility of such attempts. He must cooperate with others if the memorial was to be finished. The president, his last recourse, had turned him down.

In December Nagle and Associate Architect Howard W. Baker* of the Region Two office of the Park Service in Omaha went to Mount Rushmore to make a complete inspection. To pave the way, Arundel explained to Borglum that "the Park Service is doing this in the spirit of cooperation." Nagle again maintained that every penny should be spent on carving the faces. He believed that once they were completed, the service could justifiably request further funds for work around the memorial. Nagle and Baker also considered other matters. They wanted to know if Borglum would be retained to help develop the overall artistic plan. They recommended that a date be set for the commission to relinquish full authority to the National Park Service and suggested that eventually Mount Rushmore should be administered by the superintendent of nearby Wind Cave National Park. These

---

*In 1950, Baker became director of Region Two.

officials ordered a master plan drawn up showing all houses, roads, walks, and other features of the project.* They estimated that the remaining $107,000 would complete the faces.

Nagle had never been enthusiastic about Borglum's Hall of Records or the grand stairway. It was largely upon his and Boland's recommendations that work on these aspects of the memorial had been postponed until 1938. Nagle was still using his influence to hold Borglum in check. The principal consideration, he believed, was to finish the faces while Borglum was available. Assuming that the hall and stairway were desirable parts of the project, they did not require a nationally known sculptor to construct them. The National Park Service employed engineers and artists who were fully capable of such work and who could be employed at a much lower cost. But no one else could do Borglum's carving satisfactorily, so it was necessary to confine him to the faces. Borglum was incensed. "I know that it was their work that stopped all work on the mountain except on the heads," he wrote. Moreover, he charged them with attempts to "get physical possession of Mount Rushmore."

While these administrative adjustments were taking place, Borglum was going ahead at the mountain. He spent an average of more than $13,000 a month or a total of $161,826 during the fiscal year 1940. This was by far the largest expenditure ever made on the memorial. Borglum's honorarium alone was $28,233. On July 1, 1940, a little more than $31,000 remained to continue into 1941. Most of the large budget had been spent on the figures, for work had been largely confined to finishing and refining the faces. This was relatively expensive work, requiring additional skilled labor. Progress was not easily determined by the casual observer at this time; the *New York Times* somewhat prematurely reported on February 23, 1940, that Washington's head was "undergoing today its final buffing."

It became clear late in 1939 that the $300,000 Congress had authorized a year earlier would not even finish the figures, to say nothing of the Hall of Records, the stairway, and the inscription. In fact, by that time Borglum had abandoned the idea of an inscription on the west wall of the mountain and had decided to place it in the Hall of Records. But he was insistent on some kind of permanently

---

*A preliminary master plan was submitted in 1940, but it was not until 1948 that a completed plan, outlining current and future developments, was finished.

engraved account. "The inscription will have to go on [or in] the mountain sooner or later," he wrote. "You might as well drop a letter into the world's postal service without an address or signature, as to send that carved mountain into history without identification."

Borglum's promise to finish the memorial with current appropriations did not embarrass him when he returned to Congress for more money. A budget was worked out by Storck, Borglum, and National Park Service officials, asking for an additional $318,000 to finish the faces, the Hall of Records, and the grand stairway. Borglum estimated that $60,000 was yet necessary for completion of the figures, $80,000 for the Hall, $95,000 for the stairway, and thousands more for landscaping and miscellaneous improvements.

On May 15 the Interior Department submitted an estimate of $350,000 to the Bureau of the Budget. However, the director of the bureau recommended only $86,000 to Congress. The president supported this and wrote the Speaker of the House, "I should like to see the work at Mount Rushmore finally wound up."

It proved to be an uphill fight in Congress without the support of the president or the Bureau of the Budget. "We are having a deuce of a time getting an appropriation for Mount Rushmore," Arundel wrote. Representative Case explained to Borglum that if they received $86,000, "it will be very difficult to get any further funds from the Federal government. The committee takes the position that they have been told before that this appropriation, or that appropriation, would definitely wind up the work." Arundel and Case appeared before the House subcommittee on July 9, but they were not encouraged. If Congress continued this attitude, Arundel said, "we are in quite a pickle." On August 5 Borglum and Arundel presented their case before the subcommittee with no greater success.

Counting on past successes, Borglum appealed directly to Roosevelt. But the president thought it would be unwise to ask Congress for money to start new work "not covered by specific authorizations to date." This was especially true, he said, in the light of congressional opposition and in view of Borglum's statement to the appropriations subcommittee in 1938 that no additional funds would be requested. Borglum's careless assurances were finally bearing their bitter fruit.

Tired of unkept promises regarding the time of completion, Congress reluctantly appropriated $86,000 for the fiscal year of 1941.

This would provide the $60,000 which Borglum said would finish the heads, $15,000 for the sculptor, and $11,000 for administration. With more than $31,000 on hand July 1, a substantial budget of about $117,000 was provided. This looked like the end. The project's promoters must make the best of their last money for carving.

The attitude of national lawmakers toward granting additional money for mountain sculpture was conditioned to a large degree by world affairs. Huge expenditures for rearmament militated against further appropriations for Mount Rushmore and many other projects with which Congress had been liberal during the depression of the 1930s.

Borglum's correspondence throughout 1940 reveals growing dissatisfaction, discouragement, and anger. Such attitudes were not new to the erratic sculptor, but ill-health coupled with the closer supervising of his work added to his irritation. In March he was hospitalized for several days at Colorado Springs, and after returning home he was attended by a trained nurse. "Viking stock overdoes," he told President Roosevelt, "but it takes a lot to stop it." Yet the years of strenuous living were beginning to take their toll. He might try to fool the public by giving his age as sixty-nine, but the body which held his restless and energetic soul knew well that he was four years older.

As difficulties mounted owing to lack of money and tighter administrative control, Borglum became increasingly critical of the National Park Service. "If the Park Service people were wise," he asserted, they would "fall over themselves to help me to do the finest possible thing I'm capable of." In his annual report written in December 1939, he had aimed some of his sharpest barbs at Nagle and the service. "It is little short of absurd to apply roadbuilder practices or sophomoric engineering to the carving of a great portrait; it is precisely this kind of interference that is and has been the only persistent enemy of this memorial." He expressed deep discouragement over the reorganization order which "Burlew grafted into our life." It had been "a curse to the work" and a constant threat "to the proper fulfillment of a great undertaking," he said. Borglum confessed to Arundel in an impassioned moment that 1940 had been "one of the most troublesome, sabotage periods" in the history of his colossal work.

Borglum opened his mind and soul to Doane Robinson, who, despite his eighty-four years, was still dreaming big dreams and thinking big thoughts. He suggested to Borglum the possibility of carving a statue to the pioneer mother. Based on his own experience, Borglum was not enthusiastic. The drab, ox-like civilization of America was not conducive to artistic perfection, he declared. It was discouraging, he concluded, when one had to labor against ignoramuses who could only ask stupid questions about how long it would take, the ultimate cost, and the artist's salary. Such an atmosphere, Borglum thought, was utterly destructive to great artistic achievement.

But controversies and personality conflicts could not stop the work on the mountain. Lincoln Borglum, who had been promoted to superintendent in 1938* at a salary of $4,800 a year, was assuming more and more responsibility. Borglum's was the master hand, but details of operation were left to his son, who was growing in both artistic and administrative stature. Practically all the work was now confined to finishing and refining the faces.

Early in March 1941 Borglum went to Chicago for what his doctors said was a minor but necessary operation. He needed to recover his old vigor and energy if a successful fight was to be waged for additional funds. In February the Interior Department had submitted requests to the budget director for $278,000, including $125,000 for the stairway, $75,000 for the Hall of Records, and additional amounts for water, sewage, power, buildings, and other facilities.

But the fighting sculptor had fought his last battle. Suddenly and unexpectedly on the morning of March 6, he died of a heart attack. With seventy-four strenuous years behind him, the last sixteen of which had been devoted to Mount Rushmore, he did not live to see his great dream entirely completed. Death robbed posterity of a finished memorial, grandiose in conception, superb in execution. But the work was so near completion that Borglum could die with the exalted feeling that comes with an ambition realized.

The genius of Borglum had compelled him to accomplish an artistic work of national appeal, which would stand as long as the granite mountain endured. It was not only a memorial to American ideals and institutions; it represented the spirit, vision, and audacity of Gutzon Borglum. Although he was not America's greatest sculptor, he was the most daring and unconventional artist of his time. He expressed the reckless spirit of his generation and its cult of magnificence.

---

*Lincoln Borglum served as superintendent until June 1944.

On the day Borglum died, Russell Arundel asked Secretary Ickes if he had any objection to constructing a crypt "of a design approved by the Park Service and the Commission at an unobtrusive spot in the mountain." He explained that this would be undertaken with private funds. Secretary Ickes and members of his staff strongly opposed this suggestion, stating that it was contrary to established policy and that it would lead to innumerable requests to bury private citizens in national areas. Despite the opposition of the Interior Department, Representative Case's bill providing for the interment of Borglum's body at the scene of his greatest work was passed by Congress and was signed by the president on July 11. However, it came to nothing. Private funds for constructing a suitable crypt were not to be had. A second futile attempt was made in 1943, when a bill was passed temporarily reviving the defunct commission for that purpose. The sculptor was finally laid to rest in Forest Lawn Cemetery in Glendale, California.

Borglum's contradictory personality was not without elements of modesty. At one time Arundel and Senator Pittman had strongly urged that in some way his name be made a part of the monument itself. The sculptor replied that under no circumstances should his name go on the mountain. Despite this protest, it would have been fitting and proper to carve in some inconspicuous spot the name of Gutzon Borglum. Might not visitors ten thousand years hence ask the identity of the man who had defied convention to carve these heroic faces?

CHAPTER NINETEEN

Afterglow

A NY discussion of events which took place at Rushmore after Borglum's death seems an anticlimax to the story. But there was work yet to be done, and by good luck the plans were virtually complete. The master had lived to do the major work, and young Borglum was capable of going ahead.

The commission held a meeting on March 17, at which time the sculptor's son was asked to continue as superintendent. The executive committee was authorized to draw up a contract similar to Borglum's except that Lincoln would be paid 15 instead of 25 percent. A resolution was passed stating that the memorial would be completed "in accordance with the known plans, models, and specifications of the late Gutzon Borglum." The commission approved a budget of $205,000 for the fiscal year 1942. Shortly afterward a contract was negotiated with Lincoln Borglum.

With the sculptor gone and the national defense emergency becoming more serious, there remained only the faintest hope of obtaining any further appropriations for carving. About a week before Borglum died Arundel had written him that Roosevelt had ordered the Bureau of the Budget to reduce nondefense expenditures sharply. So far as Mount Rushmore was concerned, Congress had practically closed the treasury doors in 1940, and now with the president's economy order, they seemed to be locked. "I am getting a little jittery," Arundel wrote, "although I am doing everything humanly possible to get the appropriation." He was referring to the $300,000 which Borglum had thought was necessary to finish the memorial.

Later on March, Demaray and Director Newton B. Drury of the National Park Service appeared before the subcommittee which was considering the Interior Department appropriation bill for 1942. There was still an unexpended balance of about $50,000, and Demaray explained that after exhausting this amount, the service did not intend to undertake further work. The service was only requesting about $18,000 for administration and maintenance. Members of the subcommittee agreed that nothing more should be appropriated for carving. Congressman Scrugham went much further. "We will undoubtedly be asked . . . to provide funds for carving somebody else's head or face on another mountain," he said. "But as a matter of general policy, the initiation of similar undertakings to be paid for by the Government, should be discouraged."

Director Drury left no doubt about the position of the National Park Service: "As far as I am concerned . . . I hope this will remain as it is now, unique, and the only one of its kind." The official position of the National Park Service, Drury wrote later, was that "death stayed the hand of the artist."

Since no additional funds could be obtained except for maintenance and administration, the executive committee of the commission met in June to decide on future action. They agreed that Lincoln Borglum should be recommended as permanent superintendent and that following his appointment, all remaining functions of the commission should be transferred to the National Park Service. The hope was expressed that the service would complete the memorial at "such time and under such circumstances as may be determined by the Secretary of the Interior." The Second Deficiency Appropriation Act of 1941 legislated the commission out of existence after June 30 of the following year.

Meanwhile, Lincoln Borglum was trying to leave the memorial in the best possible condition when funds should run out. Although nothing had been appropriated for work after July 1, 1941, about $21,000 remained in the treasury, and operations continued until funds became exhausted. Final drilling was done on October 31. During early November a few men were retained to store the machinery, remove the cableway, and perform general clean-up tasks. This ended about six and one-half years of actual work extending over a fourteen-year period. During that time about 450,000 tons of stone were removed from the mountain by almost four hundred workers.

From March to November, while young Borglum was in complete charge of the work, workers concentrated on the face of Roosevelt, which was never finished; Lincoln's head was refined and brought out more fully; and Jefferson's collar was blocked out, though no work on his hand was undertaken because of the poor quality of the stone. The collar and lapels of Washington's coat were finished.

In making his final report to the commission, Lincoln Borglum stated his views regarding future operations at the monument. "With the possible exception of some more work on the hand of Lincoln to make it stand out more and to balance that part of the memorial," he said, "I do not think any more should be done on [the] figures . . ." The memorial as it stood, he believed, was just as effective as if it had been carried down to the waist as shown in the models. The Hall of Records and the stairway, however, he considered essential to the memorial's completion. Without explanatory data, "the memorial will become a riddle to people a few thousand years from now," he wrote. He recommended removing the debris below the sculptural group. This would give the figures the appearance of more height and grandeur. But these suggestions had to wait upon the uncertainties of the future.

The memorial had cost $989,992.32. This included Borglum's honorarium of about $170,000, payrolls and salaries, buildings, equipment, and all other expenditures necessary for the project. Of this amount, the old Mount Harney Memorial Association had raised $54,670.56 from large corporations which had financial interests in the Black Hills, from small local concerns, and from individuals. Citizens of Rapid City contributed $13,896.36, and those of Lead, $7,000. Hot Springs and Belle Fourche were the only other Black Hills towns which gave more than $1,000. Sioux City, Iowa, donated $1,625.

The first Mount Rushmore Commission had raised $99,709.76. The relief grant of $50,000 made up more than one-half this amount, and the remaining $49,709.76 came from Borglum, the individual commissioners, the sale of memberships in the Mount Rushmore National Memorial Society, the income from the brochures, and other sources.

The federal government was the largest contributor. Congress had appropriated $836,000, all of which was spent except $388. Three major authorizations were made: $250,000 in 1929, $200,000 in 1935, and $300,000 in 1938. A final $86,000 was appropriated in 1940 as a part of the first supplemental civil functions appropriations act, without specific previous authorization. Beginning with annual budgets of from $40,000 to $60,000, the largest expenditure was in the fiscal year 1940 when more than $161,000 was spent.

The financing of Mount Rushmore was typical of many other projects during that period. Beginning with only local support, the first move was to seek matching funds from Congress. With one foot in the proverbial door, it was just a short step for the federal government to assume full responsibility. Mount Rushmore's history demonstrates what determined and skillful senators and representatives can do in obtaining federal aid for a project in their own state. More important, perhaps, it shows the growing reliance of Americans upon their federal government.

For several years Borglum had been counting on President Roosevelt to participate in the final dedication of the memorial. Although the president refused to approve further appropriations after 1940, he did not lose interest in the project. He had not forgotten Borglum's suggestion that a climactic celebration to dedicate the completed monument should be held sometime during his administration. Before Roosevelt was elected for a third term, Borglum had thought of arranging appropriate ceremonies prior to January 3, 1941. But when the president won another four-year term, the dedication was delayed pending more complete sculpturing of the faces. Borglum's death, however, upset these plans.

It was not until the summer of 1941 that serious consideration was given to a final dedication. Someone suggested to Roosevelt that it was an ideal time to dedicate Mount Rushmore and that the program might be built around the theme of national unity. The president "plans personally to write to Wendell Willkie, asking him to make the speech," James Rowe, Jr., administrative assistant, wrote to Secretary Ickes. "He will also suggest in his invitation that he, the President, write a letter to Willkie on national unity, which Willkie would incorporate in his speech." Rowe concluded, "I also do not need to point out that the Memorial is in the heart of the Isolationist country where spadework is very much needed."

Ickes suggested that Labor Day would be an ideal time and recommended that the details for the program be made by the Region Two office of the National Park Service in Omaha. The plans went awry, however, when Willkie declined to speak and when Chief Justice Stone also refused because of pressing court duties. Roosevelt then decided to postpone the event until 1942. Meanwhile, the hounds of war were unleashed, and no dedication commensurate with the significance of the memorial was held until many years later. What about future work at Mount Rushmore? Will the memorial always be left in its unfinished condition? Why has the debris below the faces never been removed? Would it be possible to complete the figures according to Borglum's models? What about the Hall of Records and the grand stairway? These questions are upon the lips of almost every person who visits the monument. They are important questions, and the American public deserves definite answers. But some of them are not easily found.

The main problem after Borglum's death was, of course, financial. Lincoln Borglum could have finished the figures following his father's models and designs if funds had been available and if public opinion supported such a move. This is true of the Hall of Records and the grand staircase as well. Raising sufficient money to remove the debris and to do the finishing work on the figures was a difficult problem. Young Borglum once estimated that this work would cost $200,000 to $250,000, but the inflationary conditions that followed World War II would probably have greatly increased that amount.

The potential sources of money included congressional appropriations, the assessment of a small admission fee at Rushmore, and the sale of a special memorial coin or medal. The chances of getting more money from the federal government were indeed slim. World War II and the subsequent years of national emergency, huge federal expenditures, and astronomical debts reduced the chances of any windfall from this source. Although Congress appropriated millions for less worthy purposes during the turbulent and free-spending 1940s, most friends of the Rushmore memorial considered a direct appropriation most unlikely.

The idea of levying a small admission fee had originally been considered by Norbeck and Borglum. Congress consistently opposed this plan, and the basic laws of 1929 and 1938 stated, "No charge shall ever be made for admission to the memorial grounds or for viewing the memorial." However in 1941 this scheme was revived. Apparently President Roosevelt made the proposal, for on April 18 he sent a memorandum to the director of the budget suggesting that an admission fee of ten cents might be charged each visitor. This revenue could be used, he said, for physical upkeep and maintenance.

The budget director included this provision in the second deficiency appropriation bill for 1941, which contained an item of $18,000 for National Park Service administration. The language specifically authorized the secretary of the interior to "charge appropriate fees for the parking of automobiles in the Mount Rushmore National Memorial area." It was believed that this would provide some $12,000 to $13,000 a year.

When the matter was considered, Congressman Case was invited to express his views before the Interior subcommittee. "I do not like it," he frankly told his colleagues. He then filed a supplementary statement with the subcommittee chairman which stated that such a law was contrary to the spirit of the basic legislation. "I seriously question the legislative desirability of breaking faith by a rider to the very first appropriation for administration after completion of the heads," he wrote. Case felt that visitors would resent even a small charge. When the bill came up for passage, he objected to this provision and won on a point of order.

Case took the right position. Borglum had always insisted that he was building a national monument, not to individuals, but to the greatness of America. Any admission charge, even for automobile space, was out of keeping with the great purpose of the memorial. The federal government should permanently maintain it for all the people without charge, he argued.

The Mount Rushmore National Memorial Society, formed in 1930 to help finance and publicize the project, had actively explored the possibility of persuading Congress to authorize a special memorial coin or to strike a Mount Rushmore medal which might be sold at a substantial profit. In 1947 the Senate passed a bill permitting the coining of two million silver fifty-cent pieces, "carrying a replica of the memorial." These were to be sold by the society at above face value, and the proceeds were to be turned over to the National Park Service for additional work, particularly the clearing away of debris. But the measure failed in the House, and no satisfactory plan was developed to raise enough money to do the necessary work around the monument. The heroic sculptures will remain as Lincoln Borglum left them in November 1941.

The National Park Service assumed full control of the site in September 1941 when the memorial was placed under the superintendency of Wind Cave National Park. Lincoln Borglum became superintendent on October 1. The area to be administered totaled 1,800 acres. The Mount Rushmore Act of 1938 had set aside 1,500 acres of the Harney National Forest which was designated as the Mount Rushmore Memorial Reservation. Borglum believed that this area was not large enough to protect the monument properly, and in 1940 Congressman Case sponsored a bill adding 300 acres, most of which was along Senator Norbeck's scenic Iron Mountain Road. This put the most picturesque approaches to the memorial under the commission's control. Borglum's purpose was to keep commercial establishments from springing up along the entrances to Mount Rushmore.

In 1949 the Rushmore Reservation was reduced to 1,278 acres, 58 of which were state-owned. The remaining area of some 500 acres was made a part of the Norbeck Wildlife Preserve which had been recently established through the efforts of Francis Case—a proper memorial to the great conservationist.

What about additional figures? The friends of Susan B. Anthony had about given up hope of placing their heroine on Mount Rushmore. The demand to carve a head of Franklin D. Roosevelt did not die so easily. In the early planning stages, supporters of Woodrow Wilson had wanted his likeness carved, indicating that Democrats were not wholly satisfied with Borglum's selections. The idea bobbed up intermittently to include a contemporary Democrat, Franklin D. Roosevelt. Writing in the *Mitchell* (*South Dakota*) *Daily Republic* in December 1944, Jack Bailey suggested the addition of Roosevelt's figure to the Rushmore group. His remarks aroused only slight comment at the time, but after Roosevelt's death in 1945, agitation to include his portrait increased greatly. Scores of correspondents urged Representative Case to promote such a move. Secretary Ickes opposed further work, however, so nothing resulted from the Democratic pressure. Case suggested that Roosevelt's friends and admirers work toward completing the Hall of Records and place a bust there.

Borglum never seriously considered adding any more portraits to his sculptural design. He always insisted that there was insufficient rock for another figure. He referred to congressional restrictions on using funds for carving additional faces and scoffed at such proposals. He told the president in 1939 that he "would have to find stone for such a head and I have pretty nearly used it all up. Enough of that!" The suggestion really "falls within the realm of humor," he said.

Borglum repeated his opposition to carving more figures so often that his friends, both Democrats and Republicans, were well aware of his stand. He wanted no tampering with his basic design.

But the friends of Roosevelt were not deterred by the lack of stone, and in December 1949 Senator Hubert Humphrey of Minnesota, a militant New Dealer, introduced a resolution authorizing the National Park Service "to investigate the feasibility and desirability of adding to the carvings . . . at Mount Rushmore National Memorial the figure of Franklin D. Roosevelt." Although this created a flurry of activity for a short while, nothing came of the move.

One of the most interesting aspects of the story was the plan to illuminate the figures so that they might be viewed at night. Congress willingly bore this additional expense. Although Borglum had used rockets and aerial bombs to light the faces at the dedication of the Theodore Roosevelt figure in 1939, he had never indicated that he favored artificial lighting as a permanent policy.

Late in 1947 Congressman Ben F. Jensen of Iowa was traveling in South Dakota as a member of an Interior Department subcommittee. When he and Coordinating Superintendent Harry Liek left Wind Cave for Mount Rushmore, it was nearly dark. As they drove along Liek pulled out his watch and remarked, "We won't get to Mount Rushmore before dark." Jensen replied, "Well, I'd just as soon see it under the lights." Liek then explained that there were no lighting facilities. Jensen was surprised and indignant. "It's going to be lighted," he told Liek. He was distressed by the thought that thousands of people might miss seeing the memorial because they could not afford to stay overnight in the Black Hills just for that purpose. There must be an opportunity to view the portraits of these four great statesmen both day and night, he concluded.

When Jensen returned to Washington he insisted that the National Park Service provide lighting. He promised to obtain the money. The service was not overly enthusiastic about this project since it would increase administrative costs in a budget already too small. But Jensen made good his pledge. Congress provided about $50,000 to install floodlights which were turned on officially on August 1, 1950. Jensen's objective was commendable, but the sculptural effect left much to be desired. The figures were carved to take advantage of overhead, natural lighting. With floodlights shining from below and directly into the faces, the marvelous light and shadow effects which Borglum developed were lost. It was many years later before significant advancements were made to light the memorial. The aging lights installed by General Electric in 1950 were not replaced until 1990, and in 1998 further lighting improvements were made. The National Park Service continues to research lighting methods that will more closely match the natural appearance of sunlight on the faces.

It was clear by mid-century that no sculptures would be added to Mount Rushmore regardless of how distinguished any individual might be. Furthermore, it was evident that the major tasks for the National Park Service would be to provide adequate facilities in the viewing area for the rapidly increasing number of tourists, and to show the historical significance of the monument through better interpretive and educational programs.

The increasing number of visitors demonstrated that the crowds were outgrowing the rather primitive facilities provided in the 1940s. To meet the demand, the Memorial View Building was completed in August 1957, and its modern eating facilities and a gift shop afforded an excellent view of the faces. An amphitheater, also finished in 1957, was built to provide a setting for special programs and the nightly lighting ceremony held during summer evenings. Borglum's old studio soon became completely inadequate as a visitor center. In May 1963 the National Park Service finished a new building that housed administrative offices and provided a center for tourist information and services. When the original parking area, which accommodated 60 cars, became inadequate, more space was added. But it was not until July 1958 that a 400-unit parking area was finished. Even this was not enough, and space for 200 additional automobiles was added in July 1964.

Providing facilities that would meet growing tourist demands and expectations at Mount Rushmore was a constant challenge to the National Park Service whose budgets never seemed sufficient. It was not until the 1990s that funds became available to do a basic reconstruction of the visitor facilities.

Through the solicitation of private and corporate gifts, and with investments by the concessionaire, the Mount Rushmore Preservation Fund was credited with raising $56 million to improve nearly every aspect of the facilities. New structures included an information center that was completed in 1994, and a gift shop and dining room that were finished in 1996. The new amphitheater, with seating for two thousand people, opened in 1997.

Three major developments were completed in 1998. The Lincoln Borglum Museum that is below the Grand View Terrace and contains an unusual array of exhibits and displays depicting the history and development of the memorial was a great addition to the overall complex. Then new parking structures were opened that summer, providing 1,150 parking spaces, more than double the previous number. A parking charge was initiated to help pay for that facility. Also in the summer of 1998 a new Avenue of Flags was completed.

By the summer of 1998 the complex had a completely different look from what it had been earlier. To some old-timers the change was not welcome. They argued that the new facilities ruined the more natural look that had prevailed before. But however different individuals may have viewed the reconstructed visitor complex, it was impressive and was much better able to handle the growing crowds. Now visitors emerge from a modern and convenient parking lot, walk up a broad avenue on concrete and granite that leads between the gift shop and restaurant, and then proceed along the Avenue of Flags to the main viewing terrace. The faces are constantly before visitors as they walk from the parking area toward the main viewing terrace. It is an enjoyable and dramatic setting for this memorial witnessed by millions of tourists from the United States and foreign countries.

Although Borglum's idea of developing a Hall of Records in the mountain back of the faces lay dormant for many years, a few interested individuals, including some of Borglum's family, kept the mission alive. Finally, in the 1980s Borglum's daughter, Mary Ellis Borglum, began a concerted effort to win support to complete the hall. The National Park Service had never been enthusiastic about Borglum's purpose and concept for the Hall of Records but did agree that some kind of permanent identification at that location would be appropriate. Rather than complete the entire cavern that had been bored and blasted out in 1938–1939, officials agreed on a greatly reduced design that would be funded by money collected through the Mount Rushmore Preservation Fund. The plan simply called for preparing a small chamber in the entrance floor of the hall that would be four feet deep, twenty-six inches long and sixteen inches wide, a space that would hold porcelain enamel panels on which some basic United States documents would be inscribed. These documents included the Declaration of Independence, the Constitution, and other writings, a brief biography of Borglum, a brief history of the first 150 years of the United States, and materials on the four presidents whose faces graced the mountain.

On August 9, 1998, a small group gathered at the entrance to the Hall of Records and observed placement of the panels into a teakwood box that was put into a titanium vault and lowered into the granite chamber. The vault was then covered with a heavy black granite capstone with an inscription explaining how the Hall of Records relates to the sculpture. This ceremony represented a kind of closure for that part of the overall Mount Rushmore project, although it was a far cry from what the sculptor had envisioned and hoped for. The granite stairway from the base of the mountain to the Hall of Records did not receive support and remains only an unfulfilled dream of the sculptor.

During the 1990s the National Park Service not only emphasized the physical comfort and convenience of tourists, but carried on a meaningful interpretive and educational program to help visitors understand the meaning and significance of the monumental sculpture. This involved the preparation and distribution of leaflets and brochures, orientation talks, lectures, exhibits, and other educational materials. Improved education and interpretation of the memorial's fundamental significance is an ongoing goal of the National Park Service.

One important matter that was not achieved for many years was a proper dedication of the monument. At last, on July 3, 1991, fifty years after completion of the carving, a crowd of some thirty-five hundred people gathered for dedication ceremonies. President George Herbert Walker Bush was present to bring national attention to the event. In his comments President Bush praised the men whose faces graced the mountain as leaders who had "chiseled into our national soul a yearning for freedom, democracy, equality, and justice . . ." Viewers of the sculpture, he said, "see carved in stone a symbol that invokes the American character." The entire occasion was a triumphal moment in the history of Mount Rushmore.

One challenge that continually confronts the National Park Service is protection and preservation of the sculpture against the effects of nature. By the 1990s monitoring devices were installed to detect changes in the granite. Also, the original materials developed by Borglum to patch cracks were replaced with a silicone-based product that provides a more permanent but flexible seal. The National Park Service is constantly watchful of the need for any preservation measures.

Mount Rushmore's economic impact on South Dakota has been huge. This was originally predicted by both Doane Robinson and Gutzon Borglum. As the sculpture attracted more and more visitors, millions and millions of tourist dollars poured into state coffers. Motels, hotels, restaurants, automotive services and other businesses benefitted from visitors driving to Mount Rushmore and staying in the vicinity. And tax money on supplies and services purchased by these travelers boosted the state treasury. Moreover, there is no indication that the memorial will ever become an expendable resource. So long as automobile transportation is available, Americans will travel to the "Shrine of Democracy" and shower the state with dollars.

Mount Rushmore never achieved universal approval, especially in the early years, and critics were heard in both professional and lay circles. The files of Senator Francis Case reveal that South Dakotans themselves were not unanimous in their support. Early in 1940 a resident wrote that Borglum had "lotz of Gutz" and should not be given money for any more carving. A South Carolinian who had seen both Stone Mountain and Mount Rushmore sent an open letter to the *New York Times* declaring that many citizens did not admire "this type of mutilation of the noble outlines of mountains."

Ralph M. Pearson, a New York art critic, was probably the most unfriendly individual in professional circles. He described the feeling of "impotent anger" which swept over him upon first seeing the "monstrous naturalistic heads." He continued by saying of the sculpture, "Vandalism, discord, a kind of blasphemy was this presumptuous destruction." Pearson said the heads had nothing but size to recommend them. Many of his remarks were doubtless prompted by the fact that he did not share Borglum's ideas about art.

But a day spent at Mount Rushmore listening to the comments of hundreds of ordinary citizens proves conclusively that few people share the sentiments of such critics.

Borglum in the aerial tramway.

*Progress in 1939
on the Roosevelt
face.*

Workers take time to pose in front of their colossal creation.

's Photo Shop

259

Finishing touches on the monument, 1941.

Borglum's son, Lincoln, oversaw the completion of the memorial after Gutzon died.

CHAPTER TWENTY

For the Ages

"I did not, and don't intend that it shall be just a damn big thing, a three-day tourist wonder," Gutzon Borglum once said of his colossal sculpture. But despite Borglum's intentions, the majority of visitors at Mount Rushmore are most impressed by the monument's huge proportions. It is the impressiveness of mass and size which makes the memorial outstanding to most people. This is not surprising in an age which emphasizes bigness. Mount Rushmore, however, is much more than a "tourist wonder" which produces such descriptive terms as "gigantic," "enormous," "stupendous," and "massive." The monument arouses emotional and spiritual impulses in many of those who view it. The most significant thing about the memorial is not its size, but its effect upon people.

A professor from the University of Nebraska expressed a typical opinion. "I drove to Mount Rushmore," he said, "thinking it was simply another chamber of commerce promotional scheme to relieve tourists of their extra cash." But upon rounding the curve which brought the huge heads into full view, he forgot all about economics. There before him were the gigantic sixty-foot portraits, all well proportioned and blending into the mountain. The sheer bulk was impressive. But that was not the most striking feature about the sculpture or that which caused him to stretch a short visit into a much longer one.

The four heads are not simply rough portraits in stone. Borglum has projected the character and dynamic power of Washington, Jefferson, Lincoln, and Roosevelt in such a manner as to leave a lasting impression upon the observer. The one who views this monument sees more than four stone faces. He sees and feels independence, freedom, justice, equality, self-reliance, individuality, and other qualities which have characterized America, and which these four leaders personified. That is why people spend several hours, sometimes a full day, looking at the ever-enduring faces. They are gripped by the force and power of them. These faces of noble Americans, gazing eastward toward the Plains, seem to be silent guardians of the principles upon which the nation was founded and through which it has been maintained. They stimulate quiet reflection and serious meditation.

The entire setting is dramatic. Nature has blended the elements of earth, stone, trees, valleys, mountains, sky, and clouds into a panorama of beauty which no artist could ever depict so effectively on canvas. In the midst of this natural picture the sculptured figures dominate the countryside. "The noble countenances emerge from Rushmore as though the spirit of the mountain heard a human plan and itself became a human countenance," said Frank Lloyd Wright. Here is a memorial which has real meaning. Certainly, it is colossal, and in that sense spectacular and heroic. But it is not "just a damn big thing." Borglum gave Americans a work that has the impelling power that characterizes all great art.

Borglum's mountain figures are accurate sculptural reproductions. Judged in the tradition of romantic naturalism, they are good heads, powerfully modeled and skillfully executed. As a work of art, however, Mount Rushmore has never excited any particular comment in professional circles. The standard books on sculpture or other writings of critics and professionals give only scant attention to Borglum's final work. Artists do not agree that it is good simply because it is large, an important factor in the judgment of the average person. It must be added, however, that by any standards, lay or professional, the scale models are only average. If they were not signed by Gutzon Borglum, they would receive very little, if any, acclaim as a work of fine art.

Some critics assert that the main flaw in this gigantic sculpture lies in the weakness of the artistic tradition to which Borglum belonged, one largely repudiated by the so-called contemporaries of the mid-twentieth century. Most of Borglum's major work was popular because it was naturalistic. The great rank and file could appreciate his efforts because they understood them. This is true of his crowning work which has dwarfed all his other claims to fame. The eminent understandability of the memorial and its great mass and bulk account for its effect upon people.

As a patriotic shrine, Mount Rushmore has no equal in the United States. Congressman William Lemke, a great admirer of Borglum, said, "No man or woman can view this monument without becoming a better citizen for it." In the presence of the carved likenesses of American leaders, "one could be nothing else but conscious of the responsibilities and meaning of democracy," declared another onlooker. A multitude of people have given similar testimonies. Indeed, it is a monument for the ages. Mount Rushmore represents the greatness, and preserves the best traditions, of America. In conception, spirit, and size, the memorial is a vivid realization of an American dream and is the work of free men, who, aided by modern machines, stamped the earth for posterity. When Lord Halifax visited the memorial in April 1946, he called it "the most amazing, astounding thing I've ever seen."

There is a fundamental and far-reaching significance associated with mountain-carving. Mount Rushmore was Borglum's conception of art on a grand scale, equal to the other aspects of American greatness. It is a part of the American emphasis upon size and bigness. Colossal sculpture is in the tradition of the skyscraper, the forty-five thousand–ton battleship, the superhighway, the large jet airplane, the Grand Coulee Dam, or the Paul Bunyan legend. To many American citizens, the greatest things in their culture are the largest and most monumental. A book is apt to be judged by its number of pages rather than by its content; a building, by the number of stories it towers into the sky rather than by its architectural beauty. Borglum was gripped by the mania of bigness no less than other citizens of his era. Before and during the time he carved at Rushmore, Borglum constantly compared his achievement with the art of previous civilizations. He scoffed at the Sphinx, the Lion of Lucerne, and other monuments because they were not as large as the Rushmore memorial. He once boasted that if it were completed to scale, his George Washington could wade across the Hudson River and scarcely get his ankles wet.

Some writers, among them Arnold J. Toynbee, have deplored this emphasis on size and have asserted that it is a symptom heralding the decline of Western civilization. Whether this is the case only time can tell. Egypt enjoyed hundreds of years of glory and power after the Sphinx was built. In any event, Borglum believed in the importance of creating a memorial that would overshadow the works of the ancients. Regardless of the ultimate destiny of Western civilization, his sculpture will show succeeding generations that American society had reached an apex, a high point of material greatness. No one could doubt that a civilization that had carved a mountain into heroic likenesses of four men was one of power, audacity, and importance.

Only history can determine Mount Rushmore's true significance. For present generations, William Williamson made its importance clear in the early days of the memorial. "The whole project," he told his congressional colleagues in 1928, "is symbolical and allegorical. Washington symbolizes the founding of our country and the stability of our institutions; Jefferson our idealism, expansion, and love of liberty; Lincoln our altruism and sense of inseparable unity; while Roosevelt typifies the soul of America—its restless energy, rugged morality, and progressive spirit. The memorial, as a whole, will idealize all that is best in our national traditions, principles, and form of government. It will symbolize maturity, stability, noble purpose, and liberty of thought and action."

The entrance to the Hall of Records, which penetrates the mountain about seventy feet. The hall was never completed as Borglum had intended, but in 1998 an underground vault was placed in the entryway that contains reproductions of important American historical documents.

Right: Borglum's daughter, Mary Ellis Borglum Vhay, middle, poses with National Park Service staff during the dedication of the Hall of Records in 1998.

*An aerial view of the
finished sculpture.*

John A. Boland

Peter Norbeck

William Williamson

Doane Robinson

Opposite: The Shrine of Democracy. Rushmore Photo

Chronology

December 28, 1923	Colossal sculpture in the Black Hills first suggested by Doane Robinson.
September 24, 1924	Visit of sculptor Gutzon Borglum to the Black Hills to survey the possibilities of sculpture.
March 5, 1925	Passage of the law by the South Dakota Legislature permitting carving in the Black Hills. (Since the proposed area was situated in a national forest, national legislation was also enacted to allow carving.)
August 13, 1925	Theodore Shoemaker guided Gutzon Borglum to Mount Rushmore, which was tentatively chosen for the sculpture.
October 1, 1925	Dedication of Mount Rushmore as a national memorial.
1926	Rough models of the sculpture made by Borglum; efforts made to raise money for the project.
March 1, 1927	Contract made between the Mount Harney Memorial Association and Gutzon Borglum naming Borglum the sculptor and the association the supervising agency.
August 10, 1927	President Calvin Coolidge's address at Mount Rushmore supporting the work and focusing national attention on the project.
October 4, 1927	The first actual drilling.

1928	Work on the mountain halted by lack of money.
February 22, 1929	Passage of a national law authorizing (1) $250,000 on a matching basis for carving at Mount Rushmore and (2) a federal commission to administer the work.
June 6, 1929	The Mount Rushmore National Memorial Commission organized at a meeting held in the Cabinet room of the White House.
July 4, 1930	Dedication of the Washington figure.
1931	Drilling continued.
1932	Work stopped because of lack of funds.
September 1932	$50,000 secured for work at Mount Rushmore from relief grant made to South Dakota by the Reconstruction Finance Corporation.
June 10, 1933	Executive order issued by President Franklin D. Roosevelt placing Mount Rushmore under the jurisdiction of the National Park Service, Department of the Interior. No immediate administrative changes.
1934	Removal of the Jefferson figure, first started south of Washington, to present location; carving continued.
June 15, 1934	Federal legislation obtained by Senator Peter Norbeck making available the unexpended balance of the congressional authorization without matching funds from private sources.
August 24, 1935	Additional authorization of $200,000 obtained by Senator Norbeck for carving.
July 1936	Julian C. Spotts sent to Mount Rushmore by the National Park Service as resident engineer.

August 30, 1936	Visit of President Franklin D. Roosevelt to the monument for ceremonies dedicating the Jefferson figure.
September 17, 1937	Dedication of the Lincoln figure.
June 15, 1938	Passage of a new Mount Rushmore law giving Borglum practical control of the project and authorizing $300,000 additional federal aid.
July 1, 1939	The National Park Service, which had lost administrative authority under the law of 1938, assumed formal control of the project under a presidential reorganization order. Responsiblity for completing the work left to Borglum and the commission.
July 2, 1939	Formal ceremony dedicating the figure of Theodore Roosevelt.
August 1940	Final appropriation by Congress of $86,000 for Mount Rushmore. (Total federal appropriations: $836,000; total expenditure on Mount Rushmore, including money from private sources: $989,992.32. Of this sum, Borglum received about $170,000.)
March 6, 1941	Death of Borglum in Chicago. The work carried on by Lincoln Borglum, his son and assistant.
October 31, 1941	Final drilling at Mount Rushmore.
July 3, 1991	Formal official dedication of the memorial by President George H. W. Bush.

Notes on Sources

CHAPTER ONE
Robinson Papers: Doane Robinson to Lorado Taft, December 28, 1923, and January 26, 1924; Robinson to Peter Norbeck, January 26, 1924; J. B. Greene to Robinson, March 2, 1924. Norbeck Papers: Norbeck to Robinson, January 4, 1924; Robinson to Gutzon Borglum, August 20, 1924; Borglum to Robinson, August 28, 1924. *Huron Evening Huronite*, January 23 and February 14, 1924; *Rapid City Daily Journal*, February 1 and 8, 1924; *Yankton Press and Dakotan*, January 31 and February 7, 1924; *Sioux Falls Daily Argus Leader*, February 1, 1924; *Dakota Republican*, February 7, 1924; *Hot Springs Star*, February 21, 1924; Doane Robinson, "Inception and Development of the Rushmore Idea," *Black Hills Engineer* 18 (November 1930), 335.

CHAPTER TWO
Chicago *Evening Post*, October 20, 1897; *The National Cyclopedia of American Biography* 30 (New York, J. T. White and Company, 1943), 69; "The Moment of Intensity—Gutzon Borglum's Sculpture," *Current Opinion* 56 (May 1914), 379–80; George Marvin, "Gutzon Borglum, Mechanic, Horseman, Politician, and Apostle of American Art," *World's Work* 28 (June 1914), 198–200; Gutzon Borglum, "Individuality, Sincerity, and Reverence in American Art," *The Craftsman* 15 (October 1908), 3–6; Borglum, "Art That Is Real and American," *World's Work* 28 (June 1914), 200–17; Borglum, "Aesthetic Activities in America," *The Craftsman* 15 (December 1908), 301–307; Arthur Strawn, "Phidias, U.S.A.," *Outlook* 157 (January 14, 1931), 72; Rupert Hughes, "The Sculpture of Gutzon Borglum," *Appleton's Magazine* (December 1906), 709–17; *New York Times*, February 7, 1913, February 15 and 22, 1914, January 24, 1915, and May 6, 1932; *New York Sun*, February 10, 1914,

and March 25, 1938; *Washington Star*, May 6, 1934; *Toledo Morning Times*, June 14, 1934.

CHAPTER THREE

Robinson Papers: Doane Robinson to Peter Norbeck, September 28, 1924; Gutzon Borglum to Robinson, October 22 and November 21, 1924; Robinson to Borglum, November 16, 1924; Borglum to Robinson, December 2, 1924, and January 26, 1925; Norbeck to Robinson, January 20, 1925; Robinson to Mrs. Cora B. Johnson, December 2, 1924; J. B. Townley to Robinson, December 26, 1924; Mrs. Johnson to Robinson, December 6, 1924; Carl Gunderson to Norbeck, January 16, 1925; Robinson to Borglum, May 5, 1925. Norbeck Papers: Robinson to Norbeck, December 18, 1924. *Rapid City Daily Journal*, September 25 and 26, 1924, and March 11, 1946; Robinson, "Inception and Development of the Rushmore Idea," *Black Hills Engineer* 18 (November 1930), 335; *Senate Exec. Doc.* 32, 43rd Cong., 2nd sess. (1875), 5; *House Exec. Doc.* 1, 44th Cong., 1st sess., II, 1151.

CHAPTER FOUR

Norbeck Papers: Peter Norbeck to Doane Robinson, June 1, 1929; Norbeck to Hollins Randolph, April 2, 1925. Borglum Papers: Gutzon Borglum to Norbeck, April 3, 1925; Borglum Diary, entry for February 25, 1925. Robinson Papers: Borglum to Robinson, October 25, 1924; Borglum to Robinson, May 11, 1925. Gutzon Borglum, "The Confederate Memorial," *World's Work* 34 (August 1917), 437–46; James C. Derieux, "A Sculptor Who Rode to Fame on Horseback," *American Magazine* 98 (January, 1924), 12–14; *The Pepper Box* (St. Louis) 30 (November 28, 1940), 665–66; *Plutarch's Lives*, with trans. by Bernadott Perrin, Loeb Classical Library vol. 78 (New York, G. P. Putnam's Sons, 1928), 8:427; Borglum, "Engineering Problems to Be Met in Mountain Sculpture," *Black Hills Engineer* 18 (November 1930), 308–34; "The Stone Mountain Fiasco," *Plain Talk* 2 (1928), 393–99; "Uncivil War over the Confederate Memorial," *Literary Digest* 84 (March 14, 1925), 28–30; *A Statement of the Executive Committee of the Stone Mountain Confederate Monumental Association*...(pamphlet), n.p., March 14, 1925; *New York Times*, January 2, 1916, February 25, 1923, February 22, 26, 28, March 1, 3, 13, 17, 1925, and February 14, 1929; *Columbus*

(*Georgia*) *Enquirer-Sun* reprinted in *New York Times*, March 12, 1925; *Chicago Tribune*, March 3, 1925

CHAPTER FIVE

Norbeck Papers: Gutzon Borglum to Peter Norbeck, April 25, 1925; Norbeck to Borglum, April 25, 1925; Norbeck to C. M. Henry, January 21, 1925; Borglum to Norbeck, April 6, 1925. Robinson Papers: Norbeck to Doane Robinson, January 20, 1925; Borglum to Robinson, January 26, 1925; Borglum to Robinson, April 25, 1925; Borglum to Norbeck, August 28, 1925; Robinson to Borglum, October 18, 1925; Borglum to Robinson, October 28, 1925. Borglum Papers: Borglum Diary, entry for August 13, 1925; Private source: Mrs. Cora B. Johnson to Carl Gunderson, August 15, 1925; unnamed writer to Gunderson, September 25, 1925; Gunderson to Mrs. Johnson, August 18, 1925. Williamson Papers. Robinson to William Williamson, February 27, 1925. For Borglum's comments on colossal sculpture see *New York Times*, January 2, 1926, and *New York Herald Tribune*, August 21, 1927. *Rapid City Daily Journal*, August 11, 13, 19, 26, and 27, 1925; *Sioux Falls Press*, August 12 and 13, 1925; *Deadwood Pioneer-Times*, August 23, 1925. Mount Rushmore National Memorial Commission files: Gutzon Borglum, "Report Addressed to the Harney Peak Memorial Association" (1926). Interview with Theodore Shoemaker, September 7, 1950.

CHAPTER SIX

Norbeck Papers: Peter Norbeck to Doane Robinson, August 31 and October 9, 1925; Robinson to Norbeck, October 2, 1925; Herbert Myrick to Edgar B. Davis, April 9, 1927; Norbeck to Myrick, April 17, 1927; Robinson to Norbeck, September 28, 1926; Norbeck to Robinson, September 29, 1926. Robinson Papers: Gutzon Borglum to Robinson, September 5, 1925: Robinson to Edward W. Bok, November 1, 1925. Borglum Papers: Borglum to Robinson, November 16, 1926; Robinson to Borglum, November 16, 1926. *Rapid City Daily Journal*, August in September 28 and 30, October 2, 3, and 8, 1925, August 24 and September 3, 1926; *Lead Daily Call* reprinted in *Rapid City Daily Journal*, October 7, 1925. Mount Rushmore National Memorial Commission files: Gutzon Borglum, "Report Addressed to the Harney Peak Memorial Association" (1926).

CHAPTER SEVEN

Norbeck Papers: Peter Norbeck to Doane Robinson, January 15 and February 15 and 17, 1927; John A. Boland to Norbeck, February 4, 1927; C. C. Warren to Norbeck, March 23, 1927; Robinson to Norbeck, April 13, 1926; Herbert Myrick to Norbeck, March 11, 1927; Norbeck to Boland, January 25, 1927; Gutzon Borglum to Norbeck, June 7, 1927; Norbeck to Robinson, June 12, 1927; Robinson to Borglum, May 18, 1927; Borglum to Norbeck, April 1, 1927; Norbeck to Robinson, April 5 and 9, 1927; Robinson to Norbeck, June 10, 1927; Robinson to Norbeck, August 16, 1927; O. E. Rolvaag to Norbeck, September 1, 1927; Norbeck to Robinson, August 20, 1927. Borglum Papers: Borglum to Robinson, June 6 and 28, 1927; Borglum to Robinson, September 11, 1927; Robinson to Borglum, September 17, 1927. Mount Rushmore National Memorial Commission file: Borglum, "Report to the Commission," June 6, 1929, in Minutes of the First Mount Rushmore Commission, July 17, 1929; contract between Gutzon Borglum and the Mount Harney Memorial Association. *Huron Evening Huronite*, March 19, 1927; *Rapid City Daily Journal*, June 20 and August 11, 1927; William J. Bulow, "My Days with Gutzon Borglum," *Saturday Evening Post* (January 11, 1947), 106; *Art Digest* (December 15, 1926), 1; *Address of President Calvin Coolidge* (pamphlet).

CHAPTER EIGHT

Norbeck Papers: Peter Norbeck to Doane Robinson, January 2, 1928; Robinson to Norbeck, March 28, 1928; Norbeck to Robinson, May 18, 1928; Gutzon Borglum to Norbeck, May 17, 1928; Norbeck to Borglum, May 18, 1928; Norbeck to Robinson, June 2, 1928; John A. Boland to Norbeck, May 3, 1928; Norbeck to Boland, May 14, 1928; Norbeck to Borglum, January 25, 1929; Norbeck to C. J. Buell, March 15, 1929; Norbeck to Borglum, May 3, 1929; Borglum to Norbeck, June 3, 1929; Norbeck to Boland, May 17, 1929; Norbeck to Robinson, February 27 and March 1, 1929; Norbeck to C. D. Erskine, March 1, 1929; Norbeck to Calvin Coolidge, March 2, 1929; Norbeck to Robinson, June 8, 1929; Norbeck to Boland, November 19, 1929; Norbeck to D. B. Gurney, June 21, 1929. Williamson Papers: Norbeck to William Williamson,

April 7, 1928; Williamson to Robinson, July 30, 1930; Williamson Diary, entry for February 22, 1929. Mount Rushmore National Memorial Commission files: "Audit of the Tucker Account," November 20, 1929; Minutes of the Meeting of the Mount Rushmore National Memorial Commission, July 17, 1929; financial statement of the commission, November 1, 1929; E. C. Howe to Coleman Du Pont, September 5, 1929. *Congressional Record*, 70th Cong., 1st sess., May 28, 1928, 10412, and May 29, 10710; 70th Cong., 2nd sess., February 22, 1929, 4011; *United States Statutes* 45, 1300.

CHAPTER NINE

Borglum Papers: Calvin Coolidge to Gutzon Borglum, April 14, 1930; Borglum to Coolidge, April 22, 1930; Borglum to J. S. Chamberlain, June 24, 1930; "Report of the McCutcheon-Gerson Service, January 31, 1930"; undated clippings for 1930. Williamson Papers: William Williamson to J. S. Cullinan, February 22, 1930; Coolidge to Williamson, July 28, 1930. Mount Rushmore National Memorial Commission files: Minutes of the Meeting of the Commission, July 3, 1930; Cullinan to Members of the Commission, January 18, 1930; "Report of the Chairman to the Executive Committee, July 1, 1930"; Coolidge to Cullinan, April 28, 1930; Cullinan to Coolidge, May 6, 1930; Williamson to John A. Boland, August 5, 1930. *Independent Offices Appropriations Bill for 1931.* Hearings before Subcommittee of House Committee on Appropriations, 71st Cong., 2nd sess., January 10, 1930, 177ff.; *New York Mirror*, January 19, 1930; *Seattle Times*, January 26, 1930; *New York Post* reprinted in *St. Joseph (Missouri) Gazette*, February 16, 1930; *London Daily Telegraph* reprinted in *St. Joseph Gazette*, January 26, 1930; *Waterbury (Connecticut) Republican*, April 19, 1930; *Waterloo (Iowa) Courier*, May 19, 1930; *Beloit (Wisconsin) News*, May 22, 1930; *Cleveland Plain Dealer*, May 22, 1930; *Tampa (Florida) Tribune*, May 15, 1930; *Olympia (Washington) Olympian*, May 14, 1930; *Leavenworth (Kansas) Times*, May 14, 1930; *Salem (Massachusetts) News*, May 15, 1930; *Oklahoma City News*, May 15, 1930; *Los Angeles Times* reprinted in *Lead Daily Call*, May 19, 1930; *New York Times*, November 20, 1930; *Rapid City Daily Journal*, July 3 and 5, 1930; "Is It Art?" *Art Digest* (March 1, 1930), 8.

CHAPTER TEN

Mount Rushmore National Memorial Commission files: John A. Boland to Doane Robinson, March 4 and November 8, 1930; William Williamson to Boland, December 29, 1930; Gutzon Borglum to J. S. Cullinan, November 22, 1930; Borglum to Peter Norbeck, December 10, 1930; C. M. Day to Boland, March 28, 1931; Borglum to Boland, undated, 1931; Borglum to Cullinan, September 4, 1931; Boland to T. Q. Beesley, July 5, 1931; Hugo Villa to Warren E. Green, September 16, 1931; Borglum to Boland, October 12, 1931; "Report of the Chairman of the Executive Committee, July 1, 1930"; "Report of the Chairman of the Executive Committee, November 15, 1930." Williamson Papers: Boland to Cullinan, December 7, 1929; Boland to Williamson, May 3, 1930. Case Papers: Francis Case to Beesley, July 29, 1931; Case to C. M. Day, July 25, 1931, and September 15, 1932. *Rapid City Daily Journal*, April 25, 1931; *Huron Evening Huronite*, October 21, 1930; *Sioux Falls Daily Argus Leader*, September 27, 1931; *Chicago Tribune*, December 22, 1932.

CHAPTER ELEVEN

Norbeck Papers: Peter Norbeck to C. M. Day, July 23, 1932; Norbeck to Harry L. Gandy, October 17, 1935; Gutzon Borglum to Norbeck, December 16, 1930; Harold Ickes to Norbeck, August 4, 1933; Alvin Brown to William Williamson, August 7, 1933. Mount Rushmore National Memorial Commission files: Borglum to Herbert Hoover, March 7, 1932; Borglum to J. S. Cullinan, March 7, 1932; Borglum to John A. Boland, May 28, 1932; Borglum to Boland, May 4, 1932; Norbeck to Warren E. Green, September 14, 1932; Norbeck to Boland, September 21, 1932; Borglum to Cullinan, September 4, 1931; Norbeck to Borglum, October 9, 1933; Norbeck to Boland, October 7, 1933; "Financial Statement of the Mount Rushmore National Memorial Commission," October 31, 1931, to April 1, 1932; Minutes of a Meeting of the Commission, Novemeber 29, 1932; Auditor's Report, November 24, 1933; "Report of the Committee on Design and Publicity, November, 1929." Williamson Papers: William Williamson Diary, entries for June 20 and 21, 1932. National Archives, Division of Natural Resources and Records: Ray Lyman Wilbur to Cullinan,

November 22, 1929; Memorandum by Horace Albright to E. K. Burlew, undated, 1930; Memorandum for Mr. Lewis, March 13, 1930.

CHAPTER TWELVE

Norbeck Papers: John A. Boland to Peter Norbeck, May 22, 1929; Gutzon Borglum to Norbeck, June 3 and September 22, 1929; Borglum to Norbeck, October 4, 1933; Borglum to Norbeck, September 27, 1933; Borglum to Norbeck, September 14, 1933; Norbeck to Borglum, September 21, 1933; Borglum to Norbeck, September 27, 1933; Norbeck to Borglum, December 18, 1934. Borglum Papers: Borglum to Fred W. Sargent, August 16, 1934; Borglum to Herman Oliphant, August 18, 1934; Borglum to Franklin D. Roosevelt, October 14, 1933. Boland Papers: Boland to Director of the National Park Service, September 18, 1936. Mount Rushmore National Memorial Commission files: George Philip to Borglum, May 14, 1934; Borglum to Boland, September 12, 1933; annual reports of the Mount Rushmore Commission, 1931, 1932, and 1933. Spotts Papers: John A. Boland to Borglum, October 26, 1936. National Park Service files, Office of the Director: Borglum to Harry Slattery, April 7, 1936.

CHAPTER THIRTEEN

Norbeck Papers: Harold Norbeck to John A. Boland, March 22, 1934; Gutzon Borglum to Peter Norbeck, April 5, 1934; Norbeck to Borglum, April 19, 1934; Norbeck to Fred W. Sargent, April 21, 1934; Norbeck to Borglum, June 20, 1934; Norbeck to Boland, June 19, 1934; Boland to Norbeck, May 12, 1934; Norbeck to Lorine J. Spoontz, June 20, 1934; Boland to Norbeck, April 19, 1934; Norbeck to Borglum, December 18, 1934; Norbeck to Borglum, October 7, 1936; Norbeck to Boland, June 21, 1935; Boland to Norbeck, June 25, 1935; Norbeck to Boland, June 5, 1935; Norbeck to Borglum, June 13, 1935; Norbeck to Boland, June 28 and July 9, 1935; Franklin D. Roosevelt to Norbeck, July 3, 1935; Norbeck to Borglum, July 3, 1935. Borglum Papers: Borglum to Fred Sargent, August 6, 1934; Borglum to Sargent, June 29, 1934; Sargent to Borglum, July 6, 1934; J. S. Cullinan to Borglum, July 9, 1934; Borglum to Herman Oliphant, August 25, 1934. Mount Rushmore National Memorial Commission files: Norbeck,

Boland, and Borglum to Lewis Douglas, May 24, 1934; Borglum to Boland, August 8, 1934; Minutes of a Meeting of the Executive Committee, June 25, 1934. *Congressional Record*, 73rd Cong., 2nd sess., May 21, 1934, 10110, and 74th Cong., 1st sess., August 24, 1935, 14653–57; *Sixth Annual Report of the Mount Rushmore National Memorial Commission, House Doc.* 30, 74th Cong., 1st sess., 2; House Report, No. 1496, 74th Cong., 1st sess.; *Interior Department Appropriation Bill, 1936*, Hearings before Subcommittee of House Committee on Appropriations, 74th Cong., 1st sess., 59–64.

CHAPTER FOURTEEN

Norbeck Papers: Edward D. Freeland to Director of the National Park Service, October 2, 1935; William Williamson to Peter Norbeck, October 9, 1936; Borglum statement, undated; Williamson to Norbeck, September 21 and October 9, 1936. Boland Papers: Norbeck to Borglum, September 15, 1936. Borglum Papers: Gutzon Borglum to Williamson, August 12, 1935; Fred W. Sargent to Borglum, May 16, 1935; Arno B. Cammerer to Sargent, July 9, 1935; Borglum to Sargent, July 2, 1935; E. K. Burlew to Borglum, August 29, 1936. National Park Service files, Office of the Director: Borglum to Edward D. Freeland, October 14, 1935; Borglum to Harry Slattery, February 22, 1936; Memorandum for Mr. Slattery by A. E. Demaray, February 28, 1936; Slattery to Borglum, February 29, 1936; Borglum to Slattery, March 5, 1936; Borglum to John L. Nagle, November 19, 1936; Nagle to Borglum, December 7, 1936; Nagle, "Report of Visit of Inspection to Mount Rushmore National Memorial, September 12 to September 18, 1936." Spotts Papers: Julian C. Spotts to Borglum, July 15, 1936; Borglum to Spotts, July 16, 1936; Borglum to Nagle, July 16, 1936; Borglum to Spotts, August 19, 1936; Spotts to Nagle, July 5, 1936; Spotts, "Report of Operations at Mount Rushmore National Memorial for the Year of 1936." Mount Rushmore National Memorial Commission files: Auditor's Report, December 13, 1935; W. S. Tallman to Members of the Commission, December 4, 1935; Nagle to John A. Boland, October 9, 1936; Boland to Nagle, October 14, 1936. Case Papers: Borglum to Francis Case, July 29 and August 8, 1937. Franklin D. Roosevelt Papers: Memorandum by Roosevelt, August 18, 1936. *Seventh Annual Report of the Mount Rushmore National Memorial Commission,*

House Doc. 336, 74th Cong., 2nd sess.; *Interior Department Appropriation Bill, 1937,* Hearings before Subcommittee of House Committee on Appropriations, 74th Cong., 2nd sess., 66–71; *Rapid City Daily Journal,* November 7, 1935, and September 1, 1936.

CHAPTER FIFTEEN

Norbeck Papers: Gutzon Borglum to Peter Norbeck, August 13, 1936. Boland Papers: John A. Boland to Fred W. Sargent, January 9, 1937; Borglum to Boland, April 29, 1937. Borglum Paper: Borglum to Herman Oliphant, May 15, 1937. Case Papers: Francis Case to Boland, April 16, 1937; Case to Borglum, August 2, 1937. Spotts Papers: Borglum "Preamble," July 24, 1936; Borglum, "National Park Service," September 17, 1937. Mount Rushmore National Memorial Commission files: Minutes of a meeting of the Commission, July 12, 1937. National Park Service files, Office of the Director: Arno B. Cammerer, Memorandum for the Secretary, March 16, 1936; Borglum to Cammerer, May 7, 1937; Borglum to Harry Slattery, April 7, 1936; Boland to A. E. Demaray, August 4, 1936; John L. Nagle to Demaray, July 22, 1937; Julian C. Spotts to Nagle, September 10, 1937. Lincoln number of the Mount Rushmore National Memorial brochure; *Congressional Record,* 75th Cong., 1st sess., May 13, 1938, *Interior Department Appropriation Bill for 1938*; Hearings before Subcommittee of Committee on Appropriations, House of Representatives, 75th Cong., 1st sess., 105–14 and 1873–75. For Pyle's comments see *Washington Daily News,* September 23, 1936; *Rapid City Daily Journal,* December 1, 1936.

CHAPTER SIXTEEN

National Park Service Correspondence files, Office of the Director: Gutzon Borglum to Franklin D. Roosevelt, March 23, 1938; John A. Boland to Borglum, April 25, 1938; Borglum to Boland, April 26, 1938; Harold Ickes, Memorandum for Director Arno B. Cammerer, May 13, 1938; John L. Nagle, "Report on Mount Rushmore," May 28, 1938; Memorandum for Mr. A. D. Demaray by A. E. Burlew, June 14, 1938; Demaray to Edward D. Freeland, May 18, 1938; Key Pittman to Franklin D. Roosevelt, March 24, 1938; Nagle, Memorandum on Mount Rushmore, April 12, 1938. Mount Rushmore files in the Office of the Secretary of the

Interior: Borglum to E. K. Burlew, April 5 and 8, 1938; Ickes, Memorandum for Cammerer, March 26, 1938, Ickes to Roosevelt, April 23, 1938. Mount Rushmore National Memorial Commission files: Minutes of a Meeting of the Executive Committee of the Commission, April 16, 1938; Boland to L. B. Hanna, March 14, 1938; Hanna to Boland, March 19 and April 4, 1938. Spotts Papers: Julian C. Spotts to Nagle, October 2, 1937. Case Papers: Borglum to Francis Case, April 1, 1938; Boland to Case, May 6 and June 4, 1938; Case to Boland, June 7, 1938. *Mount Rushmore National Memorial Commission,* Hearings before the Committee on the Library, House of Representatives, 75th Cong., 3rd sess., 1–41; *Washington Herald,* June 28, 1938.

CHAPTER SEVENTEEN
Mount Rushmore Treasury Department files: Complete Verbatim Account of a Meeting of the Mount Rushmore National Memorial Commission, August 4, 1938; Gutzon Borglum to George Storck, November 1, 1938; Storck to Borglum, November 3, 1938; Borglum to Storck, November 7, 1938; Storck to E. F. Bartelt, October 22, 1938; Borglum to Russell Arundel, August 19 and October 14, 1938; Borglum to Franklin D. Roosevelt, June 5, 1939, and March 7, 1940. Mount Rushmore National Memorial Commission files: Borglum to Kent Keller, April 26, 1939; Borglum to Arundel, September 13, 1939. Spotts Papers: Julian C. Spotts, Daily Report for July 2 and 3, 1938; Borglum to John L. Nagle, March 24, 1937. Boland Papers: Borglum to John A. Boland, February 9, 1937. Case Papers: Francis Case to Boland, January 28, 1938. Borglum Papers: Borglum to Russell Arundel, July 19, 1938. Williamson Papers: William Williamson Diary, entry for August 4, 1938. *Interior Department Appropriation Bill for 1939,* Hearings before Subcommittee of Committee on Appropriations, House of Representatives, 75th Cong., 3rd sess., 1, 1421ff.; *Independent Offices Appropriation Bill for 1940,* Hearings before Subcommittee of Committee on Appropriations, House of Representatives, 76th Cong., 1st sess., 1191–1218; *Sioux Falls Daily Argus Leader,* August 25, 1938; *Rapid City Daily Journal,* July 3, 1939.

CHAPTER EIGHTEEN
National Park Service files, Office of the Director: Franklin D. Roosevelt, Memorandum for A. E. Demaray, June 7, 1939; Harold

L. Ickes to Roosevelt, August 29, 1939; Gutzon Borglum to E. J. Burlew, July 8, 1939; John L. Nagle, "Conditions at Mount Rushmore as of August 8, 1939"; Nagle to Director of the National Park Service, August 8, 1939; Nagle and Howard W. Baker, "Recommendations and Report on Mount Rushmore, Based on Inspection Trip of December 3–7, 1939"; Russell Arundel to Ickes, March 6, 1941; Arundel to Borglum, November 8, 1939; Roosevelt to Borglum, July 22, 1940; Borglum to Doane Robinson, November 12, 1940. Mount Rushmore National Memorial Commission files: Borglum to Arundel, March 26, 1940; Borglum to Arundel, February 9, 1939; Roosevelt to Speaker of the House, August 7, 1940; Borglum to Arundel, November 15, 1940. Mount Rushmore Treasury Department files: Borglum to Roosevelt, June 5, 1939; Borglum to George Storck, March 18, 1940; Arundel to Storck, July 10, 1940; Borglum to Roosevelt, March 7, 1940. Borglum Papers: Borglum to Key Pittman, May 26, 1939. Case Papers: Francis Case to Borglum, July 9, 1940. Roosevelt. Papers: E. M. Watson, Memorandum for Roosevelt, June 5, 1939; Harold L. Ickes to Roosevelt, August 29, 1939. Reorganization Plan No. II, *United States Statutes,* 53, 1434; *Report of the Mount Rushmore National Memorial Commission, House Doc. 664,* 76th Cong., 3rd sess.; *New York Times,* February 23, 1940.

CHAPTER NINETEEN

Mount Rushmore National Memorial Commission files: Russell Arundel to Gutzon Borglum, March 1, 1941; Minutes of a Meeting of the Executive Committee of the Mount Rushmore National Memorial Commission, June 16, 1941; Lincoln Borglum, "Report to the Members of the Mount Rushmore National Memorial Commission, November 20, 1941; Borglum to Franklin D. Roosevelt, August 2, 1939. Williamson Papers: Minutes of a Meeting of the Mount Rushmore National Memorial Commission, March 17, 1941. National Park Service files, Office of the Director: Newton B. Drury to Regional Director, Region Two, April 21, 1941; James Roweⁱ to Secretary of the Interior, July 29, 1941, Lawrence C. Merriam to Director of the National Park Service, April 2, 1942. "Ralph M. Pearson's Design Workshop," New York Public Library; *Second Deficiency Appropriation Bill for 1941,* Hearings before the Subcommittee on Appropriations,

House of Representatives, 77th Cong., 1st sess., 954–56; *Interior Department Appropriation Bill for 1942,* Hearings before the Subcommittee of the Committee on Appropriations, House of Representatives, 77th Cong., 1st sess., I, 528–29; *New York Times,* March 24, 1940.

CHAPTER TWENTY

Case Papers: William Lemke to Francis Case, August 2, 1940. *Lead Daily Call,* February 3, 1943; *Sioux Falls Daily Argus Leader,* June 2, 1941; *Rapid City Daily Journal,* April 2, 1946; *Congressional Record,* 70th Cong., 1st sess., May 28, 1928, 10391ff.

Selected Bibliography

The sources for this study have come largely from the files of the Mount Rushmore National Memorial Commission, the National Park Service records, and the private papers of the principal sponsors of the monument. The files of the first commission cover the period from June 1929 to July 1938 and are located at the Library of Congress. Those of the second commission, dealing with the work between August 1938 and November 1941, are in the Office of the Director, National Park Service, Washington, D.C.

The official National Park Service historical file on Mount Rushmore is also in the office of the director and covers the years 1933 to 1941. Between 1938 and 1941 the United States Treasury Department, through its State Accounts Office in Watertown, South Dakota, maintained a separate file. This is now located at the Library of Congress.

Private papers have yielded abundant and significant material for this work. Those of Peter Norbeck are the most complete and valuable. They deal with Rushmore matters between 1925 and 1936. The Norbeck papers are in the I. D. Weeks Library at the University of South Dakota in Vermillion. The Borglum file, which is less complete but extremely valuable, deals with the entire period between 1925 and 1941. It is now located in the Library of Congress. The major part of Doane Robinson's Rushmore file has been lost or destroyed, but some one hundred items, mostly letters, remain in the State Historical Society of South Dakota. Only part of the William Williamson files is extant, but the remaining materials are significant. They are in the I. D. Weeks Library at the University of South Dakota in Vermillion. Documents by Julian C. Spotts, covering the period from 1936 to 1938, are complete and valuable. They are in the Office of the Superintendent, Mount Rushmore National Memorial.

There are some items of interest in the Franklin D. Roosevelt Library at Hyde Park; however, the most convenient source of letters to and from Roosevelt is the Borglum papers. John A. Boland's file is duplicated elsewhere, either in the commission files or in those of the National Park Service. The papers of Francis Case are located at Black Hills State University, Spearfish, South Dakota, and at Dakota Wesleyan University in Mitchell, South Dakota, and for the most part cover the period after 1938 when he was seeking new authorizations for Mount Rushmore work. He has some letters in Custer, South Dakota, dating back to the early 1930s, which deal with Rushmore matters of those years.

UNPUBLISHED REPORTS AND DOCUMENTS

Borglum, Gutzon. "Report Addressed to the Harney Peak Memorial Association." Typewritten. 1926. Borglum Papers.

―――. "Report of Work Accomplished on the Mount Rushmore National Memorial during the Year 1930." Typewritten. Williamson Papers.

―――. "Report of Gutzon Borglum Sculptor–Engineer to the Mount Rushmore National Memorial Commission." Typewritten. Undated, probably 1934. Borglum Papers.

―――. "National Park Service." Typewritten. September 17, 1936. Spotts Papers.

―――. "Preamble." Typewritten. July 24, 1936. Spotts Papers.

Borglum, Lincoln. "Report to the Members of the Mount Rushmore Commission." Typewritten. November 20, 1941. Williamson Papers.

Minutes of the Meetings of the Mount Rushmore National Memorial Commission, 1929 to 1941.

Minutes of the Meetings of the Executive Committee of the Mount Rushmore National Memorial Commission, 1929 to 1941. The minutes of meetings held prior to August 4, 1938, are found in the first commission file, National Park Service, Region Two, Omaha, Nebraska. Copies of minutes for 1938–1941 are to be found in the second commission files in the Office of the Director, National Park Service, Washington, D.C.

Nagle, John L. "Report of Visit of Inspection to Mount Rushmore National Memorial, September 12 to September 18, 1936."

Typewritten. National Park Service. Mount Rushmore correspondence files, Office of the Director, Washington, D. C.

––––––. "Conditions at Mount Rushmore as of August 8, 1939." Typewritten. National Park Service. Mount Rushmore correspondence files, Office of the Director, Washington, D. C.

Nagle, John L., and Howard W. Baker. "Recommendations and Reports on Mount Rushmore Based on Inspection Trip on December 3–7, 1939." Typewritten. National Park Service. Mount Rushmore correspondence files, Office of the Director, Washington, D. C.

Spotts, Julian C. "Report of Operations at Mount Rushmore National Memorial for the Year of 1936." Typewritten. Spotts Papers.

––––––. "Report of Operations at Mount Rushmore National Memorial for the Year of 1937." Typewritten. Spotts Papers.

––––––. "Report of Operations at Mount Rushmore National Memorial for the Year, 1938." Typewritten. Spotts Papers.

GOVERNMENT DOCUMENTS

Annual Reports of the Mount Rushmore National Memorial Commission, 1929 to 1939. These are found in the following House Documents: *House Doc. 164.* 71st Cong., 2nd sess. (October 31, 1929); *House Doc. 656.* 71st Cong., 3rd sess. (October 31, 1930); *House Doc. 203.* 72nd Cong., 1st sess. (October 31, 1931); *House Doc. 517.* 72nd Cong., 2nd sess. (October 31, 1932); *House Doc. 228.* 73rd Cong., 2nd sess. (January 2, 1934); *House Doc. 30.* 74th Cong., 1st sess. (January 18, 1935); *House Doc. 336.* 74th Cong., 2nd sess. (January 9, 1936); *House Doc. 25.* 75th Cong., 1st sess. (February 4, 1937); *House Doc. 517.* 75th Cong., 3rd sess. (January 15, 1938); *House Doc. 22.* 76th Cong., 1st sess. (January 2, 1939); and *House Doc. 664.* 76th Cong., 3rd sess. (December 31, 1939). No annual report was published for the years 1940 and 1941.

Independent Offices Appropriation Bill for 1931. Hearings before the Subcommittee of House Committee on Appropriations, 71st Cong., 2nd sess.

Interior Department Appropriation Bill for 1936. Hearings before the Subcommittee of House Committee on Appropriations, 74th Cong., 1st sess.

Interior Department Appropriation Bill for 1937. Hearings before the Subcommittee of House Committee on Appropriations, 74th Cong., 2nd sess.

Interior Department Appropriation Bill for 1938. Hearings before the Subcommittee of House Committee on Appropriations, 75th Cong., 1st sess.

Interior Department Appropriation Bill for 1939. Hearings before the Subcommittee of House Committee on Appropriations, 75th Cong., 3rd sess.

Mount Rushmore National Memorial Commission. Hearings before the Committee on the Library. House of Representatives, 75th Cong., 3rd sess.

Independent Offices Appropriation Bill for 1940. Hearings before the Subcommittee of the Committee on Appropriations, 76th Cong., 1st sess.

Second Deficiency Appropriation Bill for 1941. Hearings before the Subcommittee of the Committee on Appropriations, 77th Cong., 1st sess.

Interior Department Appropriation Bill for 1942. Hearings before the Subcommittee of the Committee on Appropriations, 77th Cong., 1st sess.

House Reports, 1925 to 1940. House Report No. 1435. 68th Cong., 2nd sess.; No. 1800. 70th Cong., 1st sess.; No. 2618. 70th Cong., 2nd sess.; No. 1929. 73rd Cong., 2nd sess.; No. 1496. 74th Cong., 1st sess.; No. 2514. 75th Cong., 3rd sess.; No. 1757. 76th Cong., 3rd sess.

Senate Reports 1925 to 1940. Senate Report No. 1186. 68th Cong., 2nd sess.; No. 1176. 70th Cong., 1st sess.; No. 1559. 70th Cong., 3rd sess.; No. 1041. 74th Cong., 1st sess.; No. 1917. 75th Cong., 3rd sess.; No. 641. 80th Cong., 1st sess.

Federal Legislation:

43 U. S. *Stat.* 1214. Granted permission to carve in the Harney National Forest.

45 U. S. *Stat.* 1300. First basic law relating to Mount Rushmore carving.

48 U. S. *Stat.* 1223. Amended matching feature of law.

49 U. S. *Stat.* 962. Authorized $200,000 to complete Mount Rushmore.

52 U. S. *Stat.* 694. Reorganized the commission and authorized $300,000.

State Legislation:
  Chap. 232, Session Laws, 1925.
  Chap. 170, Session Laws, 1927.
  Chap. 185, Session Laws, 1929.

BOOKS

Caffin, Charles H. *American Masters of Sculpture.* New York: Doubleday, Page and Company, 1913.

Dean, Robert J. *Living Granite.* New York: The Viking Press, 1949.

Dodd, Loring Holmes. *The Golden Age of American Sculpture.* Boston: Chapman and Grimes, 1936.

McSpadden, J. Walker. *Famous Sculptors of America.* New York: Dodd, Mead and Company, 1927.

Taft, Lorado. *The History of American Sculpture.* New ed. New York: The Macmillan Company, 1930.

PERIODICALS

Borglum, Gutzon. "Art Tendencies of Our Time." *Arts and Decoration* 14 (January 1921), 194.

———. "Art That Is Real and American." *World's Work* 28 (June 1914), 200–17.

———. "Engineering Problems to Be Met in Mountain Sculpture." *Black Hills Engineer* 18 (November 1930), 308–34.

———. "Moulding a Mountain." *Forum* 70 (October 1923), 2019–26.

———. "The Confederate Memorial." *World's Work* 34 (August 1917), 437–46.

———. "What Is Beauty in Sculpture." *Black Hills Engineer* 18 (November 1930), 304–308.

Bulow, William J. "My Days with Gutzon Borglum." *Saturday Evening Post,* January 11, 1947, 24–25.

D'Emery, Charles. "Carving the Largest Monument in the World," *Mentor,* XVI (February, 1928), 42–47.

Derieux, James C. "A Sculptor Who Rode to Fame on Horseback," *American Magazine,* January, 1924, 52–54.

Hughes, Rupert. "The Sculpture of Gutzon Borglum," *Appleton's Magazine,* December 1906, 709–17.

Johnson, G. W. "Sophocles in Georgia." *Century,* September 1926, 565–71.

Lubell, S., and W. Everett. "Man Who Carves Mountains." *Reader's Digest*, May 1940, 113–15.

Kennedy, J. B. "Master of Arts." *Collier's*, December 19, 1931, 25.

Marvin, George. "Gutzon Borglum, Mechanic, Horseman, Politician, and Apostle of American Art." *World's Work* 28 (June 1914), 198–200.

Mechlin, Leila. "Gutzon Borglum, Painter and Sculptor." *International Studio* 28, supplement (April 1906), 35–43.

Myrick, Herbert. "National Monument Rushmore." *Dakota Farmer*, November 15, 1926, 998.

O'Hara, Cleophas C. "The Black Hills, Birthplace of the Americas." *Black Hills Engineer* 18 (November 1930), 301–303.

Perlman, D. "Four for the Ages." *New York Times Magazine*, August 25, 1940, 8–9.

Robinson, Doane. "Inception and Development of the Rushmore Idea." *Black Hills Engineer* 18 (November 1930), 334–43.

Strawn, Arthur. "Phidias, U.S.A." *Outlook* 157 (January 14, 1931), 72.

Thompson, Craig F. "The Stone Mountain Fiasco." *Plain Talk* 2 (1928), 393–98.

NEWSPAPERS

New York Times, 1914 to 1950.

Rapid City Daily Journal, 1924 to 1950.

Many other newspapers were used for certain periods and for specific stories, as indicated in the text. Mrs. Borglum made available hundreds of newspaper clippings covering the period between 1925 and 1941.

Index